THE ABERCROMBIE AGE

THE
ABERCROMBIE
AGE

MILLENNIAL

ASPIRATION

AND THE

PROMISE OF

CONSUMER

CULTURE

MYLES ETHAN LASCITY

The University of North Carolina Press

Chapel Hill

Set in Garamond and Trade Gothic by Copperline Book Services
Manufactured in the United States of America

Material in chapter 4 previously appeared as "Girls That Wear
Abercrombie & Fitch: Reading Fashion Branding Aesthetics
into Music Videos," *Studies in Communication Sciences* 18, no. 2
(2019): 325–37; and "Brand References and Music Video Intertextuality: Lessons from 'Summer Girls' and 'She Looks So Perfect,'" *Film, Fashion and Consumption* 6, no. 2 (2017): 105–22.

Cover art © konradbak / Adobe Stock.

Library of Congress Cataloging-in-Publication Data
Names: Lascity, Myles Ethan, author.
Title: The Abercrombie age : millennial aspiration and the promise of
    consumer culture / Myles Ethan Lascity.
Description: Chapel Hill : The University of North Carolina Press, 2024. |
    Includes bibliographical references and index.
Identifiers: LCCN 2024020859 | ISBN 9781469680903 (cloth ; alk. paper) |
    ISBN 9781469680910 (paper ; alk. paper) | ISBN 9781469680927 (epub) |
    ISBN 9781469680934 (pdf)
Subjects: LCSH: Generation Y. | Mass media and culture—United States. |
    Mass media—Moral and ethical aspects—United States. | Consumption
    (Economics)—Social aspects—United States. | Success in popular
    culture—United States. | United States—Social conditions—1980–2020. |
    BISAC: SOCIAL SCIENCE / Ethnic Studies / American / General | SOCIAL
    SCIENCE / Media Studies
Classification: LCC HQ799.2.M352 L37 2024 |
    DDC 305.2420973—dc23/eng/20240615
LC record available at https://lccn.loc.gov/2024020859

CONTENTS

ILLUSTRATIONS

ACKNOWLEDGMENTS

For a project that had been percolating for fifteen years or so, many, many people helped me think through these arguments and my analysis of these media texts both formally and informally, much of which I'm sure has made it into this book in various ways.

First and foremost, I need to thank my colleagues in the journalism division and fashion media program at SMU for picking up the slack (and my spirits) while I've worked on this project; Jenny B. Davis, Andrea Arterbery, and Jacqueline Fellows are some of the best colleagues a person can ask for. Special thanks to Melissa Chessher and Jake Batsell, who have been nothing but supportive in my research, and Tony Pederson, who helped secure a research sabbatical to get this book across the finish line.

Because of the project's long runway, I also need to acknowledge and thank many people from both my master's and doctoral programs who shaped my thinking along the way. This includes Nancy Deihl from New York University's costume studies program and my classmates there, especially Alejandra Salcedo Casas; Alexandria Hoffman, who helped me secure documents early in this process; and most notably Priscilla Chung, who has shared my ongoing fascination with Abercrombie & Fitch and shared everything and anything that discussed the brand since 2010. From Drexel University's communication, culture, and media doctoral program, thanks to D. M. Greenwell for presenting with me an *A&F Quarterly* years ago and advisers Brent Luvaas, Jordan McClain, and Joseph H. Hancock II for asking tough questions.

At the University of North Carolina Press, I am indebted to Mark Simpson-Vos for his expert support and guidance, even when I might not have been the easiest author to work with, and Dominique J. Moore, who helped shape this project early on. Additionally, I'd be remiss not to mention María Isela García, Thomas Bedenbaugh, Erin Granville, Iza Wojciechowska, and the rest of the UNC team for their assistance throughout the process and the multiple anonymous reviewers whose criticism and input undoubtedly improved the finished product.

Most notably, four colleagues (and friends) have helped shape this project more than most: Candice D. Roberts, Melinda Sebastian, Maryann R. Cairns, and Lauren Smart. Whether discussing this project with me ad nauseam, watching films with me, or reading drafts—I am forever indebted to you all.

On a personal note, I need to thank Ray for the love, support, and hours of free copy editing. And finally, as much as this is an academic pursuit, this is also a reckoning with the culture that created me, meaning I need to shout out my longtime friends—Kara, Mel, Andee, Jes, and Bex—who experienced much of this with me at the time. I wouldn't be here without your support, encouragement, and camaraderie over the years. Thank you, and I love you all.

PREFACE

This book is the end point of a project I started during my master's thesis in 2009, although we can trace my interest in Abercrombie & Fitch to the moment I saw the new hires at the Mall at Steamtown in Scranton, Pennsylvania, in 2001. That is to say, both my personal and intellectual interests here have long roots. While I put this a bit on the back burner during my doctoral program, I was able to approach it in earnest again in 2019 and 2020. That means that from the time this book's central argument was formulated to when it was written and is now hopefully being read, we collectively have experienced a global pandemic, an ongoing reckoning with race after the murder of George Floyd and the Black Lives Matter protests, the turning back of women's rights by the United States Supreme Court, an attempted coup of the US government, and an ongoing threat of right-wing authoritarianism throughout the world. (In fact, by the time someone reads this, we'll likely know whether or not Donald Trump and his authoritarian promises will be returning to power in the United States.) In light of all this upheaval, it felt almost foolish to continue with this project, as there were more important tasks to be done. What could a cultural analysis of a now-past, affective ideal possibly contribute today?

As I wrestled with this, I remembered a Stuart Hall line conveyed to me by a friend and colleague. "Against the urgency of people dying in the streets, what in God's name is the point of cultural studies?" Hall asked rhetorically at a conference on cultural studies and its legacies. Hall positioned this question toward the AIDS epidemic at the time but acknowledged that cultural studies scholars needed to operate within the tension, as the representations of the affected— and the communities from which they came—have "constitutive and political" repercussions.[1]

Although this book does not interrogate anything as serious as pandemics, abortion, police violence, or the rise of authoritarianism, it does aim to help explain how the United States got to where it is now. Broadly, I'm arguing that the frivolousness—or what critics might suggest is vapidness—of popular culture in the 1990s and early 2000s, and an overreliance on consumer culture as a tool to make political, social, and cultural change, helped pave the way to this point. As society was sold narratives that conditions would continually improve, institutions were our friends, and the immaterial constructs put upon consumable goods *meant something*, we diverted our attention away from the venues where real change is possible—politics, community, organizations. Instead, we focused on consumption as a tool to succeed in and buy our way into the American Dream. This book makes the case that these themes of consumption were especially potent for the eldest millennials like me; but of course, we were not producing the pop culture we were exposed to in our teen years.

Writing about fashion in the 1980s, philosopher Gilles Lipovetsky noted, "Under fashion's reign, democracies enjoy a universal consensus about their political institutions; ideological extremes are on the wane and pragmatism is on the rise."[2] He saw the order that fashion brought about as a stabilizing force that went hand in hand with a stable, democratic social order. Although Lipovetsky outlined several paradoxes within the system, two seem especially poignant. First, he noted that debates about ethics and specific ethical stances continue during the reign of fashion but that adherence to them will wax and wane in line with society's systemic changes. Second, rather than fashion causing the liberal order to weaken, he saw the "gaps" in the system where people find themselves "excluded" from the advertised society as the most problematic.[3] While I do not share Lipovetsky's optimism that fashion can be the answer to current problems, it does seem like it's the gap between what was promised—*advertised*, even—and what was delivered that is causing increasing harm.

As I explain in chapter 1, my interests in this book are twofold: I argue that the intertextual nature of media in the 1990s and early 2000s led to a media sphere that promoted the cultural affect of privileged frivolity and how that promise crashed against reality in various ways. While I am hardly the first writer to note increasing disillusionment with the system (journalists as diverse as Chris Hayes, Jill Filipovic, Will Bunch, and David Leonhardt have all written about it in different ways), it certainly appears that elder millennials were uniquely positioned at the cusp of a slew of changes, including the fall of the United States as a singular, global superpower and the coming climate catastrophe. As Twitter user @Merman_Melville tweeted, "Kind of bummed to have been born at the very end of the Fuck Around century just to live the rest of my life in the Find Out century."[4] Unlike younger members of the millennial generation who don't remember much (if any) of the 1990s, elder millennials remember the decade, as *BuzzFeed* and a slew of social media accounts like to remind us often. And although we might not know what lies ahead, a fear of the future seems more pronounced now than ever before in our lives.

THE ABERCROMBIE AGE

ONE

**ABERCROMBIE, ASPIRATION,
AND CONSUMER CULTURE**

In the midst of a tropical dance party, the music cuts out as everyone looks upward toward a neon green digital clock quickly counting up from 23:59:53. As the seconds pass, the sound of crickets can briefly be heard in the background, which then gives way to the clicking of cameras. As the clock turns to 00:00:00, the scene goes dark, and everything is still. With a flash of green, "2000" appears before disappearing again, taking all the surrounding electricity with it and leaving everyone in the dark once more. After a beat, "2000" reappears with an even bigger flash of the green light, and the music triumphantly returns as water sprays the crowd. One male partygoer—tanned, muscular, with frosted tips and a soul patch—pops champagne as the revelry continues.

The brief scene appears in the music video for Jennifer Lopez's hit song "Waiting for Tonight" (figure 1.1), released in 1999 as the third single from her debut album, *On the 6*. The song, and its music video, became an unofficial anthem for the turning of the 2000s, soaring up the charts to number eight on the *Billboard* Hot 100, and it is still remembered by some as the best song of Lopez's career.[1] The mix of high-tech visuals and high-octane pop-dance music was full of anticipation for the new millennium, joining a surge of popular music—from the Backstreet Boys' *Millennium* to Will Smith's *Willennium*—that marked the historic juncture. Whatever anxieties may have surrounded the coming of Y2K, pop stars and their fans expected a party.

As culture critics have begun to assess the millennial moment, the 1990s have become fixed as a time of peace and prosperity before the internet and digital communication came to dominate most aspects of everyday life and a time when the United States was the only global superpower—one isolated from outside attack.[2] Incidentally, it has become common to suggest that the spirit and feeling of the 1990s ended over a year and a half after calendars rolled over to 2000: on September 11, 2001, when terror attacks shattered the United States' sense of security and the country plunged into wars in Afghanistan and Iraq.[3] Yet as

Figure 1.1. Waiting for 2000: In the music video for "Waiting for Tonight" by Jennifer Lopez, partygoers are watching a clock count up to the new millennium. While the setting goes dark for a moment at the stroke of midnight, lights soon resume, and the party continues.

someone who lived through this period as a teenager—an elder millennial or Xennial, if you will, who was on the verge of adulthood at the turn of a new century—the narrative of rapid change doesn't ring true to me. In fact, when it comes to teen popular culture, the overriding narratives and promises for the future lasted well into the first decade of the 2000s. They only truly died at the hands of the Great Recession.

As such, this book is an examination of messages produced for teens from roughly 1995 through 2008: the films, TV shows, music videos, and fashion brands aimed at my age cohort, the elder millennials, sold a particular aspirational version of the American Dream that likely never existed in the first place but one we undoubtedly cannot meet now. Slightly too young to be considered

Generation X and yet too old to be fully millennial, my cohort lived through the digital revolution—as tech gadgets like PCs and cell phones and social media all became mainstays during our formative years—and entered adulthood at the end of the golden age of American prosperity. In the words of one writer, we are "an unclaimed, misfit micro-generation, the poor suckers in the middle—first given a sweet taste of the good life, then kicked in the face."[4] Later age cohorts, including younger millennials, barely experienced American prosperity at all.

But that is not what pop culture promised us. Like the unrealistic living conditions and high disposable income of fictional New Yorkers on television, popular culture peddled unrealistic expectations of an aspirational life made available through consumerism. Those who lived through the moment will quickly recognize examples: Cher's massive and computerized closet in *Clueless*, the success of the Rancho Carne Toros in *Bring It On*, the fanciful abodes in *The Real World*, MTV's various spring break activities, and even the eponymous Gilmore girls' lives in the quintessential New England town of Stars Hollow. This flood of popular culture production coincides with what some have called the "New Gilded Age," a time centered on business interests, such as low taxes and limited regulation, when money continued to flow to the top of a social hierarchy.[5]

The economic trends that set the stage for such optimism can be traced to Reaganism and the rise of neoliberalism in the 1980s—and are likely still going strong today.[6] Beyond the concentration of wealth and increased corporate power, the New Gilded Age was shaped by digitization and the internet revolution, leading the 1990s to be dubbed "the world's most prosperous decade."[7] This prosperity led to widespread shifts within consumerism and consumer culture as shoppers became increasingly "label-conscious" and the conspicuous consumption that had long been reserved for the upper, or "leisure," class increasingly trickled down through society.[8] At the same time, corporations helped commodify various lifestyle choices, so much so that both mainstream culture *and* the counterculture became identities to buy into. Such a dynamic stretched from teen clothiers— one could either purchase mainstream Abercrombie & Fitch and American Eagle or "rebel" at Hot Topic and Pacific Sunwear—to magazines like *Wired* and *Details* that began as countercultural publications and only ended up reinforcing the status quo.[9]

The increased role of corporate interests meant that "advertising not only occupie[d] every last negotiable public terrain, but ... penetrate[d] the cognitive process, invading consciousness to such a point that one expect[ed] and look[ed] for advertising, learned to live life as an ad, to think like an advertiser, and even to anticipate and insert oneself in successful strategies of marketing," according to writer Tom Vanderbilt in 1997.[10] Advertisers and brands increasingly found new ways to garner attention, while individual consumption choices increasingly defined us. Yet even as this dynamic reinforced conspicuous consumption, it came with a millennium-era twist. Conspicuous consumption, a term from the original Gilded Age, involved the explicit purchase and use of products that displayed wealth, but in the New Gilded Age, consumption became more stylistic and ingrained in less tangible goods.[11] (In short, a T-shirt was less about the material garment and more about the logo placed on it.) This turn of conspicuous consumption was mixed with irony and self-parody, whereby everything could be chalked up to style.[12] Much of this might be attributed to the media, which helped warp the understandings of people, places, and other social elements.[13] For brands and advertisers, especially, this shift resulted in shaping particular narratives or images—even creating fictional brand histories out of whole cloth.[14]

Perhaps nowhere was this concept illustrated better than in the way businesses gravitated toward teen popular culture during this time. With the renewed interest in the large teen demographic that was coming of age, business interests increasingly influenced cultural industries through advertising, sponsorships, and product placements.[15] Popular movies, from *Clueless* and *Scream* to *Titanic*, had teen and young adult protagonists. MTV continued to dominate the music scene and helped give birth to reality television, while an entire network—the WB—sprang up to cater to teen interests. Teens already had a long history of making themselves felt in the marketplace, from the launch of *Seventeen* magazine in the 1940s to *American Bandstand*, Beatlemania, and the miniskirt craze during the 1960s Youthquake and the rise of MTV and the Brat Pack in the 1980s. By the 1990s, teens were already a tried-and-true market segment.[16]

Throughout this book, I argue that at the turn of the millennium, teens were targeted, marketed, and sold the idea of privileged frivolity that prioritized a highly sexualized, aspirational consumer culture that emphasized what the world would, could, or *should* be—with the proper consumption.[17] This period took root in the post–Cold War mindset, in which the liberal, democratic order was the only governance option and neoliberal capitalism reigned supreme.[18] The broader political and economic trends allowed for a particular moment where the most pressing teenage concerns were social: the plots of teen films and television shows revolved around high school rituals like prom and homecoming and were heavily influenced by consumer culture and superficiality. My use of "superficiality" is not meant derogatorily; makeovers, appearances, and perceived identities were central to the plots. In this way, teen popular culture portrayed lives in which money was no object and the most pressing issues were interpersonal rather than threatening or structural. Such a focus on frivolity largely papered over deeper structural problems such as wage stagnation and concentration of wealth, which only came into focus decades later.

Privileged Frivolity as Cultural Vibe

Scholars have long recognized the power of consumer culture in US society to normalize and promote a range of socioeconomic choices, including their particular impacts on teen consumer culture.[19] Today, US teens are routinely seen not only as a potent market force but also as a promise of the future. Teenagers are "the symbol of Americans' rising aspiration, the repository of hopes, the one[s] who will realize the American dream," journalist Thomas Hine wrote in 1999. Yet the concept of "teenager" is itself relatively new. After psychologist Stanley Hall identified the teen years as a distinct phase of development in 1904, popular culture geared toward teens hit the mainstream only after World War II. *Seventeen* magazine was founded in 1944 on the premise that teens needed to be taught the proper ways to become an adult, and with its success, advertisers and marketers began to view teens as a source of revenue in the robust postwar US economy. As baby boomers upended popular culture, attention toward teens and young adults grew. Advertisers saw the rebellious, more youthful generation as a partner in arms, so to speak, against the bland conformity of adulthood, helping turn "cool" into a marketable commodity (and co-opting rebellion in the process).[20]

Teens remain valuable commercial targets because they are inherently at the forefront of any social change (by simply growing into adulthood) and because their identities are still taking shape. Further, although their world is impacted by broader social convulsions, teen consumption practices are isolated to a degree from trends because they do not have the expectations and expenses of adults. This attention becomes even more pronounced when there is a large number of teenagers, such as the baby boomers, who came of age during the 1960s and '70s, and more recently the millennials, who came of age in the late 1990s and early 2000s. In short, when there are more teens, there tends to be more popular culture—movies, TV shows, and fashion items—geared toward teenagers.

At the turn of the millennium, the message pop culture directed toward teens was that with a little money and some know-how, anyone could transform from the class nerd to the homecoming queen. And even if that failed, a better future awaited teens as they moved into adulthood; opportunities abounded for self-reinvention in college or later in their professional lives. In short, life could, or eventually would, be better, and in turn popular culture was unfailingly optimistic about the future and the power of consumer culture. While we might anchor some of that cultural affect in the John Hughes films and teen television shows of the 1980s and early 1990s, the idea grew substantially with the release of *Clueless* in 1995, thanks to its airheaded materialism. These messages gained traction in the resulting teen film cycle of 1998 and 1999, as well as the explosion of bubblegum pop music in the latter half of the '90s.

To be clear, this was a feeling embodied not only by particular popular culture products but by a logic that stretched across the landscape. The popular culture products of this era were deeply intertwined, as actors became singers, singers became actors, songs became promotional vehicles for movies, and brand sponsorships and product placements were used with vigor. Aesthetically speaking, films, television shows, and advertisements shared certain qualities like good-looking "teens" (who were frequently actors older than the characters they portrayed), picturesque high schools, and fun, sun-kissed beach trips. Although these messages were present throughout teen popular culture, only a slim subset of teens had a viable chance at living those realities. Yet that does not detract from the meaning and morals set forth in the media or from the aspirational impact. Further, despite its aspirational qualities, not everyone wanted to have this aesthetic; nonetheless, embodying its ethos—and full-fledged embrace of personal appearance and consumption—held an implicit promise of a more desirable life.

As is developed over the rest of this book, there were three distinct dimensions of privileged frivolity: (1) the embodiment of privilege, (2) the emphasis on objectification and consumer culture, and (3) a lack of consequences, leading to an unyielding optimism that promised a better future. While the three qualities are interrelated, each speaks to a different element of this particular time.

My use of "privilege" stems from Peggy McIntosh's discussion, which equates it to the taken-for-granted qualities of everyday life, such as being around similar people or being able to afford basic necessities. Unearned privilege, which "confers dominance," can take various forms—race, ethnicity, gender, sexuality, class, religion, and physical ability—and is often hard to separate from aspects like status or merit.[21] Yet my use of "privilege" is less precise and more focused on consumerist aspects.[22] Although the selection of texts used throughout this book demonstrates a systemic bias toward the white, straight, abled, conventionally attractive, and well-off, my interest is more in line with accrued capital—economic, social, and cultural—that people can draw from and transform into another form of capital. Although not analogous, privilege and capital are often closely linked—as straight, white men continue to outearn all other demographic groups.[23]

Of course, consumer culture is not just the act of buying and consuming but the contemporary understanding of how our use of goods and media helps construct our identities for ourselves and communicate those identities to others.[24] The logic of consumer culture implies that social structures or categorizations do not define individuals; instead, people can use accrued forms of capital to create desirable identities and associations. In this sense, self-objectification is a vital social process, and developing a desirable appearance and identity through consumption impacts relationships, education, and employment.[25] Regardless, a belief that consumer culture informs and can transform identities was a pronounced feature of the turn-of-the-millennium moment and was closely related to class privilege, as those with monetary means were more able to use consumption to its purported ends.

Finally, across pop culture, narratives generally worked out for the best regardless of specific events or transgressions. Essentially, teen culture showed a significant lack of consequences for acting "badly," and questionable behavior was understood to be a typical period of growth. Such problematic transgressions included serious sexual indiscretions, use of illicit drugs, and more general "poor" behavior (e.g., underage drinking, lying, and cheating). On one hand, this notion certainly plays into ideas of privilege: those who could break the laws and rules or otherwise manipulate the system without being overtly or harshly punished were usually straight, white, and affluent. On the other hand, these narratives did not explicitly acknowledge that privilege worked in such a way.

As such, the "lack of consequences" for the privileged created a naive assumption that situations would work out or eventually get better. There was an inherent optimism that nothing was too horrendous to overcome, and the high jinks would eventually be forgiven, forgotten, or otherwise left in the past. Throughout, consumer culture was lionized as a way to overcome obstacles and improve one's situation and life. More broadly, this reasoning rested on privilege and capital: having the money to buy clothing or beauty services, knowing someone who could help in the transformation, learning how to properly transform for the better, and having a culturally approved body were keys to success.

Overall, these themes promoted a particular "vibe," that is, a cultural affect reverberating through society that changes styles, activities, and modes of consumption. A term often used colloquially but gaining academic traction, "a vibe is the sympathetic resonance between a multiply-situated . . . subject and their social and material milieu," according to philosopher Robin James.[26] Essentially, vibes pull together disparate elements—geography, temporal conditions, political happenings, and material culture—to shape or "orient" people in particular ways. Vibes become most noticeable in hindsight when new consumption patterns have been adopted and a different cultural affect reigns.[27]

Toward this end, vibes share some commonality with the idea of a zeitgeist, usually defined as "the spirit of the times."[28] Both terms try to define something not quite tangible but that impacts everything around us, including how we understand ourselves, our positions within society and the world, and the opportunities available to us. For example, the clothing produced and how it is advertised to us today represents how we understand ourselves and what we can do. In this sense, aspirational marketing and branding are useless if we do not believe we can better ourselves and raise our social status.

That said, it is probably an overstatement to say that a vibe or a zeitgeist ever encompassed all of culture. The concept of a monoculture—the belief that nearly everyone within a society consumes the same products, engages in the same practices, and shares the same worldview—is one of cultural domination that exalted practices of particular groups over others. And today, targeted advertising, social media algorithms, and niche products have all but assured us that if there ever was a monoculture, it is long gone.[29] However, that does not mean there aren't overriding trends in pop culture that we may or may not be part of. The extent to which we can orient ourselves toward dominant cultural trends can help or hinder our specific goals.[30] This orientation is a form of social power that generally works to keep people in line, but it also gives people a dominant culture to "rebel" against.

For example, throughout this project, I show that the dominant teen cultural affect of privileged frivolity expressed itself through a specific aesthetic and belief system. Broadly, the bodily aesthetic of privileged frivolity involved a "natural" appearance that prioritized thinness, whiteness, and youth. Fashionable clothing took on a relaxed prep style (polos, button-downs, jeans) and beach look (camisoles, T-shirts, flip-flops). The appearance seemed jocular and fun-loving rather than serious or stressful; of course, those who easily fit the aesthetic—white, athletic teens who could physically fit into the look and pay for such clothing—had less to stress about than others who were excluded physically or financially from this space. Such teens—often seen in sun-kissed advertisements and various teen hangouts—prioritized appearance and consumption.

Even so, how we learn about these ideals is partially, if not mostly, attributed to the media. Certainly, there is a lived component—through the people we see and interact with—but the media plays an outsize role in shaping our cultural values, including idealized body types and desirable consumption patterns. The media's input is exceptionally robust for goods and notions we do not interact with in our everyday lives: knowing about a place through the media is different than living there, and "knowing" celebrities through their media appearances does not mean we actually know their personalities. While some forms of media attempt to be objective in their presentation of reality, fictional forms like movies, television shows, and advertisements often take creative license to create a more idyllic world. Advertising and branding, especially, push aspiration over reality.[31] Yet, while there is a difference between the messages created by advertisers and brands and those created by films, television shows, and other media forms, one is not necessarily "better," more poignant, or more impactful than others. In fact, what I contend throughout this book is that repetition is more important than the message itself, and when the messages align with or reflect one another, they become more impactful. During the time in question, advertisements, films, television shows, music videos, and even some news accounts aligned in their presentation, thereby ingraining the vibe of privileged frivolity into the cultural milieu. Through repetition, the portrayed ideals seemed actualizable, impacting how an audience understood the world.

It is also important to note that while the vibe of privileged frivolity was the most pronounced and dominant theme of the time, it was not the only aesthetic with overlapping intertextual elements. There were also segments of popular culture that targeted Black femininity, embodied by singers like Brandy, TLC, and Destiny's Child, as well as versions of hip-hop masculinity from Diddy's baller aesthetic to LL Cool J, FUBU, and street style. A thorough analysis of either of these threads could fill—and deserves—its own volume. Yet, what comes through in teen-centered media is that the imagined teen is largely (although not exclusively) straight, wealthy, and white. It would take until *Drumline* and

Love Don't Cost a Thing in 2002 and 2003, both starring Nick Cannon, to get teen fare that centered characters of color and into the late 2010s for teen films that revolved around gay characters.

This Book

Following in the footsteps of others who have been reevaluating the 1990s and early 2000s, this book does so by paying particular attention to the images and themes constructed and repeated throughout the teen pop culture landscape. My starting premise is that all consumable texts transmit cultural ideas to the teens of the era—regardless of artistic merit or other classification or discernment. Researchers have long known that the media passes on our cultural values, and the popular culture texts geared toward teens in the late 1990s and early 2000s are no exception.[32] From there, I make three interlinking arguments about the pop culture of the time and its lasting impact on US culture.

First, I argue that the interconnected and self-referential world of popular culture created the idea of privileged frivolity and sold elder millennials nebulous cultural narratives of what their lives could, and one day would, be if they purchased the right products and consumed the correct goods. This aspirational tale was best articulated in the brand constructs of Abercrombie & Fitch, as is explored in chapter 2, but it can be seen across the popular culture landscape.

Second, the resonance of privileged frivolity was only possible because consumer culture was in the midst of a postmodern upswing in which goods were purchased and used as much for their brand-constructed image and meaning as for their physical or use value.[33] These qualities involved tightly constructed identities and lifestyles that were largely fictional but influential nonetheless. Both academics and critics acknowledged that brand practices grew during this period, upending traditional consumerism and taking on increased prominence in education and other venues that had been shielded from capitalistic tendencies.

Finally, the promises that proper consumption would lead to success and the good life distracted from the economic and political realities at play. That is, until 2008, when the financial crisis undermined the irrational exuberance of the economy and the fragmented media landscape since then has made it nearly impossible to construct the same widespread culturally relevant images. Thanks to the neoliberal economic, social, and political forces that hindered social mobility, there is a stark disparity between what elder millennial teens were promised via the dominant and interconnecting narratives and what was delivered. I dig into this further in future chapters, but for a quick example, thanks to stagnant wages and wealth accumulation, millennials are poorer than previous generations and are unlikely to ever catch up.[34] And even traditional hallmarks of adulthood, like purchasing a home, are increasingly out of reach.[35]

To make these arguments, this project draws on a range of texts—advertisements, films, television shows, and music videos—chosen because they represent the dominant teen culture (frequently straight, white, affluent teen culture), including aspects of privileged frivolity, and their overlapping textual nature. Many of these texts share actors, narratives, settings, or other aesthetic qualities with other popular culture elements of the time. The selection is purposeful, but I believe it is wide-ranging enough to demonstrate the extent to which the ideas of privileged frivolity existed. Moreover, my analysis throughout is in the vein of cultural studies; therefore, my reading of these various texts may not be everyone's reading, and my position as a gay, white, working-class man who grew up during the period has undoubtedly influenced my analysis. For reference, I entered junior high in 1997—the same year the Backstreet Boys released their first US album—and graduated high school in 2003, the final year of Abercrombie & Fitch's iconic and divisive *A&F Quarterly*. For those a bit older than me, the 1990s might bring to mind grunge, *Reality Bites*, and the peak of Gen X. But many of us hit our prime with the boy bands, pop princesses, and *Total Request Live* mania in the closing years of the decade. Although others will have experienced these products from their own social positions and experiences, in each chapter, I attempt to provide as much detail and imagery as possible to support my readings, and I draw on the research and publications of others to underscore the differences between media presentation and reality.[36] I also share industry figures but want to underscore that my argument doesn't fully rest on the financial success (or failure) of particular objects; for example, a pop culture product like *Josie and the Pussycats* (discussed in chapter 6) was a theatrical flop and only later became a cult classic.

It is also worth noting that capturing the messages provided to a specific age cohort is a temporal undertaking, meaning that the "teens" of 1997 are not the teens of 2007 but rather the twentysomethings of 2007. As such, they officially aged out of many (although not all) teen products. To account for this change, the teen films, music, and shows specific to elder millennials (discussed in chapters 3 and 4) are focused on the late '90s and first years of the 2000s. Meanwhile, the college films (chapter 5) discussed range from 2000 through 2006, and the adult-aged films (chapter 8) range from 2002 through 2006. This selection of texts is more aligned with a cohort analysis rather than a generational or genre-specific analysis.

Throughout, the texts I examine could be seen as realistically attainable, meaning that I did not specifically engage with shows with supernatural elements like *Buffy the Vampire Slayer* or a rash of horror films released in this time frame (e.g., *Scream, I Know What You Did Last Summer, Final Destination*) that share textual elements. Additionally, I did not include texts mainly geared toward audiences other than teen/young adult elder millennials (e.g., *Titanic, Bridget Jones's Diary*). That's not to say these products do not fit into the mold—horror films of the time share many of the ideals of privileged frivolity—but they don't seem to be the best articulation for this project. Some of these may be referenced or discussed here through the work of others, but they are not my focus.

It is also important to reiterate that most texts I analyze in this book are white (if not intentionally supporting white supremacy) and heteronormative, meaning they center straight, white characters, stories, and perspectives. That is not to say all of the characters mentioned are straight and white, but these texts assume that acceptance into straight, white, and wealthy society was desirable and achievable. Relatedly, in retrospect, it seems that teen culture was implicitly white teen culture, while Black teens or queer teens were lumped into other market segments. Regardless, outside of chapter 2, where a discussion of the active discrimination at Abercrombie & Fitch places race front and center, this is a project about the promises of teen consumer culture that included the aspiration to fit into the dominant US culture. I do not intend to declare how people from different marginalized social positions understood these products or the overriding vibe of privilege frivolity; however, based on recent publications, it seems like at least some Black and Asian young people were attracted to these promises of consumer culture as well.[37]

That said, I would be remiss if I did not acknowledge that nearly all the media products are works of fiction and, as such, are allowed—if not intended—to be hyperbolic or aspirational with their messaging. I am not naive enough to think that films and other popular culture should, or even could, be wholly accurate portrayals of everyday life. Still, films and pop culture products act as conduits for cultural meaning and entice viewers into the world; even if, logically, we know what we're watching is unrealistic, it can still be aspirational. While it is nearly impossible to capture the cultural affect or feeling in the written word, and any attempt to reconstruct and interrogate a past affective moment will be underlined with some aspect of nostalgia, I am confident the array of texts analyzed here demonstrates how optimistic messages of hope and promise through consumption were constructed, ultimately crashing into the fierce economic headwinds.

Overarchingly, the messages promoted by popular culture created a dominant narrative and identity taught to *all* teens of the time. Again, that is not to say everyone *wanted* to be in the in-group or to adhere to the ideals of privileged frivolity, but thanks to these ideals' dominant presence in popular culture, people were, to a degree, forced to engage with them. For example, a teen could purchase products in an attempt to fit into the identity that popular culture encouraged, or teens could also *reject* the identity and choose to act contrarily.[38] Regardless, the narrative of identity and success through consumption provided a specific worldview for elder millennial teens. It shaped our views of the world, even if its premise is being increasingly questioned and questionable nearly two decades later.

To illustrate the extent of privileged frivolity, each chapter is centered at a particular moment, starting with the release of the first *A&F Quarterly* magalog in 1997. Acknowledging that cultural moments are messy and unable to be fully contained, each chapter represents a particular event or release but connects to other texts outside of a rigid linear sequence.[39] And while chapters are arranged chronologically, not all the popular culture products and texts are from that specific moment. This book is not a strict chronological history, but each chapter is positioned to advance my arguments.

The next chapter shows how Abercrombie & Fitch developed into a teen lifestyle brand. By reimagining a dated sporting goods store as a hip clothier, the company pushed a version of exclusionary whiteness to the forefront of culture. As a fashion brand, this marketing implicitly accepted the premise that consumers could buy into this exclusionary lifestyle—the same lifestyle shown across the pop culture landscape of the time. Chapter 3 shows how the themes of privileged frivolity were expanded on in teen films like *Cruel Intentions*, *10 Things I Hate about You*, and *She's All That*, which were influenced by the earlier success of *Clueless*. Of course, the idyllic lifestyle clashed with everyday teens' lived realities.

Chapter 4 explores the intertextual nature of popular culture at the time and how it helped create an all-encompassing media sphere that reinforced similar aesthetics and the themes of privileged frivolity. Starting with the music video for LFO's "Summer Girls," which referenced Abercrombie & Fitch, it is possible to see how songs acted as promotion, and in a world where musicians became actors, actors made cameos in music videos, and television shows featured teen retailers, everything felt interconnected. Chapter 5 then extends the ethos of privileged frivolity to college films—*The Skulls, Legally Blonde, Drumline, National*

Lampoon's Van Wilder, and *Accepted*—to show how even college became a consumer good. Perhaps even more insidiously, college was shown as a necessary consumption in order to have a "better life."

Chapter 6 demonstrates that while there were contemporaneous critiques of these messages, critiques more often reinforced the centrality of consumer culture because they ignored what made these messages powerful. Dissenters—ranging from the film *Josie and the Pussycats* to the brand-critical touchstone book *No Logo* by Naomi Klein and the television show *Daria*—missed that these products were meaningful to people; further, most forms of resistance were equally commodified, which would have supported this consumerism but looked somewhat different.

The remaining chapters examine how privileged frivolity continued as the eldest millennials grew into adulthood. Chapter 7 shows that privileged frivolity continued to be used in teen films after the September 11 attacks, albeit with a darker, more aggressive turn. And chapter 8 underscores how movies like *Sweet Home Alabama*, *The Devil Wears Prada*, and *Employee of the Month* continued to build unrealistic expectations of adult life for the eldest millennials as they entered the workforce.

The final chapter captures the end of *Total Request Live*, a cultural touchstone, and argues that its ending, along with the rise of *Twilight* and singers like Katy Perry, Lady Gaga, and Kesha, marked a turning point for teen culture that moved away from themes of popularity and conformity and toward themes of individuality and outsider status. Although this cultural transformation altered the media for later teens, the earlier messages still proved influential for elder millennials now into middle age. Specifically, the mismatch between what these formative texts promised and what was delivered in contemporary life (i.e., increasing economic instability and precarity and decreasing job prospects) has led to an overall disillusionment that reverberates to this day.

In closing, this is not a prescriptive book; thus, anyone reading for a guide to fix the current economic, political, and social challenges will likely be disappointed. Instead, this book reconsiders the past while thinking through the vibes of a particular period and how they continue to impact social life long after they have faded from public consciousness. While I imagine this book will most strongly resonate with elder millennials like me, I believe this project advances two broader implications. First, elder millennials were not the first age cohort impacted by pop culture in this way—though they may be the last, considering the current fragmentation of our media system. Pop culture's overlapping and intertextual nature was robust at the time, and vibes were impacted by geo-political, economic, and a host of other factors. I also imagine we could pinpoint vibes like Gen X cynicism and (potentially) zoomer pessimism across different eras of popular culture as well. Relatedly, it seems possible these vibes and products might be responsible for what are often considered generational differences; for example, both Gen Xers and zoomers seem to be bemused by millennials' reliance on media products as part of their ingrained personal identity. Second, this project is inherently a defense of taking "throwaway" pieces of popular culture seriously for what they affectively contribute to everyday life. It is imperative to consider that common products, which may act as background noise at first glance, have the same cultural impact as high-minded or most well-regarded works—if not more so.

TWO

BACK TO SCHOOL '97

UNDERSTANDING THE
ABERCROMBIE TEEN

Similar-looking white guys sitting on bikes holding lacrosse sticks.
A bunch of muscular guys posing in their boxers.
A bunch of shirtless guys celebrating with a football in hand.
A group of conventionally attractive white teens posing in a field.
Models posing naked in the ocean.
Models posing naked with a horse.
Models posing naked on boats.[1]

When Abercrombie & Fitch's magazine-catalog hybrid—a "magalog"—erupted onto the scene in fall 1997, it was just one of many in the marketplace. At the time, American homes were being inundated with nearly 100 catalogs a year, so retailers began adding magazine staples like lifestyle articles, photo spreads, and even advertisements for other products to cut through the clutter. It was not the first time magalogs were tried; Hermès sold ad space in its catalog as early as 1977, while brands like Lands' End and Williams Sonoma had been including editorial content for some time. Some, like Nordstrom, went as far as to collaborate with beauty magazine *Allure* and its offerings.[2]

Abercrombie & Fitch's *A&F Quarterly* (figure 2.1) sold "the Abercrombie lifestyle," according to then Abercrombie & Fitch CEO Mike Jeffries; its goal was to generate buzz and draw people into stores with a mix of risqué photography by Bruce Weber and articles that gave advice on stocking bars, reviewed craft beers, made travel suggestions, and more. By 2000, *A&F Quarterly* had become a "youth manual," in the words of *Time*'s Stacy Perman, that helped sell the brand's "technicolor teen lifestyle" to young shoppers.[3] *A&F Quarterly* went hand in hand with Abercrombie & Fitch's experiential retailing (i.e., the look and feel of the store), which turned ordinary prep clothing like polos, button-downs, and flip-flops into much more.[4]

Although Abercrombie & Fitch had a long history as a retailer before its turn toward teen clothing, it was able to repurpose its highfalutin luxury through

Figure 2.1. Judge *A&F Quarterly* by Its Covers: A sample of *A&F Quarterly* covers. *Clockwise from top left*: *Seeking Serious Fun* (Summer 1998), *Summer Dreams* (Summer 1999), *XXX* (Spring Break 2001), and *The Brightest* (Back to School 2001).

A&F Quarterly and a highly orchestrated shopping experience that included employees hired for their looks. And teens of the 1990s—still creatures of mall culture—ate it up, so much so that "Abercrombie" entered the teen lexicon as an adjective and shorthand for "popular." This popularity brought with it a darker side: one of active exclusion and outright discrimination that would get Abercrombie & Fitch sued multiple times. Nonetheless, the brand and the Abercrombie lifestyle it was selling, along with its jeans and flip-flops, continued until the mid-2010s. This chapter explores the parameters of Abercrombie & Fitch's branding to argue that it was the best encapsulation of the tenets of privileged frivolity and that it did not exist in a bubble. As we'll see in future chapters, Abercrombie & Fitch's aesthetics and messages seemed to resonate throughout the pop culture landscape, including in films, television shows, and music videos.

The Roots of Abercrombie & Fitch

Abercrombie & Fitch traces its roots to 1892 when David T. Abercrombie opened a store dedicated to outdoor sports like camping, fishing, and hunting on South Street in New York City. Joined by frequent customer Ezra T. Fitch in 1904, the "Abercrombie & Fitch" name was born. The partnership ended in 1912 when Abercrombie left the company, turning control over to Fitch. Eventually, the store settled at the intersection of Madison Avenue and Forty-Fifth Street in Manhattan, where it covered twelve floors and launched a catalog of its sought-after merchandise. Fitch stayed with the company through 1928, the same year the store merged with another New York sporting goods store and purchased a stake in a Chicago firm. Reportedly, Abercrombie & Fitch outfitted Teddy Roosevelt for safari and Adm. Richard E. Byrd for a trip to Antarctica. It sold equipment to a range of notable figures, including presidents William Howard Taft, Warren G. Harding, Herbert Hoover, and Dwight Eisenhower, Supreme Court chief justice Earl Warren, pilots Charles Lindbergh and Amelia Earhart, writer Ernest Hemingway, and Jordan's King Hussein.[5]

Through its first incarnation, Abercrombie & Fitch became a cultural reference point for its luxe atmosphere. For example, in 1929, the store helped promote a polo game between Yale and Princeton—with an accompanying gala—and in 1938, it was one of the stores chosen to demonstrate a working television. By 1956, the *New York Times* wrote that F. R. Tripler and Co., a men's clothing store, "can hold its head up in such illustrious company as Brooks Brothers and Abercrombie & Fitch." Store products appeared in *New York Times* fashion stories, and the paper even covered the opening of the company's "niche" women's department. Still, the brand remained geared toward the adult sportsperson. "We aren't out for teenage business," company president Earle Angstadt Jr. said in 1965. "Our customers are on the go and have the time and the money to enjoy travel and sport."[6]

As a sporting goods retailer, Abercrombie & Fitch expanded to nine stores—in New York City; Chicago; San Francisco; Colorado Springs; Short Hills, New Jersey; Oak Brook, Illinois; Palm Beach and Bal Harbour, Florida; and Troy, Michigan—and its sales would peak at $28 million in 1968 before sustaining consecutive annual loses between 1970 and 1975. Abercrombie & Fitch filed for bankruptcy and ended its catalog in 1976 but refocused itself on luxury sporting goods, including shooting guns, which sold for $6,500 and $7,500.

"See for yourself why there's no other store like us," an Abercrombie ad offered, according to the Associated Press. "You might say we're more than a store, we're a lifestyle."

Yet such advertising did not help save the retailer. Nor did changing its merchandise, which was dubbed "a vain effort to revive its fading image" by the *New York Times*'s Isadore Barmash. Abercrombie & Fitch would ultimately liquidate in 1977.[7]

The original chain was undercut by expanding competitors and discount and department stores' decision to start selling sporting goods. Another sporting goods chain, Houston-based Oshman's Sporting Goods, bought the Abercrombie & Fitch trademark and its customer information in 1978 for $1.5 million. Oshman's revived Abercrombie & Fitch with a store in Beverly Hills, California, and restarted Abercrombie's mail-order business in 1979; a second store opened in Dallas in 1980. The acquisition was intended to help the Oshman's chain move into the luxury arena and expand geographically. Even though Oshman's only purchased the Abercrombie & Fitch name and list of customers, it kept some aspects of the past; the relaunched catalog reportedly sold "three Abercrombie classics: a tartan plaid shirt made of a blend of Viyella cotton and wool, the Flattie Shoe, which sold 6,000 in the last Abercrombie catalog, more than any other item, and the Lifflesdale, the Scottish-made fisherman's bag."[8]

The revived Abercrombie & Fitch was "brought up to date in the style of the 1980s," according to its president Jerry L. Nanna in 1982. By then, the store had moved into the New York City suburbs and was looking to reopen near South Street and in a flagship location in Midtown Manhattan. When Nanna resigned as president in 1983 after disagreements with Oshman's leaders, Abercrombie &

Fitch had thirteen stores, with two more planned. In 1984, the brand returned to New York City with a 17,000-square-foot store at the South Street Seaport. Throughout, the brand's storied heritage would stay with it; a *New York Times* story about the revived store ran under the headline "New Stores with Old Reputations" and noted that when the original retailer closed its doors, it "signaled that an era had come to an end." The ending era, the article suggested, was one of masculine-dominated gentry and leisure.[9]

The revived Abercrombie & Fitch continued to offer sport-related goods, including stuffed animals (not the type for children), boomerangs, weightlifting sets, and clothing like safari jackets and New Balance sneakers. Yet Abercrombie & Fitch retained its identity and cultural reference point as it continued to expand through the 1980s; a television writer noted, in a review of the miniseries *Dream West*, that actor Richard Chamberlain "seems to have stepped out of an Abercrombie & Fitch ad." (The miniseries depicted American adventurer John C. Fremont's 1830s trek in the Oregon Territory.) There were twenty-seven Abercrombie & Fitch stores when Oshman's first attempted to sell the chain to a group of investors in 1987 before calling off the deal and instead selling twenty-five of the stores to the Limited, a women's apparel firm, a few months later (and closing the other two). At the time of the sale, Abercrombie & Fitch had annual sales of $50 million. The Limited said it would evaluate the business but expected to jettison some of the sports equipment from its merchandise array, such as guns, which a company representative called "an infinitesimal" part of the business.[10]

The Limited initially named Sally Frame-Kasakas as president of Abercrombie & Fitch. A former president of women's clothing chain Talbots, Frame-Kasakas wanted to update the "classics" from the store "without losing any of its customer franchise." She sought upscale customers over thirty-five who were "fashion-oriented" and saw potential in men's and women's clothing and "gifts" like globes and telescopes. Frame-Kasakas departed for Ann Taylor in 1992, and Mike Jeffries, a retail veteran with experience working in department and specialty stores and running his own short-lived brand, became president and chief executive.[11]

By the time Jeffries took over, Abercrombie & Fitch was feeling dated. "We had old clothes that no one liked," Leslee O'Neill, vice president for planning and allocation, told *Salon* in 2006. "It was a mess, a total disaster."[12]

Reportedly, Jeffries referred to Abercrombie & Fitch's target demo at the time of his arrival as "60 (or 70) to death" and wanted to appeal instead to a younger demographic by selling faded jeans and T-shirts. Abercrombie & Fitch would become associated with the "casual luxury" of polos, sweatshirts, sweaters, flip-flops, and graphic tees with the right amount of wear. "Many of its clothes look like they've spent years in [a] washing machine, then a hamper," wrote journalist Benoit Denizet-Lewis.[13]

Jeffries's idea was to make the brand "sizzle with sex," getting photographer Bruce Weber—already known for his nude photography for Calvin Klein—to shoot the company's in-store and catalog advertisements. The strategy paid off handsomely: there were thirty-five stores when Jeffries arrived in 1992 and 230 by the end of the decade, while sales jumped from $148.5 million in 1994 to $1.06 billion in 1999. The Limited spun off the Abercrombie & Fitch brand in 1998, setting the stage for its continued growth.[14]

The Abercrombie Teen Lifestyle

When Abercrombie & Fitch turned its attention to teenagers, it did so with relatively insipid clothing and tapped into an Ivy League or other "prep" style. The offerings included basics like jeans, corduroys, khakis, button-downs, and sweaters for colder times (figure 2.2); T-shirts, cargo and board shorts, flip-flops, tank tops, camisoles (for girls), and swimsuits for warmer months; and undergarments. Yet the company couldn't be mistaken for stuffier prep brands given the intentional distress of Abercrombie's gear, including "torn jeans."[15] As such, while the clothing channeled the looks at prep schools and old-school Ivy League college campuses, it did so with a youthful irreverence. Much of the clothing was not meant to look brand new or like the wearer cared too much. On one hand, Abercrombie & Fitch's clothing can be seen as a preppy take on the grunge stylings of the early 1990s. At the same time, the wear and tear speaks to the privilege involved: Abercrombie teens were not trying too hard to fit in, be cool, or take care of their clothing. They could wear something that might be wrinkled, ripped, or in not-pristine condition but had the money, background, connections, or other capital that it either did not matter or could even enhance their status.

Nevertheless, like at many fashion brands, the clothing itself was somewhat less important than the images and meaning constructed through Abercrombie & Fitch's advertising and bestowed on the garments.[16] To this end, Jeffries leaned into the experiential branding aspects of retail to turn Abercrombie & Fitch around.

"You buy into the emotional experience of a movie," Jeffries told *Time* in 2000. "And that's what we're creating. Here I am walking into a movie, and I say, 'What's going to be [at] the box office today?'"[17]

Figure 2.2. Classic Abercrombie: A photo spread from *A&F Quarterly: On the Road* (Back to School 1998) shows a range of models dressed in Abercrombie & Fitch clothing, underscoring its classic prep style.

For Jeffries, what seemed to be at the box office was sex and popularity, coded as rich-kid whiteness. In-store advertising often featured posters of shirtless, "young, White-looking" men, whose "chests remain eternally hairless, their faces blemish- and beard-free, and their abdomens muscular."[18] Abercrombie became synonymous with an idyllic teen American fantasy that squarely targeted the "cool" kids. Jeffries "resuscitated a 1990s version of a 1950s ideal" but did so with "smooth, gym-toned bodies and perfectly coifed hair," according to Denizet-Lewis. The ideal male body, as seen through the lens of Abercrombie & Fitch, was hairless with a chiseled physique popularized and forever tied to a playful adolescence better associated with high school and college.[19]

Abercrombie & Fitch became known for its constructed in-store "experience," which included a club-like atmosphere complete with dimly lit interiors, loud dance music, and heavy use of the brand's signature fragrance. "Part of Mike's genius was in pioneering the most dramatic retail theater in the business," Craig Brommers, then head of marketing at Abercrombie & Fitch, told *New York* magazine in 2014.[20] Jeffries intricately constructed Abercrombie's home office, flagship stores, and smaller, mall-based stores; under Jeffries, Abercrombie & Fitch maintained a strict "looks" policy for employees, requiring workers to play the part of an Abercrombie teen with an array of personal adornment prescriptions including specific hairstyles, limited piercings, and only "natural"-looking nail polish and makeup.[21]

Working at Abercrombie was a "status thing," according to then director of stores David Leino in 1999; employees weren't there "to fold clothes or to make money." Instead, the "models," as the company called them, were there to be eye candy for others.[22]

"That's why we hire good-looking people in our stores," Jeffries explained in 2006. "Because good-looking people attract other good-looking people, and we want to market to cool, good-looking people."

And it worked. Years earlier, a teenager had told *Fortune* of Abercrombie's in-store models, "When I saw those guys out there, my jaw just dropped." To some extent, store employees always come to embody a brand, but Abercrombie went above and beyond, choosing only employees with the "requisite looks" to portray the Abercrombie ideal. These practices would also get Abercrombie & Fitch sued multiple times for discrimination.[23]

"Candidly, we go after the cool kids. We go after the attractive all-American kid with a great attitude and a lot of friends," said Jeffries. "A lot of people don't belong [in our clothes], and they can't belong. Are we exclusionary? Absolutely."[24]

To belabor the point, Abercrombie & Fitch under Jeffries was exclusionary; not only did he say as much, but other writers and even the Supreme Court of the United States agreed. Yet Abercrombie & Fitch had long been exclusionary. The expensive sporting goods sold in its first incarnation simply gave Jeffries and brand managers material to harken back to and reuse; luxury is, by its nature, exclusionary.

Literary scholar Dwight A. McBride noted that Abercrombie & Fitch promoted a particular type of white Anglo-Saxon Protestant (WASP) aesthetic that was inherently racist and exclusionary, a point underscored in the documentary *White Hot: The Rise and Fall of Abercrombie & Fitch*.[25] Of course, this might have been expected when the company drew on a brand that outfitted wealthy and well-known Americans for safaris and other adventures. The fact that Abercrombie & Fitch discriminated in hiring and sold T-shirts that mocked nonnative English speakers of Asian descent seems to come with the territory. It's also notable that writers suggested that Jeffries and Abercrombie were reimagining the 1950s beefcake, a decade before the civil rights movement when segregation was legal and Jim Crow laws were still in effect.[26]

Abercrombie & Fitch also believed there was a group mentality and a desire to fit in with the teens the brand targeted. "These young people want to be with one another," Jeffries told *Fortune*. "That is totally different. My generation grew up as loners." Left unsaid is *who* gets to be popular. In Abercrombie & Fitch's telling, popularity was for the thin, athletic, and privileged—those who fit into the white ideals of attractiveness.[27]

Making Sense of *A&F Quarterly*

As journalists and academics have noted, *A&F Quarterly* provided an important articulation of the Abercrombie lifestyle.[28] The magalog was spearheaded by Savas Abadsidis, an intern who became the publication's editor in chief at twenty-three, after he realized that most of the ideas being floated for *A&F Quarterly* were from an adult perspective on youth—rather than from the viewpoint of its target demographic of college students. The company gave Abadsidis and two friends wide latitude and budget to put the magazine together, and the team wanted to hew as closely to the "idealized college experience as possible."[29]

While writers and critics frequently noted and took issue with the risqué content in the magalog, its mix of advertisements, pop culture reviews, and even some philosophy managed to create a multidimensional lifestyle.[30] Stephen M. Engel argued it was a "postmodern aesthetic," whereby *A&F Quarterly* sold more of an image than an actual product. Engel's argument rests on the fact that although the brand was selling clothing, its advertising created a perceived authenticity through the photography and service journalism articles that pulled various outside products and places into the "Abercrombie lifestyle." As Engel wrote:

> Through the *Quarterly*, Abercrombie & Fitch has managed to appropriate explicitly commodities it does not manufacture into its lifestyle realm. Certain books, CDs, films and even sport activities are considered indicative of the A&F lifestyle. Abercrombie does not have to trouble itself with the production of a specifically Abercrombie-labeled version of everyday items; it absorbs those already circulating in the market and makes them its own. The process is more than anything Ralph Lauren [an originator of the lifestyle brand] has achieved precisely because it is more flexible and therefore capable of absorbing a broader array of commodities and activities, i.e., books, films, albums and video games.[31]

By mediating an array of popular culture products, the Abercrombie & Fitch lifestyle helped promote—and benefit from—other items in pop culture circulation.

Although Engel suggested that items that fit into the Abercrombie lifestyle were "infinitely expansive," looking back at the period, it seems like there were particular pieces of popular culture that became tied to the lifestyle through repetition or imitation. Essentially, not everything was pulled into the Abercrombie fold, but certainly a lot of people, places, and things were. As shown in the following section, *A&F Quarterly* played with privileged ideas throughout its issues while also signaling who did and didn't belong in the lifestyle.

For those who did not live through *A&F Quarterly*'s heyday, here are a few things to keep in mind. The magalog was published between 1997 and 2003, and its quarterly releases coincided (more or less) with the beats of the academic year: in place of traditional seasons, issues were published for back to school, Christmas, spring break, and summer. The magalog featured Abercrombie & Fitch clothing and order forms, of course, and Bruce Weber's photographs, which often included teens in various stages of playful undress, as well as travel tips, celebrity interviews, and even a satirical advice column. Although the magalog (and brand overall) ostensibly targeted college students, there was a pervading moralistic concern that high schoolers might get their hands on the magazine and that the mixture of nudity and editorial themes might be too adult for them. The articles did push the envelope: the Back to School 1998 issue included cocktail recipes and a spinner to create a drinking game; the Back to School 2000 issue offered advice for visiting strip clubs; and infamously, the Christmas 2003 issue discussed group sex and featured an interview with sex educator Sari Locker in which she didn't discourage performing oral sex in public.[32]

Meet Bryan Emerson, Abercrombie Teen

Although the magalog's articles construct the idealized Abercrombie teen in a few different ways, perhaps the best articulation of this lifestyle can be found in the Christmas 2000 issue, *A Very Emerson Christmas* (figure 2.3). The issue is designed as fictional teenager Bryan Emerson's scrapbook, which features the weddings of two of his siblings and "a family-and-friend reunion of sorts and a special day of gift giving," before the Emersons and their friends "go their separate ways and redefine what it means to be a family." Bryan and his siblings—Charles, Whitney, Adam, and Michael—are shown on the cover of the magalog decorating their house in Hamilton, Massachusetts. They are all blond, white, and conventionally attractive; their home is a white, two-story colonial house.

The issue's introduction reimagines "A Visit from St. Nicholas" to introduce

Figure 2.3. *A Very Emerson Christmas*: The Christmas 2000 issue of *A&F Quarterly* was made to look like a photo album depicting the fictional Emerson family's Christmas.

the Emersons and their friends. Readers learn that the "old Lake Sedebego gang," including the siblings and many friends, are home from college. Some have returned from the West Coast or Europe, and even the Emersons' "jet-setting" friend made his way home. Two friends haven't left their hometown, although we learn that another, who's returned from parts unknown, is "raising hell as usual." The poem tells readers that the gang got back into the "swing of things," which included "late nights down at the old Adam's Apple on Montgomery Street, bonfire beach parties at Acadia, boogie down nights at our place with Mom working the taps and chatting everybody up, while Dad stumbled around with his big beer-soaked grin, mucking it up like he was still one of the boys."[33]

On an economic level, we can tell this group of friends is likely middle class to wealthy, since they are attending colleges all across the country—at places like Wellesley or the fictional Academy of Arts in New York and San Francisco Arts Institute—and are in Europe or otherwise "jet-setting," all activities poorer adults wouldn't be able to partake in.[34] Throughout the issue, we learn more about the Emersons and their friends' social background, which is shown to be privileged, as the group engages in seemingly monied activities, like a beachside clambake, horseback riding, and polo. Meanwhile, one of the Emerson children—seemingly Adam—receives a Jeep Wrangler for Christmas in one of the photo spreads.[35]

Diversity of any type is somewhat hard to come by. We find out that B. D. Stanton, one of the two friends who "never left," runs "his own appliance repair shop out of an old ice cream parlor," which speaks to a blue-collar or working-class status. And the only two people of color in the scrapbook are friends Marley Wright and Otis Jefferies; Marley makes three appearances in the 280-plus-page issue, while Otis makes only one. Interestingly, there are not one but two weddings among the Emerson children during this Christmas break: Charles and his new wife, Faith, are married by a priest, and Whitney and her wife, Beth, are wedded by a rabbi. Given the limited attention paid to class, race, and sexuality, all of these instances seem tokenized, and, even if not purely tokenized, they all fit into the Abercrombie ideals of slim or fit, natural looking, and conventionally or "naturally" attractive.

Finally, if the WASP heritage was not on display enough in the Emerson family, there is a three-page spread about Jonas Raleigh, a professional polo player and Whitney's high school love interest and direct descendant of Sir Walter Raleigh. Readers are told that Sir Raleigh was "a classic playboy . . . reputed philanderer and wild wonder with the women" and that "Jonas was definitely a chip off the old block."[36]

Boundary Pushing in *A&F Quarterly*

Through Bryan Emerson's fictional scrapbook, *A&F Quarterly* helps set boundaries about who fits into the Abercrombie identity, and it also manages to push boundaries of acceptability. The lack of representation is perhaps the most apparent boundary established; most pictures are of conventionally attractive, fair-skinned white people (figure 2.4). As noted above, there is limited representation of people of color. While B. D. Stanton can be understood as working class, he still looks like the Emersons and their better-off friends. Even Whitney's sexuality is barely mentioned until the wedding photograph, which is more than three-quarters of the way through the magalog and is accompanied by an image of an RSVP card with the options "Yes! I'd love to see two women get married!," "No . . . I'm liberal, but not that liberal," and "Sorry . . . I know I am missing the party of the year, but I can't make it." Perhaps a reflection of the time, but even the symbolic inclusion of a lesbian couple is treated as potentially divisive.

Two recurring *A&F Quarterly* features—Ask A&F (in *A Very Emerson Christmas*, it's Ask Santa) and Where the Wild Things Are—appear in this issue that also serve to police boundaries about who fits into the Abercrombie lifestyle. The advice column is satirical and frequently makes fun of people who wouldn't belong. For example, in the Ask Santa column, "Melissa from Muncie, Indiana," writes, "I recently told my boyfriend that we had to get married by the time we're 22, and he has to promise to have at least three kids and two houses, or I won't sleep with him. I'm still waiting for him to respond. What should I expect?"[37] Santa responds, "A studio apartment and a lot of cats." The joke is that the demanding Melissa won't find love through her current method, and if she doesn't loosen up, she will be alone forever.

While that might have been good advice, responses to "Todd from Burlington, Vermont," and "Amy from Missouri" are more direct. Todd decides he is going to bake cookies rather than purchase gifts for Christmas, and Santa tells him that it's possible his mom "would be happy with a bag of your broken, overcooked oatmeal raisins. Then again, she might think you a cheap piece of crap. Why take the chance?" Meanwhile, Amy notes that the son of her aunt's boyfriend is hot, and she wants to know if it's okay to date him. Santa responds, "I think you're in the clear on this one, unless your aunt and her boyfriend get married. Then you'd be dating your cousin. And that's bad. Although you *are* from Missouri . . ." Taken together, this advice signals who fits into the Abercrombie lifestyle. You can't be overly demanding or too driven by marriage and children (such as Melissa); you

Figure 2.4. (*Above and facing*) Scenes from an Abercrombie Magalog: Photo spreads in *A&F Quarterly: A Very Emerson Christmas* (Christmas 2000) show how white and WASPy the magalog was.

The Quarry Clan
at Halibut Point Quarry
December 21, 2000

need to buy things, or else people will think less of you (e.g., Todd); and people from less cosmopolitan places are implied to be incestuous.[38]

Comparatively, Where the Wild Things Are is explicit about who does not fit into the Abercrombie lifestyle (figure 2.5). This issue's installment asks, "Why does the local mall become such a daunting place between Thanksgiving and New Year's? Because the freaks come out." Among the four "holiday shopper" types to watch out for are "Mall Santa," "Bargain Shopper," "Harried Parent," and "Ruthless Shopper." Each is depicted in caricature and described in the tone

Figure 2.5. Wild Things: The Where the Wild Things Are feature in each *A&F Quarterly* issue often featured stereotypes of annoying or "uncool" people one might run into. This installment is from *A&F Quarterly: A Very Emerson Christmas* (Christmas 2000).

of a nature field guide, including each individual's habitat, identifying characteristics, habits, occupations, and even "similar species."

The descriptions take on exclusionary tones. The Bargain Shopper, who is shown as an old woman and is said to generally work as a "librarian" or "civil service worker," is described as someone who "avoids the food court by brown-bagging her own lunch" and "spends free time sucking up your tax dollars with Medicare and Social Security payments." Meanwhile, the Ruthless Shopper only shops on Christmas Eve and "rushes through stores in a consumer frenzy, ripping presents off shelves and out of children's hands"; he also stole "a parking space from a paraplegic widow." The contempt for these various identities is apparent, with the underlying message "Don't be them."[39]

These two features appear in every issue of *A&F Quarterly*, though the above instances were holiday themed. *A Very Emerson Christmas* had fewer journalistic articles, focusing instead on celebrity interviews and reviews. Other issues offered more in the way of travel tips and the like, which helped give Abercrombie a specific set of class connotations. The Summer 2000 issue offered travel stories from

Figure 2.8. Abercrombie's Big Guys: The "Big Guy Contest" photo spread from *A&F Quarterly: Wild and Willing* showed conventionally attractive, good-looking teens enjoying the beach, but almost no one was a person of color.

Figure 2.9. Front and Center: In a photo spread from *A&F Quarterly: About Love . . .* (Spring Break 2002), six white models play music in front of an all-Black gospel choir.

Figure 2.10. Abercrombie's on a Boat: This photospread from *A&F Quarterly*'s Summer 2001 issue shows three white teens sailing with an all-white boat crew.

Abercrombie, through its strategy of marketing "the good white life" in what is already a deeply racist society, has convinced a U.S. public—white (some young, some not so young), some people of color and gay men—that if we buy their label, we are really buying membership into a privileged fraternity that has eluded us all for so long, even if for such vastly different reasons. In order for such a marketing strategy to work, in all of the diverse ways that this one clearly does, the consumer must necessarily bring to his or her understanding of A&F, and what association with the brand offers him or her, a fundamentally racist belief that this lifestyle—this young, white, natural, all-American, upper-class lifestyle—being offered by the label is what we all either are, aspire to be or are hopelessly alienated from ever being.[42]

Although I broadly agree with McBride's assessment of the situation—including that people were taught to desire this aesthetic that is so closely linked to whiteness—we must remember that consumer decisions are complicated and can be impacted by many factors. For example, Phil Yu, of the blog *Angry Asian Man*, wrote that when Abercrombie & Fitch released a line of T-shirts seemingly poking fun at Asian Americans, emblazoned with slogans and logos for fictional establishments (e.g., Wong Brothers Laundry: TWO WONGS CAN MAKE IT WHITE; or Pizza Dojo: EAT IN OR WOK OUT and YOU LOVE LONG TIME), he was skeptical Asian American college students would care, but the ferocity of the backlash surprised him. "These shirts hit a nerve," he wrote.

> On the other hand, it made sense. Abercrombie & Fitch's core demographic was college youth. . . . At my midwestern college, where Greek life was a prominent part of the social scene, Abercrombie felt like part of the starter kit. Throw on a North Face jacket and a pair of New Balance and you had the standard uniform. For some Asian American college students, the Asian-themed shirts probably felt like a betrayal and a wake-up call. Abercrombie might have wanted young people to buy and wear their clothes, but they wanted the right kind of young people, if their catalogs weren't already a dead giveaway. Pretty young white people running through a field. Pretty young white people sitting on a fence. Pretty young white people kicking back in a giant tractor tire. Not you, Asians.[43]

As *Washington Post* columnist Robin Givhan offers in *White Hot*, "The story of Abercrombie is essentially an incredible indictment of where our culture was. . . .

It was a culture that enthusiastically embraced a nearly all sort of WASPy vision of the world. It was a culture that defined beauty as thin and white and young, and it was a culture that was very happy to exclude people."

At the end of the day, brands cannot be wholly created through marketing materials, and they draw on other cultural meanings and products. The success of Abercrombie & Fitch cannot simply be attributed to Jeffries's (begrudgingly) shrewd marketing or Abadsidis's controversial magalog; instead, as Givhan noted, it played into the broader popular culture as well. In the case of Abercrombie & Fitch, this helped give meaning to a particular white aesthetic through basic apparel items like jeans, flip-flops, T-shirts, polos, and camisoles.

Conclusion

Even though Abercrombie & Fitch discontinued *A&F Quarterly* after its Christmas 2003 issue, the brand's sexualized images, half-naked models, and heavily scented stores were already ingrained in the American cultural milieu. Ultimately, brand sales would peak twice: first in 2007 at roughly $3.7 billion before sliding and then again in 2012 with just over $4.5 billion in sales.[44] The company's numbers, however, obscure the impact of the solo Abercrombie & Fitch brand, as they include the firm's other brands (Hollister, Abercrombie Kids, and Gilly Hicks). There were 362 Abercrombie & Fitch stores in November 2007, but that number dropped to 280 by January 2012 and slid to 250 in January 2015. After that, company financials combined Abercrombie & Fitch and Abercrombie Kids numbers in filings, obscuring when the brand bottomed out.[45] Jeffries departed the company in December 2014 amid the company's continued financial struggles.[46]

Yet, as Givhan noted, brands do not grow in a vacuum, and Abercrombie & Fitch's particular exclusionary branding could only work as long as teen popular culture was on the same page. As we'll see in the following chapters, teen films and television also reflected the primarily white consumer ethos of privileged frivolity that made Abercrombie & Fitch's branding possible; essentially, teens were told that as long as they were young, privileged, and good looking, they could do no wrong. And, just as important, teens could buy their way into that privilege.

THREE SPRING BREAK '99

CRUEL INTENTIONS
AND THE MILLENNIUM
HIGH SCHOOL FILM

The rivalry between stepsiblings Kathryn (Sarah Michelle Gellar) and Sebastian (Ryan Phillippe) reaches new heights in the exposition of *Cruel Intentions*. After reading the *Seventeen* magazine article "Why I Plan to Wait," announcing the public virginity pledge taken by Annette Hargrove (Reese Witherspoon), the daughter of their new headmaster, Sebastian announces his intent to seduce Annette, whom he calls "a paradigm of chastity and virtue." An incredulous Kathryn tells him Annette is out of his league, and Sebastian retorts by asking if she wants to wager on it.

Kathryn tells him she'll think about it, then calls him back into the room shortly afterward to suggest terms for the bet. "If I win, then that hot little car of yours is mine," Kathryn says, referring to the 1956 Jaguar roadster convertible viewers just saw Sebastian drive home from his therapy session. And if he wins, Kathryn offers seductively, "I'll give you something you've been obsessing about ever since our parents got married."

"Be more specific," Sebastian demands.

"In English," Kathryn states matter-of-factly, as she is perched upon her bed, "I'll fuck your brains out."

Sebastian pushes back on why Kathryn thinks that would be a bet he'd willingly take, and she informs him, "Because I'm the only person you can't have, and it kills you."

After Sebastian rejects the bet, Kathryn lies back on the bed and purrs, "You can put it anywhere."

Making a facial expression showing his desire to "put it anywhere," Sebastian turns around with a smile and tells Kathryn, "You got yourself a bet, baby" (figure 3.1).

And thus the animating plot point of *Cruel Intentions* is set.

The film, an adaptation of the book *Dangerous Liaisons*, hit the big screen on March 5, 1999—amid what critic Brian Raftery has called "the Best Movie Year Ever."[1] It was just one of a series of teen movies at the time to reinterpret a classic work. After the success of *Clueless* in 1995, an update of Jane Austen's *Emma*, the next several years saw teen updates of *The Taming of the Shrew* (*10 Things I Hate about You*), *Pygmalion* (*She's All That*), *A Midsummer Night's Dream* (*Get Over It*), and *Othello* (*O*). Other teen fare at the turn of the millennium, like the movie *Drive Me Crazy*, riffed on the book *How I Created My Perfect Prom Date* by Todd Strasser, while the movies *American Pie, Varsity Blues, Bring It On*, and *Save the Last Dance* opted for new material but recycled much of the same tropes, discourse, and aesthetics.

Following media theorist Hilary Radner's assertion that "cinema is perhaps the most logical arena in which to analyze dominant trends in popular thought because feature-length films provide a dense articulation of the contemporaneous discursive formations," this chapter explores the teen films of the late 1990s and the earliest years of the 2000s to show that these movies repeat many of the same identities, storylines, anxieties, and aesthetics of the privileged teen found in other areas of popular culture.[2] In particular, this chapter argues that these themes started with *Clueless*, and the cycle of teen films that followed helped articulate the themes of privileged frivolity; through consumer culture and objectification, all things were possible, and regardless of teens' actions, everything would work out in the end. Implicitly or explicitly, the teens in these movies were primarily sheltered from more significant concerns and instead were focused on more garden-variety high school problems like friendship and romance. The freedom and possibility during one's high school years, as portrayed in pop culture, stands in contrast to the lived experience of teens, who were dealing with increasing restrictions, from the push for school uniforms to learning to live in a post-Columbine education system.

Teen Films at the Millennium

Overall, teen films have been well studied, and many discussions have tried to define *what* makes a teen film and how it can be categorized.[3] Such questions are not unique to teen films; genre remains a highly disputed organizing convention, with the general acknowledgment that such delineations and expectations are apt to change over time.[4] Because of these changes, what exactly constitutes a teen film—or any genre piece, for that matter—is up for debate.

Figure 3.1. Sex and *Seventeen*: In an opening scene of *Cruel Intentions*, Kathryn learns of the new head-master's daughter from an essay in *Seventeen* magazine, which prompts her to make a sexual bet with her stepbrother, Sebastian.

To avoid getting too bogged down in theoretical definitions, I am following media scholar Catherine Driscoll's discursive approach to teen films and examining the themes and messages therein rather than conducting more formal analyses of an entire genre. Likewise, I adhere to her demarcation of teen films as those intended "*for* adolescents" rather than featuring teenagers; I also abide by media scholar Valerie Wee's suggestion that teen media products have more to do with themes and messages contained within than with specific subject matter.[5] Under these parameters, not all films *about* people ages thirteen to nineteen are *for* that group. Likewise, films about characters older or younger (although generally older) can be intended for consumption by teens. Further, my goal here is not to catalog all of the teen films from the time or argue that they all supported themes of privileged frivolity—but to provide enough examples to show that the tenets were widespread.[6]

Scholars have traced teen films back to the 1920s and 1930s, yet interest in and production of them ebbs and flows over time; there have been peaks in teen cinema since the commercialization of films in the 1950s, and interest in teen films in the 1980s grew so much that the decade is considered a golden age.[7] Moreover, after the successful release of a genre film, a cycle may develop that "establishes the images, plot formulas, and themes" for successive films, thus making the first film something of a prototype, shaping future films in its image.[8]

While the John Hughes canon (e.g., *Sixteen Candles*, *Pretty in Pink*, and *The Breakfast Club*) came to define the teen films of the 1980s through shared actors, tropes, and aesthetics, this chapter explores how *Clueless* informed the teen films of the late 1990s and early 2000s.[9] While identity issues had been central to teen films for some time, the movies coming in the wake of *Clueless* often centered the popular cliques and told stories about "fitting in" through the proper means of consumption while also resting on a bed of privilege, which helped characters escape repercussions for poor behavior.[10]

Clueless's Privileged Frivolity

In *Clueless* (1995), we meet Cher Horowitz (Alicia Silverstone), a ditz with a heart of gold, who lives in the lap of luxury provided by her loving and hardworking lawyer father. The film follows Cher and her friend Dionne (Stacey Dash) as they play matchmaker; first they set up two teachers and then give new girl Tai (Brittany Murphy) a makeover and try to set her up with a popular guy rather than the stoner (Breckin Meyer) she's interested in. At the same time, the film shows Cher's personal tribulations in love as she tries to date Christian, who she realizes is gay, and ultimately falls in love with her college-aged, former stepbrother Josh (Paul Rudd), who's been helping Cher's dad prepare for a big case.

Yet the influence of *Clueless* comes less from the storyline and more from the accoutrements of Cher's lived lifestyle. As the movie begins, Cher tells the audience that she has a "way normal life for a teenage girl." However, Cher's life is really one of leisure and consumption and nearly devoid of consequences.

Cher's charmed life runs the entire length of the film. From the opening, Cher is assisted by her desktop computer to select the perfect outfit from her mechanized closet. And while this seems laughably naive in hindsight, it read as fanciful yet aspirational at the time.[11] Cher's house is large and impressive, with its grand staircase and a massive painting of Cher's deceased mother hanging in the foyer. We also see Cher's family wealth play out in her car (she has a new Jeep even though she doesn't have a license yet), her cell phone (the mere fact that she had one in 1995), and her ability to wear Alaïa (a high-end brand) to a high school party.

The assumption that consumerism directly impacts identity is developed throughout: during Tai's makeover, Cher gets her to replace flannel shirts with more traditionally feminine attire, and later Josh insults Cher's patronage of Contempo Casuals (a popular mall clothing store of the time). Other scenes make the entanglement of consumption and identity even more explicit. For example, when Dionne confronts her boyfriend Murray (Donald Faison) about cheating, it is because she found a "cheap Kmart hair extension" in his car. When Murray says it must be Dionne's, she hits him with it and says, "I do not wear polyester hair, okay? Unlike some people I know, like Shawanna." Later, when Cher is trying to figure out why Christian isn't interested in her, Murray tells her that Christian is a "disco-dancing, Oscar-Wilde-reading, Streisand-ticket-holding friend of Dorothy." (For those who might not be familiar with 1990s slang, this means he's gay.) In both cases, the film underscores that consumption and consumer habits speak directly to personal identity, whether by wearing a cheap hair extension (and thus being low class) or liking dance music and a host of specific artists (which implies his sexual orientation).

Additionally, much of the film purports that there are no consequences for actions, or at the very least, the repercussions are negligible. Consider the following examples.

First, early in the film, Cher is shown driving her new white Jeep Wrangler without having a license, taking out flowerpots and car mirrors in the process. Eventually, when her father receives a second notice of a parking ticket Cher accrued, he realizes she has been driving illegally and forbids her from driving without a licensed driver in the car. The damage to the Jeep is never discussed, *and* even when Cher isn't allowed to drive, she commandeers Josh to teach her.

Second, throughout, Cher is shown as a subpar student: she badly botches a speech on Haitian refugees and otherwise receives average (or worse) grades. Rather than accept the grades, Cher "negotiates," as she tells her father, getting various teachers to improve her grades by lying or otherwise garnering sympathy.

Third, when Cher attempts to convince Christian of her ability to be a homemaker by baking cookies, she doesn't cut the premade cookie dough and later forgets they are in the oven until the smoke detector goes off. But, fear not, the cookie dough is burnt and the kitchen is filled with smoke, but otherwise, nothing is bothered.

In fact, the film's main plot is predicated on the instances in which Cher has to deal with the repercussions of her actions. For example, Tai begins to eclipse Cher's popularity and wants to date Josh. When Cher rebuffs Tai's request to set them up, Tai mocks Cher as a "virgin who can't drive." Finally, after Cher tries to help her dad's legal team but sorts files incorrectly, she is verbally admonished by a lawyer. Josh steps in to defend Cher, and she realizes her true feelings for Josh . . . leading to the questionably incestuous ending everyone has come to know and love.

Clueless as a Pivotal Teen Film

The intermingling of privilege, consumer culture, and minimization of consequences present in *Clueless* defined many teen films in the following cycle, which conspicuously conspired to teach protagonists something "profound" about themselves. Aesthetically, *Clueless* maintained some of the look and feel of John Hughes films, such as by including pop songs like "Just a Girl" by No Doubt and "Supermodel" by Jill Sobule. *Clueless* also seems to have been playing into some of the teen television tropes of the time, like those of Aaron Spelling's *Beverly Hills, 90210*, and shares ideas with "chick flicks," or films that follow independent, single women learning they can be self-sufficient often through "consumerism and sexual practice."[12] Unlike that of the protagonists in films like *Pretty Woman* and *Legally Blonde* and TV shows like *Sex and the City*, Cher's romantic arc outshines her need to be self-sufficient; however, the movie also makes it clear that Cher is insulated from monetary concerns thanks to her father's wealth. Regardless of the particularities, *Clueless* imbued viewers with the idea that a makeover and shopping trip were the path to self-actualization, and en route, the movie reimagined teen films as interpretations of classic stories in the lives of pretty, privileged teens living in a consumer culture.

To see this in force, consider *10 Things I Hate about You* (1999), a millennial retelling of *The Taming of the Shrew*. The film revolves around outcast Kat (Julia Stiles), her popular younger sister, Bianca (Larisa Oleynik), and their overly restrictive father, who decrees that Bianca can date only when Kat does; the assumption is that Kat won't date anytime soon due to her stern, man-hating exterior. However, as both Joey (Andrew Keegan) and Cameron (Joseph Gordon-Levitt) pursue Bianca, each convinces Patrick (Heath Ledger) to take Kat out at various times. Throughout the film, we learn that Kat developed her standoffish persona as a defense mechanism after dating, sleeping with, and being dumped by Joey. These storylines come to a head at the prom, where Bianca shuns Joey for Cameron, leading an angry Joey to expose that he paid Patrick to bring Kat. After Kat's initial heartbreak, she later announces her love for Patrick during a class poetry assignment. By the film's end, Kat is accepted to and plans to attend Sarah Lawrence College with her father's blessing, and she reconciles with Patrick.

There are several commonalities between *Clueless* and *10 Things I Hate about You*. While Kat and Bianca are not portrayed as being as wealthy as Cher, their family is not hurting for money; their father is an obstetrician, money is never an object of discussion, and even during talk of Kat's upcoming college departure, her father's concern with Sarah Lawrence is the distance—not the price. Moreover, we find out the differences between Kat and Bianca are superficial, and even though Kat is standoffish, she assumed that persona after being naive (like Bianca) and getting hurt. While Kat doesn't have an explicit makeover, the implication is that she could quickly adopt Bianca's persona if she wanted; thus, the exterior is broadly shallow. Finally, there is a lack of consequences throughout. When Kat gets drunk at a party, Patrick takes care of her with little blowback besides embarrassment and a hangover. Later, Patrick commandeers the public address system to apologize to Kat, and when he gets detention, Kat flashes the teacher to get him out of it. Ultimately, the only character who pays for their actions is Joey, who, after hitting Cameron at prom, is punched several times by Bianca and humiliated because he was beaten up by a girl.

In another example, as mentioned at the start of the chapter, *Cruel Intentions* revolved around a bet between stepsiblings Kathryn and Sebastian, both students at a Manhattan prep school. For her part, Kathryn was playing host to Cecile (Selma Blair) while also planning to backstab her to get revenge on an ex. Sebastian, meanwhile, was interested in keeping his reputation as a womanizer. Throughout the film, Sebastian engages in a raft of inappropriate to (what would now be considered) illegal activities, including seducing, photographing, and posting naked photos of his psychiatrist's daughter online (played by Tara Reid); enlisting Blaine (Joshua Jackson) to help him blackmail Greg (Eric Mabius), a closeted gay student, to get his assistance in courting Annette; and lying to Cecile to get her drunk and pressuring her into allowing him to perform oral sex on her. Then, after wooing and sleeping with Annette, Sebastian breaks up with her at Kathryn's prodding.

Unlike *Clueless*, where Cher gets off mostly scot-free, the characters in *Cruel Intentions* do get their comeuppances.[13] After a physical confrontation between Sebastian and Cecile's music teacher and lover, Ronald (Sean Patrick Thomas), Annette gets pushed into the path of an oncoming car. Having realized his love for her, Sebastian shoves Annette out of the way, sacrificing his life to save her. Then, at his memorial service, Annette exposes Kathryn's drug abuse and manipulation of Sebastian, thanks to a detailed journal Sebastian kept and gave Annette before his death. Still, Sebastian is not remembered for his terrible actions but lauded as a martyr, and Kathryn loses her privileged position at the top of the school hierarchy.

In addition to somewhat similar themes in plot, characters, and settings, both *10 Things I Hate about You* and *Cruel Intentions* followed *Clueless*'s mold when it came to aesthetics and reliance on pop music. *10 Things I Hate about You* featured the song "I Want You to Want Me" and "Cruel to Be Kind," both covered by the alternative group Letters to Cleo. *Cruel Intentions* featured "Praise You" by Fatboy Slim, "Coffee & TV" by Blur, "Lovefool" by the Cardigans, and "Bitter Sweet Symphony" by the Verve. The merging of popular songs and films gave wider circulation and promotion to both but also worked to unite disparate pieces of popular culture (more on this in chapter 4).

Yet *10 Things I Hate about You* and *Cruel Intentions* are hardly the only films to share commonalities with *Clueless*'s themes and production elements. A raft of movies can be seen repeating the ideas of privilege, consumerism, and lack of consequences, even if these elements fit together in slightly different ways.

PRIVILEGE

Although *Clueless* and *Cruel Intentions* likely feature some of the wealthiest characters from these films, several others deal with different forms of privilege, often as the film's animating feature. To reiterate, my use of "privilege" here closely aligns with accrued capital—economic, social, and cultural—that people can draw on in times of need.[14] Again, capital is not entirely analogous to racial or sexual privilege. Yet these categories are linked—those with privilege would be more likely to hold various forms of capital and vice versa. For example, in *She's All That* (1999), the attractive, all-American jock Zack (Freddie Prinze Jr.) bets Dean (Paul Walker) that he can turn the less affluent outcast Laney (Rachael Leigh Cook) into the prom queen. As a retelling of *Pygmalion* and *My Fair Lady*, this trope has long roots in Hollywood films.[15] Although the transformation is framed as turning the unpopular outcast into the epitome of popular, there are underlying class elements as Laney is shown having an unflattering after-school job.

Meanwhile, economic and racial privilege motivate the plot in *Bring It On* (2000). Torrance (Kirsten Dunst), the newly installed head cheerleader of the defending high school national champs, the Rancho Carne Toros, is confronted by the realization that the former head cheerleader—known as Big Red—was stealing routines from the East Compton cheer squad. After various confrontations with the East Compton Clovers squad, led by Isis (Gabrielle Union), it becomes clear that the Clovers didn't expose the theft sooner because they do not have the resources to compete at the national level. Feeling guilty, Torrance gets her dad's company to sponsor the Clovers; however, Isis rejects the offer and instead asks an Oprah-like talk show host to pay for the team's entrance to the national competition—which she does.

For its part, *Varsity Blues* (1999) turns its attention toward geographic differences and provincialism. The movies mentioned above are set in major metro areas like Los Angeles and other cities in Southern California (*Clueless, She's All That, Bring It On*), New York City (*Cruel Intentions*), and Seattle (*10 Things I Hate about You*); in comparison, *Varsity Blues* takes place in West Canaan, Texas. Although fictional, West Canaan is a small town where high school football is an all-encompassing pastime thanks to the tyrannical coach Bud Kilmer (Jon Voight). Mox (James Van Der Beek) dreams of escaping to Brown University, but that path is put into doubt when he becomes a first-string quarterback after the star, Lance (Paul Walker), is injured. To get Mox to toe the team's line and win at all costs, Kilmer threatens to change Mox's academic transcripts to hinder his escape. Likewise, Darcy (Ali Larter) underscores the characters' desperate desire to leave small West Canaan. Although she was dating Lance before his injury, she suddenly tries to sleep with Mox, using her "famous whipped cream bikini." While Mox is surprised by her sudden interest, she tells him she was only dating Lance because it was a way for her to escape.

Finally, *Save the Last Dance* (2001) also hits on several of these dynamics. In it, dancer Sara (Julia Stiles) falls during her Juilliard audition at the same time as her mom dies in a car crash. As a result, Sara moves in with her estranged father in South Side, Chicago, a poor and predominantly Black community. Sara becomes friends with Chenille (Kerry Washington) and eventually begins dating Chenille's brother, Derek (Sean Patrick Thomas), who aspires to attend Georgetown University to become a pediatrician. Throughout, the film manages to intertwine economic, racial, and geographic privilege issues in a fish-out-of-water romance.

CONSUMER CULTURE

These various forms of privilege contribute to the more pronounced portrayal of consumer culture wherein consumption helps construct our identities for ourselves and others, implying that traditional structures like class, race, and gender do not constrain us.[16] For example, in *Clueless*, no one *explicitly* says Cher is desirable because of her family's money; Cher's identity is couched in her appearance and fashion sense. This is something seen throughout the teen films of this era.

Zack in *She's All That* just happens to be the good-looking, popular jock, while Laney is the nerdy, poorer artist. Left unsaid is that the ability to succeed in sports takes a certain amount of capital and that, within a consumer society, we value some activities over others. However, that is hardly the film's only portrayal of consumer culture. The fact that Zack attempts—and largely succeeds—in turning Laney into a popular student through a makeover and a new dress speaks to the valorization of consumer culture. Even more to the point, the film's plot is set in motion because Zack's girlfriend Taylor breaks up with him to start dating a cast member of *The Real World*, whom she meets at an *MTV Spring Break* event. The cast member, Brock (Matthew Lillard), is seen as immature but desirable because he's "famous"; there's a cultural capital that comes with being on a hit reality show.

Further, the idea of the bet between Zack and Dean speaks to the monetization of interpersonal relationships. While the bet in *She's All That* is more about pride and cultural cachet (spoiler alert: viewers eventually learn that if he loses the bet, Zack will attend graduation naked), the bet in *Cruel Intentions* is more monetized: Kathryn will receive an expensive car if she wins. The linkage of money and romantic relationships is explicit in *10 Things I Hate about You*, where Patrick is paid to take Kat out. While Patrick makes it clear he continues to date Kat because he likes her rather than for the money, the message remains that money—or the promise of money—can undergird romantic relationships.

Yet some of these films also explore the limits of consumer culture. After Torrance and her friends in *Bring It On* are upstaged by the Clovers and realize they need a new cheer routine, they attempt to do what anyone steeped in consumer culture would do: buy it. At the behest of Torrance's placating and uninterested boyfriend, the Toros hire a mean-spirited but supposedly brilliant choreographer to teach the team a new routine. While doing so is frowned upon in the cheerleading world, the desperate team follows through with it—and they're horrified at the regional competition to find out the choreographer also sold the same routine to another school. Technically, it is not against the rules, so the team can compete at the national competition, but they must learn *another* new routine (which they do). The storyline indicates that not everything can be bought, or at the very least, while most things may be purchased, consumer culture ensures they are not unique to you. Still, that the team can clear their schedules to learn multiple new routines and draw on various dance styles implies an ability to turn economic capital (including time) into cultural capital (knowledge of dance routines) and capitalize on it through competition.

LACK OF CONSEQUENCES

Bring It On's (relative) lack of consequences truly drives home the privilege involved. Despite (1) stealing cheer routines for years and (2) buying a routine performed by other schools, the Toros can still advance to the national competition because of their accrued capital in the form of a previous win. Though the team finishes second to the Clovers in the national competition, the film implies an uneven playing field; placing second "teaches" the Toros that creativity and teamwork are noble goals and centers the redemption narrative of the rich, white squad over the wronged Black team.

In both *She's All That* and *10 Things I Hate about You*, the offending parties—Zack and Patrick—are forgiven for manipulating the objects of their affection. Notably, these are both young men manipulating young women (rather than vice versa). Importantly, because Zack and Patrick develop real feelings and are genuinely sorry for their "bad" actions, Laney and Kat, respectively, forgive them. Like Cher in *Clueless*, they can be forgiven because their bad actions are relatively innocuous, not malicious, and contained in the relationship sphere. This logic only partially applies to Sebastian in *Cruel Intentions* and doesn't cover the scheming Kathryn—both of whom had been deliberately harmful in their actions.

Yet in these films, the lack of consequences extends quite far if no ill was *intended*. Sebastian ultimately does pay a price for his actions—tragically, after he realizes his mistakes. However, to understand the extent here, let's consider Sebastian's earlier action of photographing his therapist's daughter naked and posting the photos online—for fun. What today would be viewed as a problematic and potentially illegal act (especially if the girl in question was underage, as the film implies) is played for laughs. The angry therapist is mocked, as Sebastian is seen as untouchable—even by a famous, professional adult—and then he jokes to Kathryn that it was deserved because the therapist was overcharging.

And that's the last viewers hear about it.

A similar situation plays out in *American Pie* (1999), where Jim (Jason Biggs) sets up a webcam to spy on the undressing foreign exchange student Nadia (Shannon Elizabeth). The encounter turns "comical" after Nadia tries to have sex with Jim, but he cannot adequately perform and prematurely ejaculates—*twice*! While Jim intended to share the link only with his friends so they could spy on a naked Nadia, he inadvertently shared the webcam link with the entire school, leading to his extensive embarrassment. Never mind that Nadia didn't even know she was being watched; because of the video (and her sexual activity), her sponsors send her back to eastern Europe, not to be heard from for the rest of the film.[17] (The character is even left out of the two sequels, not reappearing until the final film in the franchise, *American Reunion*, in 2012.)

Admittedly, some of these transgressions are relatively harmless and play into a list of expectations for teens. The average underage drinking party—as shown in *She's All That*, *10 Things I Hate about You*, and *American Pie*—may not need a moralistic comeuppance; however, seeing no repercussions for sexual transgressions (or, for that matter, when one of the *American Pie* teens sleeps with the MILF, played by Jennifer Coolidge) feels especially stark decades later. Whether intentionally harmful (Sebastian) or naively sophomoric (Jim), these indiscretions would have lasting effects that these films wave away because well-off white guys committed them.

Considering Millennial High School Life

Granted, the makers of films cannot control how audiences are going to view them. Perhaps this is most obviously notable in *Clueless*. Like its reference material, *Emma*, *Clueless* is intended to be a satire, as critic Jen Chaney argues—albeit one where the protagonist *tries* to become a better person.[18] That seems to be a pretty generous reading of the situation; Cher might have grown throughout *Clueless*, but it is hard to say she learned any lessons outside of realizing her true feelings for Josh. More importantly, one would be hard-pressed to suggest that much of the satire was picked up on by the public as the film's catchphrases entered the public lexicon, and Cher's fashion sense *still* influences designers and contemporary popular culture (for reference, see Iggy Azalea's music video for "Fancy").[19] Even when read as (minimally) satirical, it has also become something to emulate.

Moreover, the movie's choice to center teen life on high school socializing is not surprising, given how the teen demographic developed. However, *Clueless* and the films that followed showed a *particular* version of high school life. Education— the actual learning done in school—was often minimized in favor of other aspects of teen life. While *Clueless* is initially motivated by Cher's quest for better grades, she is clearly a poor student attempting to skate by. Ultimately only a handful of these movies' characters plan to attend "good" colleges: Derek in *Save the Last Dance* plans to attend Georgetown; Kat in *10 Things I Hate about You* moves to Sarah Lawrence; Vicki in *American Pie* goes to Cornell; and Mox in *Varsity Blues* strives for Brown. While I address the presentation of college consumption more in chapter 5, for now, it's just important to note that college is understood as a natural progression of teen life—even if characters aren't that interested in learning.

Instead, schools are vast open-air ecosystems where teens congregate outside before and after school hours—or during school hours, as lunch is frequently eaten outside at sun-kissed tables (figure 3.2). Students can use cell phones in the halls (*Clueless*) and skip class to make grand gestures of love (*10 Things I Hate about You*). *Save the Last Dance* is an exception to this rule with its portrayal of an inner-city school, which is probably a more realistic representation of the schools most teens actually attended but is also represented as an undesirable deviation. Moreover, *Never Been Kissed* (1998), in which Josie (Drew Barrymore) is a newspaper copy editor returning to high school undercover to report on the popular students, takes permissiveness to an extreme. In it, both Josie and her brother (David Arquette)—two twentysomethings—inconspicuously enroll in high school, seemingly without parents. In the world of such films, however, that is not especially surprising; parents are either permissive (*American Pie, Get Over It*) or absent (*Cruel Intentions, Bring It On*). And even when authority figures are present (*Clueless, 10 Things I Hate about You*), they are not all-knowing or infallible. There is give-and-take between the parents and teens, in which teens generally handle things for themselves.

Still, school is largely seen as a distraction from the other events in teens' lives. Instead, students play sports (*Varsity Blues, Bring It On, American Pie, 10 Things I Hate about You, She's All That*), float between house parties (*Clueless, 10 Things I Hate about You, She's All That, American Pie*) and proms and dances (*She's All That, 10 Things I Hate about You, Drive Me Crazy, American Pie, Never Been Kissed*) (figure 3.3), and engage in other leisure-type activities, from going to the beach (*She's All That*) to putting on a play (*Get Over It*). Notably, few teens have after-school jobs, and when they do, the jobs are used more or less as a source of humor, as Laney's job is in *She's All That*. Nonetheless, teen employment after

Figure 3.2. Sunny Highs: Movie scenes depicted high schools as having wide-open outdoor spaces and accessibility. *Top left*, Tai holds court at an outdoor lunch table in *Clueless*. *Top right*, Zack talks to his friends as they walk through the school in *She's All That*. *Bottom*, Cameron is being shown the grounds in *10 Things I Hate about You*.

Figure 3.3. The Requisite Dance: Films often featured fantastic scenes of teens dancing, like the party scene in *Clueless* (*top left*). In *She's All That* (*top right*) and *10 Things I Hate about You*, the dance scenes were set at the school's prom.

World War II drove the increased economic and cultural attention paid to teenagers; in 1998, 44.3 percent of teens had a job.[20] That number increased to 57 percent in the summer.[21] However, according to these teen films, jobs were for poor losers.

Even more importantly, these films show teens engaging in significantly more "adult" activity than is typical for their age and education level. While the underage drinking party is something of a rite of passage for teens, in *10 Things I Hate about You*, Kat and Patrick go to a club—a place Kat seems to go frequently. While technically Kat could be over eighteen, she would still be underage for most venues. More to the point, the characters in *Get Over It* attend an underground sex club that police raid while Berke (Ben Foster) is in a compromising position (figure 3.4). Again, age remains a bit of a gray area here, but in the logic of the films, it's not unrealistic that these characters would be underage. Characters who seem too mature for their age certainly fits with the themes of *Cruel Intentions*, as high school student Sebastian is suave enough to seduce and manipulate a variety of young women and make risky (and risqué) bets with his cokehead stepsister. More surprising, in *Save the Last Dance*, Derek is asked to participate in a drive-by shooting. Overall, these examples range from unlikely to extreme.

These dynamics raise another issue: how those who deviated from the "norm" were portrayed in these films. For the most part, teens throughout these films were straight, white, nondisabled, and conventionally attractive. However, some notable exceptions still mold to the broad idealized outline of the time. Dionne and her boyfriend Murray in *Clueless* might be the most prominent example; despite the scene mentioned above involving hair extensions, as well as Murray's laughable play toward a "thuggish" masculinity in calling Dionne "woman," both very clearly fit into the same world as Cher with their accoutrements of wealth—from Dionne's convertible to Murray's braces. Similar dynamics show that Bianca's best friend, Chastity (Gabrielle Union), in *10 Things I Hate about You*, and Ronald, in *Cruel Intentions*, who are both Black, have some element of class privilege.

Ronald provides a pivotal insight here. He is a classically trained musician hired by Bunny Caldwell (Christine Baranski) to give music lessons to Cecile. But after Kathryn exposes that Ronald and Cecile are dating, Bunny confronts Ronald, demanding, "I got you off the streets, and this is how you repay me?"

"Got me off the streets?" an incredulous Ronald responds. "I live at Fifty-Ninth

Figure 3.4. Teens in Adult Spaces: High school characters frequently engaging in activities that are potentially illegal. *Top*, Kat and Patrick are at a bar to see a band in *10 Things I Hate about You*. *Bottom*, in *Get Over It*, Berke is publicly dominated at an underground sex club.

and Park." Earlier in the film, viewers also learn that Ronald is attending Juilliard Pre-College; he is hardly from "the streets," despite Bunny's racist assumption.

While this scene depicts Bunny's racism, it also underscores cinematic depictions of race at the time. With the exceptions of Ronald, Chastity, and Dionne, Black characters are shown in relatively desperate situations in the "inner city." Such portrayals are explicit in *Save the Last Dance* and integral to *Bring It On*—even if in the latter it's not quite *shown* as such, since few scenes take place in East Compton.

Throughout these films, Black characters are usually in supporting roles. Some notable exceptions include Sean Patrick Thomas in *Save the Last Dance* and Brandy (star of TV's *Moesha*) in the horror sequel *I Still Know What You Did Last Summer*. Arguably Gabrielle Union stars in *Bring It On*, but the story centers the white Toros squad (Kirsten Dunst and Eliza Dushku) rather than the aggrieved Clovers. Singers Kimberly "Lil' Kim" Jones and Usher were in *She's All That* and Sisqo was in *Get Over It*, but they had bit parts. It wouldn't be until 2002 that Nick Cannon would star in the college film *Drumline* with Zoe Saldaña (more on that film in chapter 6) and in *Love Don't Cost a Thing* in 2003 with Christina Milian.

Such marginalization is similarly true for other racial and sexual minorities, when they are shown at all. In *Bring It On*, Whitney (Nicole Bilderback) is Asian American but very much fits in with the rest of the cheer squad. The actress also had a minor role in *Clueless* and the TV show *Dawson's Creek*, showing her ability to fit into this mold across media products. Meanwhile, gay characters are somewhat more complicated, although they, too, fit into a similar physical mold. There are two gay characters in the films throughout this chapter: Blaine (Joshua Jackson) in *Cruel Intentions* and Les (Huntley Ritter) in *Bring It On*. Blaine is an unscrupulous friend who helps set up the football player he's been sleeping with to be blackmailed by Sebastian. Meanwhile, while cheerleader Les's sexuality is noted (as he and Jan, a second, and straight, male cheerleader, are usually questioned about their sexuality), there is no actual discussion of his sex life (just an acknowledgment that he "speaks fag" fluently). There are no prominent lesbian characters in these films, although girl-on-girl interactions are played up for titillation; the most prominent (and ridiculed) example is a scene in *Cruel Intentions* in which Kathryn teaches Cecile how to kiss.[22]

By and large, these differences are not interrogated or usually even noticed. When these characters' lived experiences get invoked, it is often done in a separating or disparaging manner. Both *Save the Last Dance* and *Bring It On* construct the Black experience as different and more troubled than that of their white counterparts; when characters of color have capital (economic, social, or cultural), race is hardly mentioned. *Cruel Intentions* is the exception, but that film places the racism on Bunny Caldwell—even though Kathryn and Sebastian are weaponizing the racism and social dynamics of an interracial relationship to hurt Cecile.

Juxtaposing Fiction with Reality

These films lean heavily into the tenets of privileged frivolity, especially the idea that nothing is too serious and everything will work out in the end. Though there are significant conflicts—such as in *Varsity Blues* and *Save the Last Dance*—the films get resolved in feel-good ways; even in *Cruel Intentions* "justice" is ultimately served to the least sympathetic characters. Moreover, most of these films—*Clueless, 10 Things I Hate about You, She's All That, American Pie, Drive Me Crazy, Bring It On*, and *Get Over It*—take place in picturesque high school settings where the problems are superficial *and* social. These films rarely examine structural and financial issues, but when finances are an issue, the problems are attributed mainly to Black characters. (Laney in *She's All That* might be the most prominent exception, although money isn't portrayed as her biggest obstacle.) Communities have money, parents have money, and teens have money—without needing to work for it!

Yet the idea that everyone attends a "good," well-funded school was (and remains) pure fiction. Despite attention and even legal action in the early 1990s, funding today remains disparate among urban, suburban, and rural schools. Part of this has been blamed on "local control," which, thanks to the United States' long history of racial segregation and redlining, allows areas with the financial means and economic valuations to contribute more than others. The ability to move to neighborhoods with "good" schools is what economist Elizabeth Currid-Halkett called "inconspicuous consumption"—the things we consume that are not obvious.[23]

However, it was more than just structural elements that did not live up to what was portrayed on-screen. For example, a far cry from the movies' sprawling open campuses in sunny California, in 2000 nearly 66 percent of high school districts and more than 73 percent of high schools had "closed-campus policies," where students could not leave the building during the day, according to the Centers for Disease Control and Prevention (CDC).[24] And movement was not the only freedom restricted for students; more than 10 percent of high schools required students to wear uniforms, while nearly 87 percent of high schools had some dress code. President Bill Clinton was calling for schools to institute uniforms—something that had not previously been commonplace in US schools.[25]

There was also a disparity between on-screen and real-life teen activities. In a 1999 survey, the CDC found that while 81 percent of students had tried alcohol during their lifetime, only 50 percent of students surveyed had had at least one alcoholic beverage in the month before the survey, and less than a third (31.5 percent) had had more than five drinks in the preceding month.[26] While some students might have been drinking frequently, they would have been a minority—although we would not know that from the frequency of house parties in teen films.

The same might be said for romantic relationships, which were underscored in nearly every film. In comparison, in 1999, almost half (49.9 percent) of high school students reported ever having sex, according to the CDC, with Black students significantly more likely to report having sex than white and Hispanic students (71.2 percent versus 45.1 percent and 54.1 percent, respectively). Moreover, only 36.3 percent of students had claimed to have sex in the preceding three months.

Finally, financially speaking, the median household income was $40,800 in 1999, with the income for a married couple pegged at $56,800. Adjusting for inflation, income levels were higher than ever and had been building for five consecutive years, according to the US Census Bureau. Even so, considering that in 1995 more than half of US families had less than $1,000 in financial assets, most teens weren't living the lives presented in these films. And, as already mentioned, while the after-school job was a rarity on-screen, more than half of teens were in the labor force in 1999.[27]

All told, we can see how these films did not line up with reality—or at least *all* reality. By and large, the stories on-screen were of teens who were more popular and whose families had more money than most. Most high school students were drinking less, were less sexually active, and had less family income than these films would lead viewers to believe. Yet these films, broadly framed, suggested to teens that a makeover and better consumption choices could make them popular, setting them on a path to both current and future happiness.

One final difference that must be noted between on-screen representations of high school and the lived experiences of teens is the growing threat and acknowledgment of violence and, especially, mass shootings during this time. The Columbine High School massacre in Littleton, Colorado, occurred on April 20, 1999. Twelve students and two teachers were killed in what, then, was a shocking attack. It occurred in the middle of this teen film cycle, and studio executives acknowledged the violence by delaying the film *O*, which starred Julia Stiles and Josh Hartnett, for more than a year because of its content.[28] Yet teen films—that is, those geared toward a teen audience—did not acknowledge the realities of stricter dress codes, increased regulations, and now common practices like active shooter drills.

Conclusion

This chapter explored how the films associated with the *Clueless* film cycle repeated many of the tropes and aesthetics surrounding privileged frivolity. These films told stories of teens acting with an independence and autonomy that was not available to most teens at the time and engaging in mature activities, from drinking alcohol to visiting sex clubs. These films promoted the idea that consumer culture and personal objectification were keys to desirability and success without acknowledging the privileges that allowed these social dynamics to thrive. Moreover, characters used their privilege to escape consequences, even when their actions were misguided, harmful, and even illegal. In the next chapter, we'll see how intertextuality between music, television, and film helped connect pop culture products and helped move themes of privileged frivolity from the big screen and the mall into teenagers' homes.

FOUR

SUMMER '99

"SUMMER GIRLS" AND
INTERTEXTUAL TEEN TV

For nearly a decade, the MTV studios at 1515 Broadway in New York City's Times Square had been a prime destination for teens. Overlooking Broadway and Seventh Avenue, host Carson Daly counted down the day's most popular music videos on *Total Request Live* (*TRL*), a show that would become MTV's flagship. Daly was joined by musical acts, other celebrities, and, eventually, an in-house studio audience, as fans—primarily teens—would gather on the street below with signs to gawk, scream, and potentially catch a glimpse of their idols (figure 4.1). In many ways, the gatherings constituted a younger, hipper, and later-in-the-day version of those who gathered in Rockefeller Plaza for NBC's *Today* show. Eventually, MTV would lean into the phenomenon with three seasons of *Wanna Be a VJ*, a show where aspiring hosts auditioned to be the channel's next video jockey. Winners, including Jesse Camp and Thalia DaCosta, acted as side-kicks to Daly, introducing videos and interacting with fans outside the studio.

The success of *TRL* helped make MTV relevant to a new generation. While people had declared "I want my MTV" in the 1980s, *TRL* helped keep the channel cool at the turn of the millennium. The early years of the show helped launch the careers of boy bands like 'N Sync and the Backstreet Boys, pop princesses like Britney Spears, Christina Aguilera, Jessica Simpson, and Mandy Moore, rapper Eminem, and girl group Destiny's Child.

In the summer of 1999, the world of fashion and *TRL* collided with the release of LFO's "Summer Girls." The song was the trio's first (and biggest) hit, becoming a "song of the summer." Most memorably, the song name-dropped Abercrombie & Fitch in its refrain, giving the brand a boost of publicity. The cultural connection between the song and the Abercrombie brand was so extensive that when the retailer ran into financial trouble in 2016—roughly seventeen years after the song's release—CNN Money referenced it in a headline: "Summer Girls No Longer Shop at Abercrombie & Fitch."[1] Setting aside the repetition of the brand

Figure 4.1. Live from Times Square: Music fans flocked to the *TRL* studios during the show's run, as featured in the *Frontline* documentary "The Merchants of Cool" (*top row*) and the *Music Box* episode on Woodstock '99 (*bottom row*).

name in the song's refrain, the music video could have been ripped from Abercrombie's marketing materials—although much the same could be said for music videos at the time by the likes of Britney Spears, Christina Aguilera, and 98°, too. While some viewed the Abercrombie & Fitch reference by LFO skeptically, suspecting it to be product placement, the store and the band denied any financial relationship.[2]

Yet whether it was product placement is beside the point. As this chapter shows, teen popular culture was highly self-referential in the late 1990s and early 2000s, which worked to blend disparate texts through overt references or aesthetic mimicry. Intertextuality—the use of one text (or a piece of a text) by another—has long roots in the culture industries and has been seen as crucial to popular culture and postmodern aesthetics.[3] And television was (and remains) an essential site for identity construction, including fashion and dress.[4] This chapter argues that a closely woven intertextuality connected a host of popular culture products and made a tightly intertwined, culturally constituted world. While intertextuality may not be unique to the popular culture products of this socio-cultural moment, the frequency and depth of it appear to be.

Considering Intertextuality

Before diving into these particular texts, it's important to take a step back and consider intertextuality. Put simply, intertextuality is the inclusion and use of a text within another text.[5] Perhaps most commonly, this occurs when one piece of writing quotes another piece of writing, but it can also be encountered when a song samples another or when a film or television show references another. The depth of inclusion and use of the original text can vary, but one must often understand the referenced text to fully appreciate the new text.

To be more concrete, let's return to *She's All That*, a film discussed in the previous chapter. While the main plot revolves around popular jock Zack transforming art nerd Laney, the story is set into motion when Zack's girlfriend Taylor dumps him for Brock, a cast member on MTV's *The Real World*. While someone could watch the film and understand that Taylor left Zack for someone else, knowing that *The Real World* was a popular reality show that helped establish the genre and aired on MTV through much of the 1990s and 2000s adds depth to the story and to Brock's assumed desirability. Now, Taylor is not just dumping Zack for some random guy but leaving Zack for Brock, someone in the midst of his fifteen minutes of fame. Familiarity with *The Real World* adds an element of celebrity culture and closely links the film's characters to MTV and its related shows. Yet intertextuality does not need to be so blatant, either. As discussed in the last chapter, *She's All That* used the plot of *Pygmalion*, *Clueless* used the story of *Emma*, and *10 Things I Hate about You* used the narrative of *The Taming of the Shrew*; these are also forms of intertextuality.

Media researchers have also explored the somewhat similar concept of para-textuality, which considers all the elements that give a primary text its meaning. For example, a trailer for *She's All That* or a movie poster for *10 Things I Hate about You* can inform the audience how they should read the text (is it a comedy or a drama?), and even elements such as titles can tell audiences how to understand a product. Even branding has been compared to paratextuality because advertisements and other forms of communication provide information and meaning about goods while maintaining a distance from the material products themselves. For example, the magalog and other branding decisions undertaken by Abercrombie & Fitch, discussed in chapter 2, provided texts that constantly referenced the company's material goods, that is, the clothing sold by the store. In many ways, brands and their products are a series of paratexts that are constantly being referenced and re-referenced.[6]

Ultimately, brands are particular cultural objects because while they can be referenced in other forms of popular culture—as a form of intertextuality—the meaning of the brand *itself* is constantly in flux and linked to a series of other texts. To this end, a brand reference is always a dialogic process where the brand's meaning is at once used and transformed. In the last chapter, I mentioned that *Clueless*'s Cher shops at the clothing store Contempo Casuals, as noted in the movie. When her stepbrother Josh uses the name of the store as an insult, it implies that people who shop are frivolous and superficial because it connects a mass-market retailer with the flighty Cher. Yet Cher's patronage of the store provides a paratextual relationship for the brand because she gives an identity to the type of people who shop there, thus informing the brand's image for viewers.

Girls Who Wear Abercrombie & Fitch

With intertextual/paratextual dynamics in mind, it is possible to consider LFO's reference to Abercrombie & Fitch in "Summer Girls." Released on the band's self-titled debut album, the song became LFO's defining hit, reaching number three on the *Billboard* Hot 100 chart. The album, which also featured the single "Girl on TV," would ultimately hit number twenty-one on the *Billboard* 200. "Summer Girls" remains a cultural touchstone and is held in relatively high esteem, with *Rolling Stone* ranking it as one of the best "summer songs" and one of the best songs released by a boy band. Rob Harvilla of the *Ringer* even wrote that the song exemplifies many of the pop hits with nonsensical lyrics in 1999.[7]

For the uninitiated, "Summer Girls" was stuffed full of pop culture references; the lyrics were reportedly full of inside jokes, but the song is best remembered for the line "When I met you I said my name is Rich / You look like a girl from Abercrombie & Fitch" and for the refrain, which repeated, "I like girls that wear Abercrombie & Fitch." During the peak of the song's popularity, LFO lead singer Rich Cronin explained that the song was about a girl he met in the summer of 1993 who "always [wore] Abercrombie & Fitch." (Notably, Jeffries had taken over the brand in 1992.) Later, in a 2005 interview with Boston.com, Cronin further explained, "'Summer Girls' was all about a summer on the Cape. . . . I never thought that anyone besides my close friends would ever hear it."[8]

Interestingly, the reincarnation of Abercrombie & Fitch as a teen retailer was not exactly common teen knowledge when "Summer Girls" took the music world by storm. For example, the song was my first introduction to the brand—an experience others shared.[9] At the time of its popularity, a marketing professor noted that the song would likely help the brand because it was building name recognition. However, an Abercrombie & Fitch spokesman suggested the brand was already well known by many teens.[10] (They were probably cooler than me.) Still, the song helped promote the brand among the *TRL* audience, and it did not hurt that the music video mimicked Abercrombie & Fitch's marketing aesthetics.

The video (figure 4.2), directed by Marcus Raboy, begins with a group of conventionally attractive young women arriving at a beach house in a classic black convertible, where the members of LFO are anticipating them. Three young, thin, attractive, white women clad in swimsuits or other midriff-bearing outfits climb out of the car and meet the band members on the porch. The group members, who are also young, attractive, and white, are dressed in more conservative attire, namely cargo and khaki pants and pullover shirts. It's evident that everyone is excited to see one another, as the newly arrived women eagerly hug and jump on the men. Throughout the song, the video returns to this scene in which the dancing around the car becomes more excited.

Then the video transitions to its second setting: a boardwalk, which becomes its focal point. First, the band and their friends are walking in a large group along the boardwalk; a second scene features the band sitting on a picnic table; a third shows the band singing from on top of the boardwalk stalls.[11] At various points, a group of primarily young women—again, thin, attractive, predominantly white, and dressed in somewhat revealing clothing—huddles around the band. At other points, the entire group walks along the boardwalk in various states of physical entanglement—holding hands, arms wrapped around one another—and gesturing suggestively. Through one scene, the group watches a series of breakdancers— the most notable men in the video besides the band members.

When the band is on top of the boardwalk stalls, they are wearing Abercrombie & Fitch–like clothing. Cronin wears khaki pants and a blue sweater; Brad Fischetti has on army-green cargo pants and a matching T-shirt; and Devin Lima is clad in black pants and a subdued yellow-green T-shirt. Outfits change, but the overall feel remains; when the band is walking down the boardwalk with the broader group of young people, Rich is wearing an orange T-shirt and black

Figure 4.2. Summer Fun: The music video for "Summer Girls" by LFO shows the band and a group of young people enjoying a summer day at the beach.

pants, Devin is wearing a fitted blue T-shirt and tan cargo pants, and Brad is wearing a sleeveless undershirt and black pants.[12] Perhaps more importantly, the young women with the men—the girls who look like they shop at Abercrombie & Fitch, if you will—are wearing various outfits, including fitted crop tops, capri pants, shorts, and camisoles, that mirror the store's offerings. In another scene, the young people are dancing at the ocean's edge as the waves roll in around them, soaking their pants and skirts; they are unmoved, though, because they are having too much fun. And as day turns into night, the beachgoers huddle in towels and hooded sweatshirts around a campfire on the beach.

Further, these characters align with the Abercrombie aesthetic. As mentioned in chapter 2, the brand targeted "cool, good-looking people" at the expense of those who didn't fit that mold.[13] The video shows much of the same. Everyone fits traditional stereotypes of attractiveness; the young women are thin, and the young men are muscular. Further, most of the young adults are white. There are few people of color portrayed in the video, a young woman of ambiguous ethnicity being the most prominent. While one of the breakdancers appears to be Black, and there appear to be one or two other people of color in the crowd, they play no extended role in the video and still largely fit into the "natural" white beauty standards espoused elsewhere.

Having fun is also the primary activity and narrative in the video. Essentially, "Summer Girls" portrays little activity beyond singing and having fun—whether at the beach house, on the boardwalk, or on the beach. And even the settings seem to reference Abercrombie & Fitch. Similar beach scenes can be found throughout the magalog's run. In the Spring Break 1999 issue, the cover featured a model holding a surfboard overhead while standing on a beach, many of the photo spreads took place on or near beaches, and several articles dealt with surfing, beach life, or travel to beach locales.[14] A&F Quarterly's Summer 1999 edition, titled Summer Dreams, repeated many of these themes. The cover was black-and-white and featured a model on a tropical beach. Palm trees and sand featured prominently in photo spreads and articles about the difference between the beach and the pool and about beaches in Thailand.[15]

Intertextuality and Teen TV at the Turn of the Millennium

Such intertextuality is common in popular culture, but music videos are uniquely dependent on the process to tell a story; even though they rely on a mixture of narrative, video editing, characters, settings, props, and sound for their meaning,

Figure 4.3. Stars On-Screen: Melissa Joan Hart and Adrian Grenier, the stars of the film *Drive Me Crazy*, appear in the music video for "(You Drive Me) Crazy" by Britney Spears; the song was included in the film's soundtrack.

the situation is somewhat different from that of film and television, as videos jump between scenes and settings.[16] In this way, intertextuality in music videos becomes paramount, as it requires significant overlap to make sense of what is happening.[17] Yet music videos of the late 1990s and early 2000s also developed various forms of external intertextuality. Both actor cameos and film clips became common material for cross-promotion.

Consider some of these examples: Britney Spears's third single, "(You Drive Me) Crazy," was featured in the movie *Drive Me Crazy*, which starred Melissa Joan Hart and Adrian Grenier; both stars made cameos in the song's music video, providing a prime source of intertextuality to link the film and the song (figure 4.3). Elsewhere, LFO followed up "Summer Girls" with the song "Girl on TV," in which the group sang about having a crush on a famous actress, played by Jennifer Love Hewitt, a star of the show *Party of Five* and the horror film *I Know What You Did Last Summer*. (Hewitt was dating Cronin at the time.) Hewitt herself released the song "How Do I Deal" for the movie sequel *I Still Know What You Did Last Summer*, and the music video featured clips from the film.

Figure 4.4. A Genie in Abercrombie Pants: *Top*, in a screenshot from the music video for Christina Aguilera's "Genie in Bottle," the singer is wearing a pair of Abercrombie & Fitch parachute pants. *Bottom*, the same pants are in *A&F Quarterly*'s spring break 1999 edition, *Spring Fever*.

Yet not all of the intertextuality was so obvious. First, as noted elsewhere, various music videos reflected Abercrombie & Fitch aesthetics. In Christina Aguilera's music video for "Genie in a Bottle," the singer wears a pair of orange parachute pants with a stitched dragon on the back of one leg—a garment sold in *A&F Quarterly* (figure 4.4); other videos from Aguilera and others simply used clothing similar in style to Abercrombie & Fitch clothes (e.g., camisoles and sweaters) or similar hazy aesthetics, settings, and props. Scenes ranged from

Figure 4.5. Beaches Everywhere: Beaches were common backdrops for music videos of the era, including those for "Another Dumb Blonde" by Hoku (*top left*); "Sometimes" (*top right*) and "Don't Let Me Be the Last to Know" (*bottom left*) by Britney Spears; and "Genie in Bottle" by Christina Aguilera (*bottom right*).

beaches (especially) to carnivals and schools, while props included surfboards and vehicles. The repetition of similar clothing, settings, and props (figure 4.5) helped link these videos into something of a coherent world for teens, as did their inclusion in *TRL*.[18]

At the time, *TRL* had helped restore the popularity of music videos to MTV and was one of the main venues for bubblegum pop sounds in the final years of the 1990s. The show "was one of the first truly interactive television shows," according to MTV, "utilizing the synergy of the internet and television to countdown the top music videos of the day."[19] *TRL* targeted a high school audience; it aired in the afternoon—at 3:00 p.m. in the summer and 3:30 p.m. during the school year—and boosted ratings by 52 percent among twelve-to-thirty-four-year-olds in its first quarter. The show's popularity peaked in 1999 and 2000, averaging over 700,000 viewers daily. Although ratings would fall over the following years, it was not until 2008 that MTV pulled the plug on the show.[20] Even so, *TRL* remains a historic high point of MTV's success, so much so that the channel revived the name in 2017 (with lackluster results). Yet during its heyday, *TRL* helped package music videos into a program for consumption.

Critics—notably Douglas Rushkoff in "The Merchants of Cool," an episode of the PBS documentary series *Frontline*—took issue with MTV's overt and circular commercialism during *TRL*'s peak.[21] I examine this criticism more in chapter 5, but it's important to remember that MTV wasn't the only network to target teens. Starting in 1990, upstart network Fox proved that teen-centered television could work thanks to the success of *Beverly Hills, 90210* (1990–2000). Other networks had been incorporating teen perspectives into sitcoms. Still, the nighttime soap opera feel of *90210* would come to define teen television shows, including *Party of Five* (1994–2000) and the short-lived ABC show *My So-Called Life* (1994–95).[22] Though Fox abandoned the teen market, hoping to attract a wider audience, Warner Bros. hired Jamie Kellner, the executive who started Fox in the 1980s, to launch the WB. Rather than go head-to-head with traditional broadcast networks that targeted adults between eighteen and forty-nine, the new network aimed for a younger demo: twelve-to-thirty-four-year-olds. Beginning in January 1995, the WB first featured wholesome, family-friendly content. Its heavy teen focus started with the success of *Buffy the Vampire Slayer* in 1997. The series was based on the 1992 film of the same name and starred Sarah Michelle Gellar as the titular character and Alyson Hannigan as her friend Willow. Other teen-focused shows followed, including *Felicity, Popular, Roswell*, and of course, *Dawson's Creek*, widely seen as the quintessential teen show of the time. These shows had all premiered by 1999 and ran through the early 2000s. Along with dropping the family-friendly moniker, the WB found success through sex-related and other "adult" storylines in their teen shows.[23]

By the time the WB came to dominate teen TV, the teen genre had already begun to change. As mentioned in the last chapter, teen-genre products have "more to do with lifestyle and shared cultural interest" and a "range of idealized qualities such as vitality, excitement, vigor, promise, and cutting-edge interests" rather than focusing squarely on an age-specific demo.[24] For example, *Felicity* featured a college student in New York, and *Gilmore Girls* featured young mother Lorelai as much as her teen daughter, Rory. Moreover, to be taken more seriously, teen television shows drew on film production techniques, including

Figure 4.6. Films in *Dawson's Creek*: Movie posters in *Dawson's Creek* provide a key aspect of intertextuality. Posters for *I Know What You Did Last Summer* can be seen in the video store where Dawson and Pacey work (*top*), while Dawson's room (*bottom*) is an homage to Steven Spielberg with posters for *Indiana Jones and the Last Crusade, ET,* and *The Color Purple,* pictured, but also *Jaws, Jurassic Park,* and *Schindler's List.*

single-camera formats, aiming for a more textured look that prioritized aesthetics over clarity.[25]

These shows frequently relied on intertextuality. In the words of media scholar Valerie Wee, "The WB's television series were media texts that obsessively discussed other media texts." Specifically, *Dawson's Creek* (1998–2004) was rife with intertextuality, as protagonist Dawson (James Van Der Beek) was an aspiring filmmaker and general film junkie. Dawson's room featured classic movie posters for the likes of *Jaws,* and contemporary promotions for films such as *I Know What You Did Last Summer* can be seen in the video store where Dawson and his friend Pacey (Joshua Jackson) worked (figure 4.6). Moreover, an entire episode mimicked the plot of *Scream*—as characters reflexively noted the coincidences. Wee argues that this intertextuality is part of how *Dawson's Creek* and similar shows helped turn themselves into "quality" programs.[26]

Moreover, the WB shows often referenced one another; for example, Pacey in *Dawson's Creek* explained plot points of *Buffy the Vampire Slayer*, and a *Buffy* character watched *Dawson's Creek* in the series. Rather than just promoting the other shows or placing these characters in the same universe, the referencing and inclusion imply that the characters are fans of the other shows; Pacey wouldn't be familiar with *Buffy* unless he were a regular viewer. This interplay helped consolidate the WB teen brand during its peak of influence, promoting multiple series and keeping teen viewers within the network's programming, according to Wee.[27]

In addition to the intertextual references, the WB shows also became known for overt commercialization and product placement. While *Dawson's Creek* included some promotional elements and was costumed by J.Crew (in early seasons) and American Eagle (in later seasons), its much-derided and short-lived spin-off, *Young Americans* (2000), was overtly sponsored by Coke. As the *Wall Street Journal* noted at the time, having a show sponsored by a brand wasn't new—but product placement was becoming increasingly common at the turn of the millennium.[28]

To recap some of the intertextual workings, teen TV shows (1) used aesthetics similar to those in films, (2) included references to other television and cinematic productions, and (3) used fashion products that teens could purchase at their local malls. Moreover, many of the actors from these shows would go on to star in teen films: *Dawson's Creek*'s James Van Der Beek starred in *Varsity Blues*, and Joshua Jackson appeared in *The Skulls*, *Urban Legend*, and *Cruel Intentions*; Sarah Michelle Gellar of *Buffy the Vampire Slayer* headlined *I Know What You Did Last Summer* and *Cruel Intentions*, while Alyson Hannigan, also of *Buffy*, was in *American Pie*. Further, like teen movies, shows used popular music—*Dawson's Creek*'s theme song was "I Don't Want to Wait" by Paula Cole—and several series released soundtracks, helping to closely connect music and television. Finally, there was even an overlap in settings, as *Dawson's Creek*, *Young Americans*, and *Gilmore Girls* all took place in New England—with teens in *Young Americans* and *Gilmore Girls* attending private high schools. Perhaps more specifically, *Dawson's Creek* was set in the New England town of Capeside (but was filmed in Wilmington, North Carolina), lending itself to the beach-style town present throughout the films and music videos of the time. Incidentally, LFO's "Summer Girls" was penned about a girl from "the Cape"—the type of girl that might appear in *Dawson's Creek*.

Living Like Adults

Intertextual elements helped connect this variety of shows, films, and music videos. In doing so, they helped promote the idea of privileged frivolity: a privileged social position, reliance on consumer culture, and lack of consequences. Even though *Beverly Hills, 90210* pioneered some of these elements, *Dawson's Creek*, like teen films of the late 1990s, seemed to drive headlong into portraying teens like full-fledged adults.

In *90210*, the plot initially centered siblings Brenda and Brandon Walsh (Shannen Doherty and Jason Priestly) in a fish-out-of-water story when they move from Minnesota to Southern California. Brenda transforms herself from a straight-A nerd to a fun-loving party girl with the help of new friend Kelly (Jennie Garth), while Brandon joins the school newspaper and becomes friends with tough guy Dylan (Luke Perry). The contrast between Brenda and Brandon and their new-found classmates is stark: Brandon drives a brown Chevette, a small, cheap car that was technically half Brenda's, while the class has a valet for the affluent students who drive high-end cars like BMWs and Corvettes.[29]

Although *90210* was not a ratings smash, it became appointment television for its teen and college-aged audience. Fans discussed the show with one another; some recorded and rewatched episodes; and it even spawned an early webpage dedicated to hating Brenda. In these ways, the show was a clear precursor to *Dawson's Creek*, which also became a teen touchstone during its run and whose fandom extended to other media, too.[30] While there are entire volumes written on the series, I'm not interested in all of the comparisons, but there seems to be an obvious maturation of the "teen" and of "teen life" that happens between *90210* and *Dawson's Creek*.

Rather than using *90210*'s new-school setup, *Dawson's Creek* featured three longtime friends—Dawson (Van Der Beek), Pacey (Jackson), and Joey (Katie Holmes)—and newcomer Jen (Michelle Williams). Unlike the *90210* characters, who were rich while having parents who ranged from absentee to relatively permissive, the *Dawson's Creek* characters were slightly more troubled. Dawson's parents were recovering from a bout of infidelity; Pacey did not get along with his family; and Joey's mother died while her father was in jail for drug dealing, leading her to live with her older sister, Bessie. Jen lived with her strict, conservative grandparents after getting in some "trouble" when living with her parents in New York City.

Although *90210* would become well known for dealing with serious issues in a somewhat heavy-handed, moralistic way, *Dawson's Creek* treated its characters more like adults from the start. Consider this comparison: In an early episode of *90210*, Kelly helps Brenda forge a driver's license and get into a club. When the bouncer realizes Kelly's ID is fake, he doesn't let her in, leaving Brenda alone in the club. After being ditched, Brenda is approached by Jason, an adult lawyer who offers to buy her a drink. Brenda lies and tells him she is a student at UCLA who just moved with her sorority sisters from Minnesota. When Jason takes her back to his place, Brenda rebuffs his advances, and he agrees to take it slow. Later, Jason introduces Brenda to his friends, takes her out for fancy dinners, and tells her the last woman he went on three dates with he lived with for eleven months. Brenda, thinking there might be a full-fledged relationship, reveals she's a high school student, leading Jason to angrily break off the relationship and threaten to sue her parents.

Meanwhile, the pilot of *Dawson's Creek* sets up an illicit affair between Pacey and his English teacher, Tamara. The relationship comes about after Tamara flirts with Pacey while renting *The Graduate* from the video store where he works, only for him to end up in her class the next day. Eventually, they end up kissing and, after some back-and-forth, have sex. Tamara is conflicted about the situation, and rumors about the relationship spread throughout the high school. Although Tamara breaks things off, she is still called before the school board to answer for the rumors. Pacey intervenes to tell the school board he made up the relationship to impress the other students, and Tamara escapes punishment and leaves Capeside for Rochester, New York.[31] Although she briefly returns in season two (much to Pacey's surprise), they do not rekindle a romantic relationship.

Moreover, in a later episode, Dawson, Pacey, and Jen's ex-boyfriend Billy travel to Providence, Rhode Island, to go to a bar—no questions asked. At the bar, Dawson flirts with a college film major, and she offers to take him home (an offer he ultimately rejects).[32] But there is little pretense about the characters being able to hold their own with adults and, in some cases, even acting more mature than the adults around them.

Ultimately, while *90210* might have exaggerated Jason's reaction to finding out his date was underage, the series acknowledged that Brenda and her classmates were legally children. Comparatively, *Dawson's Creek* treats its characters as though they are older and essentially drops the pretense of needing to fake their age; moreover, the fact that both a college student and even a teacher found high school students interesting and mature enough to potentially sleep with seems to strain credulity. Granted, part of this change might be the movement from female protagonists (e.g., Brenda and Kelly) to male protagonists (e.g., Dawson and Pacey), but it also seems to speak to the conflicted space of teens in the 1990s. The plot of accidentally sleeping with a high schooler also made an appearance in *Friends*, and sex between teachers and students made national news in 1997 when teacher Mary Kay Letourneau was charged with raping a thirteen-year-old student (whom she would go on to marry two years later).[33]

Privileged Frivolity and the American Dream

One significant holdover from *90210* in the teen shows that came in its wake is the focus on consumer culture. From the start of *90210*, consumption is prized, as Brenda complains about not having the right clothes for her first day at a new school, and as mentioned above, the distinction between vehicles clearly sets the newcomers apart. While *Dawson's Creek* was not as overt about consumption, it played an essential role in the show, especially regarding other media texts and how they helped define Dawson's identity as an aspiring filmmaker.

Moreover, *Dawson's Creek* broadly supported class and capitalistic structures in American society. Media scholar Lori Bindig shows that the series specifically upheld the "American Dream," which she breaks down into four components: (1) the United States is a classless society; (2) the United States is a middle-class nation; (3) everyone is getting richer; and (4) everyone has an equal chance at success. Joey's story arc throughout the show—as a poor teen from a broken home who succeeds through intelligence, hard work, and perseverance—directly promotes the national myth even though, in reality, few people will surpass the class status of their parents.[34]

To see how consumption is the largely unspoken aspect of the American Dream, we can compare Joey to Rory Gilmore from *Gilmore Girls*. In *Dawson's Creek*, the characters attend a public high school, and Joey is driven to improve her life through educational success. Her drive is a foil to Pacey, who doesn't believe he can do better and ultimately slacks off. But Joey wants to go to college and believes scholarships are the only way she can manage it—a bet that eventually pays off by the series' end when she attends a school in Boston.

In comparison, *Gilmore Girls* (2000–2007) provides an alternative message about class. Set in the quaint town of Stars Hollow, the show follows mother Lorelai (Lauren Graham) and daughter Rory (Alexis Bledel) through their daily lives. At the start of the series, Lorelai runs the town's inn while Rory gets accepted into the private Chilton Academy. Unable to pay the cost of the school, Lorelai turns to her estranged parents—Emily and Richard—for financial assistance. Lorelai, who came from a privileged upbringing, had previously left home after getting pregnant with Rory at sixteen. For her part, Lorelai worked her way up from maid to manager and eventual owner of the inn—without her parents' help. However, she was unable to fully work herself into the upper-class echelon through hard work alone; she still needed her parents' help to pay for Rory's private school. Throughout the series (and subsequent Netflix specials), Rory graduates Chilton as valedictorian, attends Yale, and becomes a successful journalist.

Broadly, Joey and Rory provide conflicting messages: Joey works hard in school and gets into college. While there is some trepidation about her ability to pay for college—Dawson helps her out at one point—she's getting a "good" education despite her family situation. Rory, who also works hard, succeeds in her private school and ultimately gets into Yale, but much of this comes because of her grandparents' financial support. While Rory might have achieved this without their support, that wasn't tested. And if we're being honest, statistically speaking, private school students have a far better chance at reaching the Ivy League than their public school counterparts; according to *Slate*, only 7 percent of students attended a private college in 2019, but roughly 40 percent of Harvard's admissions came from private high schools.[35] As a foil, *Gilmore Girls* exposes some of the myths that *Dawson's Creek* supports. First, *Gilmore Girls* shows that the United States is very much a class-based society, and even though her parents' old money might be stifling to Lorelai, it's a boon to Rory's future. It also shows that not everyone has an equal chance of success. Certainly, Rory was able to get into Chilton on her own accord, but her attendance would have been a hardship—if not impossible—without her grandparents' wealth.

At the same time, these stories overlap in the idea that education is a vehicle of *consumption*. As we'll explore in chapter 5, college holds a particular place in the American imagination as both a formative and a cherished time of life that also acts as a means of bettering one's social status. Students are expected to engage in and pay for college—a form of consumption—if they want any chance to better themselves, and college is considered an investment that will pay dividends later in life. While Rory was bright and promising, she and her mother faced the prospect of paying for high school to help her get into an Ivy League college. And both Rory and Joey needed to pay for college once they got there.

Conclusion

To bring this discussion full circle, one of *TRL*'s most popular music videos was 1998's " . . . Baby One More Time" by Britney Spears, which showed the singer as a student at a private high school—schoolgirl skirt and sweater included. Spears's video not only reflected the private school feel of *Gilmore Girls* but, through its interspersed scenes, reflected other aspects of high school life as well—not all that different from those discussed in the previous chapters. And as the teenage Spears played a prominent role in the video's creation, it is perhaps not surprising that it captured the teen zeitgeist so thoroughly.[36]

More importantly, as this chapter has shown, television provided a prime site for intertextuality that helped define teen life as a time of privileged frivolity and blended messaging from the fictional and lived worlds. Whether through music videos that referenced and reflected the advertising images of Abercrombie & Fitch, television series that used cinematic techniques, or films and TV shows that used pop music as a paratext for entry, television was the glue that held these images together. MTV and the WB tapped into a teen market and sold fictional and idealized lifestyles of frivolity and consumption without concern; privileged frivolity appeared on television sets weekly—or even daily, in the case of *TRL* music videos.

Thus far, we've examined how the idea of privileged frivolity was made possible by social conditions, used in brand messages, and promoted through film and television. This chapter showed how intertextuality and self-references tightly connected the popular culture ecosystem. In the next chapter, we turn our attention to the college films of the early aughts. Not only do these share the aesthetics of late-1990s teen films and television shows, but the college films underscore how higher education, too, was conceived as a commodity consumed for personal betterment.

FIVE SPRING BREAK '00

THE SKULLS AND THE MILLENNIAL COLLEGE EXPERIENCE

Is America really a class society?" a professor dryly asks his students huddled around a long wooden table. "Or is it the meritocracy we're taught it is since kindergarten?"

As the professor asks the question, senior Luke McNamara (Joshua Jackson) is more interested in a law school brochure outlining the $45,000 tuition. Sensing Luke is not engaged in the discussion, the professor peers down the table and asks, "Mr. McNamara?"

After being caught off guard by the question, Luke recovers, asserting, "Actually, I believe that it's both, sir."

"How can it be both?" the professor asks.

"Well, it's been my experience that merit is rewarded with wealth, and with wealth comes class," Luke responds.

"Nice recovery, Mr. McNamara," the professor concedes to the chuckle of the class.

The scene is one of the first in the opening of *The Skulls*, released in theaters on March 31, 2000. In the opening sequence, viewers see Luke working in the school's cafeteria, defending his friend Chloe (Leslie Bibb) from an arrogant sophomore, and then racing his bike across campus to make this seminar. We know that Luke is attending a prestigious Ivy League school, not only because the title card implies as much but also because of the Gothic architecture shown across campus and the wood paneling and furniture in the classroom.

In the American popular imagination, college has become a life stage after high school, while also credited with driving economic mobility. As such, the college experience is paradoxically presented as carefree and visceral (think: *Animal House*) but also deeply serious and cerebral. It not only remains a rite of passage but is also shown as the best—if not only—way to get ahead and better yourself and your social status.

Although the public once saw higher education as a social good in the United States, eventually colleges, administrators, and politicians who oversee many universities "created a privatized regime with a diploma as a golden ticket," according to journalist Will Bunch.[1] In this way, colleges and universities have increasingly succumbed to neoliberalism in their modes of operation, wherein schools are run more like businesses than educational facilities—and students are treated more like customers.[2] While critics have lambasted some universities for excessive amenities like rock climbing walls or the notorious "lazy river," it has also become clear that a "college experience" of game days and partying rivals, if not overshadows, the education.[3] Still, college is understood and portrayed as an entry fee into the good life.

With that promise in mind, the cost of college has exploded in recent decades. The average price of college is now more than $36,000 a year and more than $145,000 for a four-year degree. For four-year private schools—the type often valorized in entertainment media and that represent the "typical" college experience in the public imagination—that number is even higher: roughly $54,500 a year, or a staggering $218,000 for four years.[4] And this number does not include the massive interest students and families might accrue while trying to pay this off.

To be clear, I am not trying to dismiss students as consumers; if they will be paying off a six-figure debt for the rest of their lives, they should get what they want from their college experience.[5] What seems problematic is the idea that a college education—and a specific type of college education—has been presented as the only road to future success. Research has shown that elite colleges (i.e., the Ivies and other private schools like Stanford, Duke, and the University of Chicago) are more likely to admit students from the top 0.1 percent, which impacts future employment opportunities and future earnings; attending a prestigious undergraduate school increases the likelihood of attending "top" graduate schools and getting a job at "prestigious" organizations (e.g., national news organizations), and such graduates are overrepresented in both business and political leadership.[6]

This chapter argues that popular culture portrayed the consumption of college—that is, paying for and attending a school and undertaking all the activities that go with it—as the path to success. Those who could not attend college—due to choice or outright rejection—were destined to struggle. The type of college life portrayed in these films was not simply—or even *mainly*—about education but about going to a "good" college with history and traditions. Ultimately, this chapter argues that these presentations supported broader cultural assumptions that valorized attendance at picturesque, private, elite schools, thereby diminishing other forms of postsecondary education like community colleges, technical training, and regional public institutions. Decades later, the ramifications of these narratives are still playing out, from the college admissions scandal of the 2010s to the questioning of legacy admissions following the ending of race-based affirmative action.

Welcome to College

Compared to teen films, college films have not received nearly the same scholarly attention; this dearth of research is likely due to college's contested place in the social order and the relatively small number of stories explicitly set at or about college. Still, since colleges serve educational and social functions similar to high schools, it is easy to see how they also fit within the teen genre, as they often deal with issues of romance, socialization, and self-discovery.[7] In high school films, college is essentially an end point: somewhere someone ultimately gets to. As discussed in chapter 3, elite colleges were a destination that would provide freedom for otherwise restricted teens. In *10 Things I Hate about You*, Kat was eager to flee her overprotective father by attending Sarah Lawrence, a school across the country from her Washington State home. Mox in *Varsity Blues* saw Brown University as a way out of his football-worshipping provincial town. For others, college simply represented a chance to start over: Vicky in *American Pie* was not escaping, but she left her boyfriend behind as she went off to Cornell. Even nonelite colleges were a place to grow, change, and leave your old life behind (for good or ill), as Torrance's boyfriend did in *Bring It On*.

College films of the early 2000s ranged from dramas (*The Skulls*) to party films (*Van Wilder*), rom-coms (*Down to You* and *Loser*) and general comedies (*Legally Blonde, Accepted*, and *The House Bunny*). Throughout, college is seen as a space for self-exploration and an investment, or consumable, that one must make to have a successful adulthood. This sentiment is displayed explicitly and implicitly, but it also becomes apparent that college is filled with gatekeeping at several levels. Although success is not guaranteed, with the right mix of privileged frivolity, college can be a place for a person to find themselves and set the stage to achieve their dreams.

Nowhere is this better represented than in *The Skulls*, which made $535 million domestically and $15.7 million globally at the box office but managed to spawn two direct-to-video sequels.[8] In the film, Luke is a townie who earned his way into the prestigious university and is a dedicated member of the rowing team. Luke is clearly different because he works at the dining hall, compared to the wealthy kids he serves. Viewers learn that Luke is obsessed with getting invited to join the Skulls, the most prestigious secret society at the school.

And thanks to Luke's grades and success in rowing, he nets an invite.

Luke overcomes a series of ordeals to get inducted and gets partnered with Caleb Mandrake (Paul Walker), the son of federal judge and current Skulls chair Litten Mandrake (Craig T. Nelson). Membership in the Skulls comes with handsome rewards, including an expensive car and thousands of dollars—money Luke needs to finance his future. The time Luke spends with the Skulls and the society's secretive nature leads to strained relationships with Chloe and his best friend, Will (Hill Harper).

The situation gets worse when Will, a reporter for the campus newspaper, is killed after infiltrating the Skulls' lair. As Luke pieces together the circumstances of Will's death, the Skulls ruling board has him involuntarily committed to a psychiatric hospital—requiring Chloe to rescue him—and Luke comes to understand that the only way out of the group is to challenge Caleb to a duel. Ultimately, Caleb cannot bring himself to kill Luke and instead shoots his father to protect Luke. After winning his freedom, Luke chooses to walk away from the organization even though it means rejecting the money, connections, and road to the "good life" the Skulls offered.

The film is heavily indebted to the ethos of privileged frivolity, especially the idea that wealth and privilege lead to increased consumption and insulation from nearly all consequences. Membership in the Skulls comes with obvious financial rewards and a host of social connections. Senior members of the society are senators, judges, and even the university provost. Early in the film, when Will questions why Luke wants to be part of a secret society, Luke explains, "I'd join the Girl Scouts if they paid for grad school, which the Skulls supposedly do." He adds that if he wants to go to Harvard Law, even with scholarships and financial aid, he would owe upward of $100,000.

Needing to pay for college is just one of the ways consumption as a means for self-improvement is embedded in the film. As mentioned in the introduction to this chapter, Luke is attempting to work his way through an Ivy League school and get into law school—two things that are nearly impossible without wealth. Money and the ability to pay are as important as merit or drive. Further, as poor

meet him at his high school graduation, where he praises his mother for getting him to graduate. Later, he tells his absent father (who is working as a subway attendant and didn't attend his graduation) about his success. At Atlanta A&T, Devon is a talented drummer who is too cocky and unwilling to "pay his dues" as a lower-string member of the band. He butts heads with Sean Taylor (Leonard Roberts), the drumline leader, who tries to "break" Devon to get him to fall in line with the band. Devon's cockiness prompts a fight between his band and a competing troupe, straining his budding relationship with Laila (Zoe Saldaña) and getting him kicked off the team. While Devon flirts with the idea of joining the rival team, he recoils when the leader wants him to divulge A&T's plans for the upcoming marching band competition, the BET Big Southern Classic. Instead, Devon's estranged father sends him a series of cassettes, which inspire Devon to create a new drum arrangement, after which he reunites with Sean, who helps him get reinstated to the A&T band. Happily, A&T wins the competition.

Like the other films, *Drumline* also takes place at a prestigious and picturesque university. In both *Drumline* and *Legally Blonde*, the protagonists must revamp themselves to succeed in a new environment. However, while Elle can reimagine herself through consumption and is ultimately successful *because* of her prior knowledge, Devon is shown to need to conform to succeed. While that is a somewhat common trope in competition films (see also *Bring It On* and *Pitch Perfect* for very different examples), Devon's conformity is more corporeal. For instance, when Devon doesn't learn the band rules, his punishment is having his head shaved. Moreover, Devon can be truly successful only after he learns how to properly conform, keeping his ego in check and working with others. While Elle successfully challenges the dominant, even predatory ethos, Devon must subjugate himself to have a happy ending.

Taking together the films mentioned above, we can see how privilege (or lack thereof) shapes each protagonist. Elle is a white twentysomething woman supported by wealthy parents; this gives her the resources to break out of the mold. And Luke, as a young, working-class white man, sees money as the key to future success, although he ultimately finds the (figurative) price too high and rejects it. Comparatively, Devon is a fresh-out-of-high-school Black man. His options are either to conform to the expectations of the drumline, which also allows him to attend college, or not, which would mean he would not be able to stay at school. Collectively, these films demonstrate the interconnection of privilege, consumption, and consequence.

What Does College Look Like, Anyhow?

Visually speaking, we might have a sense of what a college campus looks like: old brick buildings for classes and residences surrounding sprawling lawns where students can gather, as many had before them. Films around the turn of the millennium were more than happy to oblige in this regard, depicting picturesque college experiences (figure 5.1). Even in the cases of *National Lampoon's Van Wilder* and *Accepted*, where the main characters are understood to be less driven, aspirational and prestigious schools relied on heritage and tradition.

National Lampoon's Van Wilder (2002) follows student Van Wilder (Ryan Reynolds) during his seventh year at the fictional Coolidge College.[9] Viewers are introduced to the college in the opening scenes during the campus's first day of the school year. An anonymous tour guide quizzes first-years as they walk past brick buildings and green lawns. "Coolidge College was established in eighteen . . . Who knows this?" she asks. "It was in your freshman facts!"

Meanwhile, Van's voice-over explains that the new year brings a new student body (emphasis on the "body"). He adds, "As for me, well, I like to start off each semester with a, well, with a certain time-honored tradition, a ritual, if you will, that allows me to get my head in the right place." The scene cuts to Van standing provocatively above an older Asian woman and strongly implies she is performing oral sex; instead, she is tailoring a new pair of pants for Van—while sucking on a lollipop.

Although filled with sexual double entendres, both scenes set up Coolidge College. It's a historic institution (although the first-year students don't know the year it was founded, it's more than 100 years old), and Van's soliloquy plays up the ideas of "time-honored" traditions and "rituals" that only come from places with storied histories. The scene echoes the real-life Ivy League schools in *Legally Blonde* and *The Skulls* and the equally prestigious (if fictional) Atlanta A&T in *Drumline*.

In the rest of *Van Wilder*, viewers learn that Van may be in his seventh year but he is also the big man on campus: he's made friends with the security guards and organizes social events across campus, including a Naked Run and a fundraiser for the swim team. He even holds tryouts for someone to be his assistant. (The role eventually goes to Taj, played by Kal Penn.) Yet when Van's father finds out he is *still* paying for his son's education after Van should have graduated, he arrives at the college to cut him off. "I'm sorry, son," Van's father tells him after

Figure 5.1. Picture-Perfect Colleges: Idyllic (and similar) college settings are seen in various movies, including (*clockwise from top left*) Yale University as shown in *The Skulls*; Coolidge College in *Van Wilder*; Atlanta A&T University in *Drumline*; and Harmon College in *Accepted*.

crashing a pajama party, "but sometimes in life, you have to realize a poor investment and simply cut your losses."

As Van embarks on various schemes to raise the money to stay in college with the help of Taj and his friend Hutch (Teck Holmes, of *The Real World: Hawaii* fame), a tenacious reporter for the campus newspaper, Gwen (Tara Reid), is assigned to profile him. Van is reluctant, but Gwen's perseverance wears him down and he slowly opens up to her. He seems wise beyond his years and wants to support those less fortunate—that is, popular—than him. A love triangle develops between Van, Gwen, and her boyfriend Richard, a frat boy planning to go to medical school who is staid, boring, and disrespectful to women—including Gwen. Van's fun-loving and open life stands in comparison to that of Gwen's parents, which is the future life she and Richard had been planning. Eventually, the rivalry between Richard and Van comes to a head after Richard sneaks children into Van's party, which nearly gets Van expelled. Instead, Van convinces the disciplinary board—including an older woman he slept with—to force him to graduate instead.

Throughout the film, consumption plays out on two levels. First, regarding personal consumption, Van is undoubtedly cool because of his ability to spend money and (initially) consume without care. His dorm apartment is enormous and decked out with fantastic furniture and even a cigarette machine that dispenses condoms. From the start, viewers see that money is not a concern for Van. Further, during her reporting, Gwen points out that while many people go to college wanting to graduate and make money, Van is not eager to move into the real world. In essence, his consumption of college life is seemingly an end in itself.

The role, intention, and consumption of college underscores the entire film *Accepted* (2007), which follows Bartleby Gaines (Justin Long), a mediocre but enterprising student who does not get into a college and inadvertently starts his own. Bartleby's best friend, Sherman Schrader (Jonah Hill), is set on becoming the "fourth generation" of his family to go to nearby Harmon College; meanwhile, all eight colleges Bartleby applied to reject him—including his "safety school."

In breaking the news to his parents, Bartleby initially tries to spin not going to college by pointing out they would be paying $80,000 for him to go to school for four years, whereas he could work and *make* $80,000 instead. He calls it "fiscally irresponsible" to go to school when he could be working, but his father does not buy the argument.

"Okay, cut the crap, Bartleby. Society has rules," his father begins. "And the first rule is you go to college. You want a happy and successful life? You go to college. If you want to be somebody, you go to college!"

Bartleby's disappointed and rueful mother says, "I knew we should've started preparing for college in junior high."

Trying to lessen his parents' disappointment, Bartleby decides to fake acceptance to a fictional college, the South Harmon Institute of Technology. However, after Schrader makes a working website offering acceptance to all who apply, Bartleby encounters dozens of students who want to go to college to forge a better life for themselves but were rejected from other schools. Even some of Bartleby's better-prepared friends were unable to attend other schools due to sports injuries or having set their sights solely on Yale. Ultimately, Bartleby leases a former asylum and launches a fake school with the tuition money the "accepted" students are willing to pay.

Throughout *Accepted*, Bartleby's South Harmon Institute of Technology is contrasted with Harmon College, which Schrader, Bartleby's love interest Monica (Blake Lively), and her boyfriend Hoyt Ambrose (Travis Van Winkle) attend. Yet the prestigious Harmon College is not all it is purported to be: Schrader attempts to pledge a fraternity and is humiliated in a number of ways; Monica learns about the convoluted nature of academia when she can't get into the photography classes she wants; and the president of the college recruits Hoyt's help in his quest to purchase land near campus (including the area where Bartleby set up the South Harmon Institute of Technology), level the buildings, and make a grand entryway to compete with the campuses of Yale, Princeton, and Stanford.

Since Bartleby does not have the qualifications (or the appropriate resources) to establish a place of higher learning, he asks the students what they want to learn and ends up with an unconventional curriculum that includes meditation, skateboarding, cooking, and just walking around thinking. As the dean and sole faculty member of the school, Ben (Lewis Black), a former college professor who "burned out," explains to Bartleby, "People forget the most important rule: college is a service industry. . . . As in 'serve us' as opposed to the other way around. . . . They all paid to come here. . . . They all paid for an experience."

This exchange is hardly the only critique of the higher education system embedded in *Accepted*. At one point, Ben suggests that the entire point of the American education system is to turn students into producers and consumers, and in another scene, Rory (Maria Thayer) states that she was not accepted to Yale because there were "too many rich kids with mediocre grades and well-connected parents this year." In this vein, all of the students who end up at Bartleby's South Harmon Institute of Technology admit that they applied to other (i.e., better and real) colleges but were rejected. Instead, the students at South Harmon— shown to be an array of misfits, including one man with ADD (now ADHD) and a stripper who became a "college girl"—feel accepted *somewhere*. The premise is that being rejected from school(s) is a hurtful and othering process that makes outsiders feel less than. Ultimately, after being sued by Harmon College, Bartleby's new school receives provisional accreditation from the education board, allowing the experiment of nontraditional education to continue.

Image and Reality of College

Accepted's critiques of contemporary higher education were poignant in many ways: the academic criticism of college as a service industry; the fact that well-connected and wealthy families are able to impact admissions; and even the pressure families face to prepare students increasingly early for the admission process. However, the film also plays into traditional assumptions and discourses around education. First, *Accepted* assumes and treats college admissions as a particularly opaque process (which it is) but also one with an incredible amount of gatekeeping that keeps slackers like Bartleby or other "undesirable" students, such as those dealing with disabilities or in a socially maligned career, from ever bettering themselves. Likewise, college is portrayed as a one-shot chance: either you go directly from high school to college or you're lost forever.

It's important to underscore that neither of these points are true. While elite colleges traditionally accept a tiny number of applicants—often the wealthy and well-connected—there are a host of colleges that have near-universal acceptance. There are, of course, for-profit colleges without standards, but public universities like the University of Maryland and Pennsylvania State University have acceptance rates of 44 percent and 55 percent, respectively, and other state schools like Michigan State and Arizona State accept upward of 88 percent of applicants. Some schools, like the University of Texas at El Paso and the University of Mississippi, even have acceptance rates in the high 90s to 100 percent. These colleges might not be as prestigious as the Ivies and other elite schools, which arguably give students the best chance of high-profile future success, but these schools still provide appropriate and regulated four-year degrees.[10]

Furthermore, even if someone *did* get rejected from all eight schools they applied to—there's always next year! Or next semester! The life-or-(might-as-well-be-)death stakes are frequent narrative tropes that do not map onto the real world. There are gap years and community college opportunities, not to mention that less than 38 percent of *all* Americans older than twenty-five hold a bachelor's degree (or better), meaning that 62 percent of people in the United States are living without a bachelor's degree.[11] Again, while those with a degree tend to make more money over a lifetime, portraying the situation as "straight from high school to college or bust" is incorrect at best and deeply flawed. Nonetheless, this is what millennials were sold: do well in high school to get into (and pay for) a good college, or your life will suck.

That wasn't always the belief. Decades earlier, higher education was considered a public good that would help the United States stay ahead of rivals. As such, states funded higher education, helping to make state schools affordable (and they still have relatively high acceptance rates). But funding began to dry up in the 1980s, shifting the cost of college onto students and, increasingly, parents. Moreover, attending prestigious colleges became a commodity people were willing to pay for. Colleges became more expensive, and at the same time, higher education became necessary for economic advancement.[12]

Toward this end, attending a good, prestigious college became closely tied to someone's identity and their parents.[13] This view was not because of better education per se but rather because attendance would lead to better wages and purchasing power throughout life.[14] Some have called this the "commodification of higher education," describing the turn of higher education toward becoming a service industry rather than being a necessary public good.[15] Perhaps unsurprisingly, this change has gone hand-in-hand with colleges' pursuit of prestige—in the form of better rankings—and the perception that graduates of prestigious universities are more employable.[16]

This development also speaks to schools' attempts to attract students through better "rankings" and better accommodations and parents' desire to push their children into ever more extracurricular activities, hoping to score a sought-after spot in these schools. Both of these issues are mocked in *Accepted*, but they persist nonetheless. Look no further than the Varsity Blues scandal, where well-off parents were willing to pay (and cheat) to ensure their children got into the best colleges.[17] In hindsight, *Accepted* was especially poignant in this regard: as noted earlier, Rory incisively attributed her rejection from Yale to "too many rich kids with mediocre grades and well-connected parents."

On the other end of the spectrum, when organizations take the commodification of education to the extreme, students have been preyed on by for-profit colleges that provide substandard education and large bills. Like other higher education institutions, predatory schools sell the idea that they provide a better life for students, but they often hoodwink them into useless diploma mills that leave them in debt and no better off than before.[18] The collapse of some for-profit colleges—as well as the US Department of Education's recognition that these schools had been preying on students (hence the forgiveness of those student loans)—underscores the risks of seeing and selling degrees as a ticket to a better life.[19]

Yet it is hardly only predatory, for-profit schools that saddle students with debt. Even traditional schools can leave students in debt. According to the Education Data Initiative, 43.6 million borrowers have some student loan debt, with the average borrower owing more than $37,000. On average, women are more likely to take federal student loans than men, and Black student borrowers are most likely to use federal loans; on average, Black borrowers owe $25,000 more than their white counterparts, and they are more likely to owe more four years after graduation than they initially borrowed.[20] Many prestigious schools also offer (relatively useless) master's degrees, which stick students with massive debt.[21]

The cost of higher education for students has been growing substantially since the 2000s, spurred by "cheap" federal loans that have buried students in debt. While it remains true that college graduates will make more over their lifetimes than those without a college degree, some have questioned whether college is a sound investment. Such questions are bound to arise when education is pitched only in financial terms and as a ticket to a nebulous "better life." Further, increasingly those who cannot earn a college degree—because they can't afford it, don't get in, or simply choose not to—feel excluded from these purportedly better futures.[22] The films discussed here—especially *Accepted* but also *Drumline* and *The Skulls*—reflect the idea that college is a make-or-break decision.

That's not to say the projected image of college in these films was perfect; subordinating oneself to an academic system (and secret societies and fraternities) seemed arduous at best, but it was ultimately shown to prepare people for "good" white-collar careers (discussed further in chapter 8). Yet in these films, the stately universities and the decades of investment and history seem worth it if the outcome is a better future. In *Accepted*, after Monica cannot take the classes she wants (without fully understanding why), she gives up on the prestigious Harmon College and decides to take a chance on Bartleby's endeavor.

Yet there is also a united message across these films that warns people that appearances can be deceiving. In *The Skulls* and *Legally Blonde*, the message is that the old boys' club isn't willing to protect those not in the in-group, while both *Van Wilder* and *Accepted* suggest that idolized fraternity brothers—the *height* of privileged frivolity—are duplicitous, self-absorbed, and arguably evil.[23] This moral also works against conformity, suggesting that learning to be "true to yourself" (whatever that means) allows someone to grow and achieve fully, though, of course, all these films underscore the need to learn to work within the system before you can truly break out of it.

Conclusion

Consuming college to better one's position in society has perverse effects on all involved. Those who can afford it continue to go to idyllic, prestigious schools, and well-off families who can pay for help—legal or illegal—can get students into the "top" schools. Moreover, the idea that those who receive a college degree from a traditional school are not just better educated but somehow inherently smarter or meritorious drives a wedge between the "college educated" and those who are not. This myth has exerted pressure downward onto high school students and their families. Not only that, the idea that talented, deserving kids from all backgrounds can gain entry into the best colleges seems to have been a sham all along; the wealthiest are overrepresented at prestigious colleges, even before considering the privileges they were afforded before reaching college, like tutors and private schooling.

In the same way that the movies discussed in this chapter question some cultural narratives, the following chapter turns its attention further to critiques presented in popular culture texts at the turn of the millennium to understand why many of those critiques failed to put an end to the consumer and brand culture they were criticizing. Much like these college films—in which protagonists must engage with capitalist, consumer-driven systems to escape without a ready alternative—the critiques largely missed the point and reified the overarching structures.

SIX

SPRING BREAK '01

JOSIE AND THE PUSSYCATS
AND OTHER CRITIQUES

When MegaRecords executive Wyatt Frame visits Riverdale's massive record store to look for new talent in *Josie and the Pussycats*, he sees an opportunity to "test" a new song: "'Round the World" by the recently missing boy band DuJour. After the store's resident DJ agrees to play the song on the in-store sound system, customers quickly express their love for the song: a trio of girls declares it's DuJour's "best song ever!" One fan continues, "If I don't buy it, everyone is going to hate me!"

"Totally!" her friend eagerly agrees.

"And I also want orange shoes!" the third girl adds, while the other two quickly agree, and they decide, "Orange is the new pink." (Elle Woods would disagree.)

Other shoppers came to similar conclusions; one was "sick of their Reebok sweats" and wanted Puma sweatpants instead, while a different shopper said he "gotta buy a pack of Zima"—even though he didn't drink.

Wyatt (Alan Cumming) is happy with the response to the song; that is, until one young woman isn't sold.

"I think that song sucks," says the teen who is wearing a black T-shirt over a gray waffle thermal shirt with dark eyeliner and lipstick, a thick black choker, and a roller-chain bracelet. "I plug my ears when crap like that comes on," she tells Wyatt.

After he points out that everyone else seems to like it, she continues, "That's because they're mindless drones who will gobble up anything you tell them is cool."

"I see! Wow! You're a free thinker, aren't you?" Wyatt asks with mock amusement. "I'd love to talk to you some more. People in the recording industry, like me, always want to hear the opinion of individuals like yourself . . . to find out what we're doing wrong."

"Yeah, right," the girl says. "How much time do you have?"

After Wyatt assures her that he has all the time she wants to talk, he whispers into his wrist, "Smells like teen spirit" (in an apparent reference to Nirvana and the rebellious grunge scene from the early 1990s), and escorts the girl down a darkened stairwell to an emergency exit. They walk toward a set of emergency doors that Wyatt pushes open, and just as the girl is about to talk, a white van pulls up, snatches the girl, and drives off as Wyatt watches and deadpans, "Gosh, that's fascinating." As he pauses, the camera continues to look out the double doors and across an alleyway, showing an MTV logo and the web address mtv.com in large black letters.

And the girl is never heard from again.

The scene is just one of many in *Josie and the Pussycats* (2001) that lampoons the brand culture at the turn of the millennium (figure 6.1). Based on the fictional band from the *Archie* comics, the film follows Josie (Rachael Leigh Cook), Melody (Tara Reid), and Valerie (Rosario Dawson) as they are discovered by Wyatt and become an overnight success, only to learn of a dark secret and (essentially) save the world.

Unlike much of the teen-centric fare I discussed in previous chapters that centered and helped construct the ideals of privileged frivolity, there were plenty of contemporary detractors in popular culture—as *Josie and the Pussycats* clearly shows—to mixed popularity. Films like *Josie and the Pussycats* and *Not Another Teen Movie*, the satirical band 2ge+her, and the TV show *Daria* all lampooned the rampant commercialization and perceived vapidness of the products sold to teens. More in-depth critiques came from the *Frontline* documentary episode "The Merchants of Cool" and various mass-market books, including *No Logo* by Naomi Klein and *Branded* by Alissa Quart. Some of these works provided astute analyses and insights into the cultural and economic conditions of the time—many of which are still valid today—but ultimately were not enough to end the consumerism and overall ethos of the time. In short, like the detractor Wyatt unceremoniously carted away, criticisms fell by the wayside and consumer lifestyles rolled on.

The following pages examine some of these critiques in turn; however, this chapter makes two points. First, consumerism and brand culture were not only presented to teens of the time but also actively critiqued; as such, this underscores the centrality of the ideas during the late 1990s and early 2000s. These themes and brand practices were not limited or otherwise inconspicuous but were present, widely noted, and, to some extent, debated. Yet as *Josie* and the other texts demonstrate, these critiques continued to play into the double bind of neoliberal consumer culture, whereby *different* identities and lifestyles still uphold the

Figure 6.1. Brand-New Mockery: Scenes from *Josie and the Pussycats* satirize pop culture in the early 2000s. At top left, the fictional boy band DuJour performs in a thinly veiled reference to the Backstreet Boys. At left, both DuJour's private plane (*middle*) and Josie and the Pussycats' private plane (*bottom*) are decked out with brand logos. At right, a punk or goth character complains about the music (*top*), and after she is unceremoniously carted off, the mtv.com web address is clearly visible on screen (*bottom*).

same overriding ethos. Second, these critiques largely missed that these products are, by default, meaningful to their audience. Even if cultural industry products are highly promotional, they remain valuable to their audience without an alternative.

Reading *Josie* as a Critique

The tongue-in-cheek critique of consumer culture is present throughout *Josie and the Pussycats*. The film reimagined the comic book characters—who had already appeared in a short-lived animated TV show in 1970—and updated them for the new millennium. The film starts by following the boy band DuJour—a thinly veiled reference to the Backstreet Boys, complete with screaming fans and a private jet.[1] Three of the four DuJour members are played by well-known actors: Donald Faison and Breckin Meyer (who were both in *Clueless*) and Seth Green (of *Can't Hardly Wait*). The fans are all dressed in bright pink and have signs professing their love of the band or their favorite member. Product placements pack the jet—a hint of what's to come in the rest of the film. Target logos adorn the plane's interior and boxes of Bounce fabric softener sheets hang on the wall, while a bottle of Ivory dishwashing soap sits nonchalantly against the plane wall. Marco (Meyer) complains to Wyatt that the picture of him on a "limited edition" Coke can doesn't accurately depict his face, and Travis (Green) complains that Marco took his signature pose during appearances on *Total Request Live* and the Kids' Choice Awards and on the cover of *Seventeen*.

However, things turn sinister when band member Les (Alexander Martin) questions Wyatt about a "really strange background track" the band heard on one of the latest remixes. Wyatt listens and tells the group he doesn't know what it is but will find out. He walks into the cockpit where he says to the pilot, "Take the Chevy to the levee" (a reference to Don McLean's "American Pie," about the plane crash that killed Buddy Holly, Ritchie Valens, and the Big Bopper), and Wyatt and the pilot strap on parachutes and jump out of the plane—apparently leaving DuJour to die. When Wyatt lands near the welcome sign of Riverdale, he tells someone on his cell phone, "It looks like we need a new band."

Meanwhile, news of DuJour's disappearance is announced in an MTV News alert—anchored by actual MTV journalist Serena Altschul—which notes the band's label, MegaRecords, hadn't released a statement but did release a "limited-edition commemorative box set, complete with a CD-ROM history of DuJour." Josie, Val, and Melody, who are watching the news, are upset by "what seems to be another rock-and-roll tragedy," in Altschul's words.

That opening sets the stage for several critiques of pop culture throughout the film. Wyatt stumbles upon Josie and the Pussycats, who are playing on a street corner, and turns them into the biggest band in the world, with a number one hit song and all the brand sponsorships that can be stuffed on the girls' Motorola-themed plane. Seemingly, the film critiques both the constructed (and purportedly disposable) pop culture *and* the prominence of branding and consumerism while also lampooning the idea that media products can alter tastes and purchases.

To better explain, after Wyatt finds Josie and the Pussycats, they turn into near-literal overnight sensations thanks to him and MegaRecords CEO Fiona

(Parker Posey). Within a week, they record an album and see it rise to the top of the *Billboard* charts. At the same time, Fiona is demonstrating to political leaders from around the world how the record company can insert subliminal messages into music that can force people to act. When leaders ask Fiona how they can control the musicians, she flippantly answers, "Ever wonder why so many rock stars die in plane crashes?" She goes on to say that "the possibilities are endless," from drug overdoses to "bankruptcy, shocking scandals, and religious conversions," and that they even "created a highly rated TV show just to explain what happens to these people."

That show? VH1's *Behind the Music*, which ran from 1997 to 2014.

To this end, the film embodies one of the oldest critiques of pop culture: that it is commercially produced and easily replaced.[2] Yet the film was also sending up the number of musical groups that had been assembled for commercial purposes, a cohort that was enjoying its peak in the late 1990s and early years of the 2000s. Massively successful groups like the Spice Girls, Backstreet Boys, and 'N Sync had been famously assembled by managers, and by 2000, the reality show *Making the Band* had raised the curtain on such processes. (*American Idol* wouldn't debut until June 2002, over a year after *Josie and the Pussycats'* release.) Further, the emphasis on production techniques rather than musical talent or skill underscored the standardization and disposability of artists; there's always someone new to replace the last artist.

Second, the film critiqued the rise of branding and sponsorships and the intertwining of popular and consumer culture. The overriding idea is that these musical products are created only to sell more goods. For instance, in DuJour's plane and throughout Josie and the Pussycats' rise, dozens of products and brands are seen in the film.[3] Some of this is very clearly deliberate, like the brand placements inside the planes, the Steve Madden store in front of which Josie and the Pussycats initially play, and DuJour's discussion about their Coke cans. But some were seemingly incidental. For example, an advertisement for Josie and the Pussycats is put up in Times Square, which necessitates the inclusion of other ads to both seem realistic and highlight the band's popularity.

The final send-up is of subliminal messaging; the idea is that advertisements can supposedly be inserted into cultural products without consumers' knowledge, leading to automatic changes in consumer action. It's this final bit of lampooning that muddles the earlier critiques. For example, we see subliminal advertising working in the film—inducing fans to switch from pink to orange or to buy Zima when they don't drink—and the process is also used to cause a rift between Josie and her bandmates. Yet this is fictional and conspiratorial (as was the idea that musicians' deaths were elaborately orchestrated), and there is little evidence that subliminal advertising can change behaviors.[4] While subliminal messaging is used as an over-the-top plot device, the question becomes, Who *exactly* is being ridiculed? Is the film criticizing the commercialization of popular culture and its corruption by brands? Or is it satirizing the *critics* as pearl-clutchers who don't understand reality?

The second way these critiques become muddled is that by the end of the film, everyone learns that both Fiona and Wyatt were outcasts in high school who embarked on this project to get people to like them. (Fiona's severe lisp is exposed, as is Wyatt's albinism.) The two realize that they had gone to the same high school before each of them moved and changed their name and identity—and that they are in love with each other. In the film, the US government also knows about the subliminal advertising because it helps the economy—an educational video featuring a cameo by actor Eugene Levy says as much—but the government officials act surprised to find out about the activity and let Fiona and Wyatt take the fall.

Alexandra Cabot (Missi Pyle), the sister of Josie and the Pussycats' manager, captures the limits of these critiques. "So, what's the moral of the story here?" Alexandra asks. "Freaks should date other freaks?"

"I think the moral of the story is that you should be happy with who you are," Alexander, her brother, responds. "This whole time, we've been spending money on expensive clothes trying to impress people. It never made me happy. No . . . happiness is on the inside. I'm not this. I'm not what I wear. I'm not what I wear!"

At best, we can chalk this up to the naive belief that there is some "authenticity" outside of the oppressive consumer culture, but the film complicated much of that supposed moral. Fiona and Wyatt both found more widespread acceptance through money and the accompanying consumer culture; for a time, they were no longer "freaks," to use Alexandra's word. While Fiona's and Wyatt's intentions might ultimately have been "bad," consumer culture worked to make them cooler and popular. Similarly, Josie and the Pussycats had been playing in empty bowling alleys before Wyatt found them; with the help of MegaRecords, they were playing to a sold-out stadium. After the scheme is exposed, the band plays their original music—rather than the music MegaRecords helped them produce—and they bring the crowd along, but the band would never have reached the same levels of success without the corporate machine. In short, *Josie and the Pussycats'* critique is superficial at best.

Understanding the Critique

Ultimately, *Josie and the Pussycats* was a box office failure—earning only $4.56 million its opening week and less than $15 million during its box office run—although its directors believe the disappointing sales were because it was marketed to preteens.[5] Indeed, the film has become a cult classic and even had a reunion show in Los Angeles in 2017.[6] Yet it was hardly the only criticism of the consumer culture of the time; in fact, wider-ranging critiques have come in the form of journalism since the late 1980s. Anticapitalist publications like the *Baffler*, a magazine of "left-wing" criticism and cultural analysis, and *Adbusters*, a Canadian magazine, were started in opposition to advertising and capitalism more broadly in 1988 and 1989, respectively. Moreover, books like *No Logo* by Naomi Klein, published in 1999, criticized brands for taking over public spaces—in terms of ads, guerilla marketing tactics, and the corporatization of physical areas—and for hollowing out material production to a series of contractors, paving the way for opaque and exploitative factory conditions.[7] And Alissa Quart's *Branded: The Buying and Selling of Teenagers* (2003) critiqued consumer culture's focus on teenagers as a market demographic, noting branding's increased presence in entertainment and education.[8] Many of the above publications took issue with branding's impact on social aspects of life, and Klein and Quart both specifically asked what happens when corporations control space and culture for corporate profits—themes that play into the messages of *Josie and the Pussycats*.[9] In the film, an employee from Steve Madden threatens to call the police because the band is playing on the sidewalk outside the store, a scene that could be ripped from Klein's book.

Further, "The Merchants of Cool," an episode of the PBS documentary series *Frontline*, reported by Douglas Rushkoff, also took issue with the way pop culture and brands targeted teens.[10] Looking at media channels like MTV, Rushkoff noted that cynicism underlined much of teen culture in the late 1990s, and satirical references to making money were at the forefront of the culture, but that satire *still made money*. Like Quart, Rushkoff noted that teens were learning to perform for the media. Teenagers would appear in person at MTV events and shows, where the channel recorded, edited, and packaged such event content for the air, thereby selling it to other teens.

To Rushkoff's argument, *Josie and the Pussycats* centers MTV as a prime venue for "controlling" teens. Not only does the film use MTV News alerts to advance the plot, but it also features *Total Request Live* host Carson Daly. Val and Melody are ostensibly invited to be on the show, but in reality they are being set up to be killed by Daly and *another* Carson Daly, played by *Saturday Night Live* alum Aries Spears. When fighting with Melody, Daly says, "You know, if I wasn't a key player in this whole conspiracy to brainwash the youth of America with pop music, like, we could totally date." (Part of the joke was that Daly *did* date Reid.) And as discussed in chapter 4, MTV was a prime site for intertextuality that helped connect the various venues of popular and brand culture.

Still, this hardly started in the 1990s, as *Josie and the Pussycats* tongue-in-cheekily showed. According to *Baffler* cofounder, historian, and cultural critic Thomas Frank, during the 1960s and '70s, advertising executives saw countercultural movements "not as an enemy to be undermined or a threat to consumer culture but as a hopeful sign" against the establishment, which preached conformity, hard work, and corporatism.[11] While advertising was successful in latching on to countercultural ethos and ideas, the result was a type of vapid, yet inescapable, commercialism; it's perhaps no surprise that the *Baffler* released a collection of essays in 1997 under the title *Commodify Your Dissent*.[12]

To be clear, much of the criticism here was spot on and has influenced my thinking on the time period and consumer culture at large. Yet, these critiques fell flat. As philosophers Joseph Heath and Andrew Potter point out, many countercultural criticisms inadvertently reify consumerism because they miss the individuality people see in mass-produced goods.[13] And that is part of the problem of the critiques from that time. Their assumption was that consumerism, brand culture, and even popular culture were vapid, replaceable, and otherwise devoid of meaning. It's the unspoken truth of the entirety of *Josie and the Pussycats* and underlies a good deal of cultural criticism. Even if we accept the myth that there is some deeper authenticity outside of consumer culture, it has not been the dominant mode for decades—especially for teens.[14]

Regardless, what has been derided as commercial, superficial, and meaningless is simply a different type of cultural knowledge. Unsurprisingly, consumer culture, which has been closely associated with women and teens, has been derided as unimportant and inauthentic, but what's left if the superficial is meaningless?

An example of finding all of it meaningless is in *Branded*, where Quart argues that several of the films I discussed in chapter 3 were more shallow and less interesting than the John Hughes teen films of the 1980s because they were more interested in the "in crowd." According to Quart, the earlier films had some redeeming qualities where the characters learned more profound lessons and spent less time at the mall.[15] While my reading of the films in chapter 3 agrees with Quart about the prominence of consumer culture messaging, that does not make the movies unimportant or uninteresting. And, even if they *are* less interesting, as Quart asserts, they were (and perhaps remain) guideposts for those of us who grew up with them.

Satirizing Privileged Frivolity

The animated MTV show *Daria* (1997–2002), which ran for five seasons and spawned two television movies, offers one of the most prominent critiques of the superficiality of consumer culture at the turn of the millennium. The show was a spin-off of the popular 1990s show *Beavis and Butt-Head* and followed social outcast Daria Morgendorffer as she moved from Highland (the setting of *Beavis and Butt-Head*) to Lawndale. Daria becomes friends with Jane Lane, a budding artist, and deals with the perceived idiocy of her classmates, especially football player Kevin and cheerleader Brittany, while navigating the frequent hypocrisy and cluelessness of her parents, Helen and Jake. While Daria has several foils in the show (intelligence versus ignorance between Daria and Kevin/Brittany; youthful clarity versus practical adulthood between her and her parents), Daria's main counterpart is her fashion-obsessed younger sister, Quinn (figure 6.2).

The older Daria looks at the world cynically, if not entirely pessimistically, usually speaking in a monotone voice and with biting sarcasm. She is a brunette and wears thick-rimmed glasses, a green jacket, a black skirt, and combat boots. Although often implored to care more about her looks or other "popular" pastimes, Daria is a voice of reason in an otherwise crazy world. (This is underscored by the fictional show *Sick, Sad World*, which Daria often watches.) In the show's early seasons, Daria develops a crush on Jane's older brother, Trent, who lives the life of a "rock star" (e.g., sleeping in late, staying up all night) and plays in the fledgling band Mystic Spiral. Later, a love triangle develops when Jane begins to date Tom, who develops feelings for Daria instead. Tom goes to prep school and has a wealthy family, so the fact that Daria and Jane are both interested in him underscores the desirability of a particular type of privilege.

Yet, comparatively, Quinn is the younger and more popular Morgendorffer sister. She is vice president of the school's fashion club, whose members include club president Sandi, secretary Stacy, and treasurer Tiffany. The four girls of the fashion club shop frequently and discuss insignificant things related to fashion, and their interactions are often filled with passive-aggressive barbs aimed at one another. Quinn is courted by three football players—Joey, Jeffy, and Jamie—

Figure 6.2. Animated Duo: In "Malled," Daria (*right*), finds out her sister, Quinn (*left*), skipped school to go to the Mall of the Millennium with the rest of the fashion club. Daria and Jane (*center*) are there as part of a class field trip.

who fight for Quinn's attention and whom she often plays against one another. Moreover, Quinn offers blunt or offensive statements about her sister's appearance and lack of popularity, which Daria usually mocks sarcastically.

Daria's general wry cynicism is the guiding point of criticism about the superficiality of then-contemporary teen life. As such, the intersections of privilege, consumerism, and lack of consequences are not only expected but also ridiculed. Lawndale is a middle- or upper-middle-class town; Daria's parents are a lawyer (Helen) and consultant (Jake), and some of her classmates are even better off. For example, when Daria and Jane go to a party at Brittany's house, we learn that she lives in a private community, complete with a security guard who monitors visitors. Meanwhile, Brittany is stressed because she thinks people will judge her house since her parents haven't had the Jacuzzi installed yet. The satirical nature comes full circle when Brittany apologizes about the Jacuzzi. Jodie Landon, one of the more diligent and insightful students at the high school, responds sarcastically, "It's okay. The wall-to-wall carpeting in the bathroom makes up for it."

Most characters are also white: only Jodie and her boyfriend, football player Mack, are Black, and Quinn's friend and fellow fashion club member Tiffany is seemingly Asian American. Jane's brother, Trent, a struggling musician, is perhaps the poorest person on the show; while he drives a broken-down car, he lives with Jane and her parents and sleeps all day while playing in a band. Even though he has little money, this is part of his alternative cred. The rest of the school drives nice cars; at one point, Quinn rates the guys she's dating and assigns extra points if they have a convertible. In another episode, most of the characters go to a music festival and their wealth (or lack thereof) is displayed in car form: Kevin drives his friends in a Jeep, Sandi takes the fashion club in an Eclipse convertible, and Jane and Daria ride in the unsecured back of a beat-up van Trent borrowed from his bandmate.

At various points, *Daria* lampoons consumerism, especially regarding school. In the episode "Malled," a teacher asks for a "concrete representation" of economic theories. After being called on, Daria deadpans, "If we're talking concrete, I'd have to go with the repository of human greed and debasement: the mall."[16] The teacher eagerly agrees with Daria's example and decides the class should visit the Mall of the Millennium—a reference to the Mall of America—over the protests of Daria and Jane. The students meet with executives from the mall, who attempt to use the students as a focus group, unbeknownst to the students or teacher.

The focus group ruse is exposed when Daria turns off the lights and reveals executives standing behind a two-way mirror. After the exposure, Jodie presses the executives and threatens to alert the media about the ploy. An executive offers them a free yogurt and ten dollars in merchandise, which Jodie and Jane reject as insulting. The executive then offers everyone twenty-dollar merchandise vouchers, and Daria protests, saying, "You don't get it. There's a principle involved."

"No there isn't," Jodie rebuffs Daria before she and the rest of the class eagerly take the coupons.

"So much for idealistic youth," Daria deadpans as Jane reminds her that it's twenty dollars.

A second episode, "This Year's Model," features a modeling agency that has paid the school to use its students as potential new models and to award one student a modeling contract. When the principal announces the arrangement, Daria asks, "Isn't modeling about dropping out of school to pursue a career based solely on your youth and looks, both of which are inevitably declared over by age twenty-five?"

"And don't fashion people squander their lives loudly, worshipping all that is superficial and meaningless while the planet keeps riding a roller coaster to hell?" Jane adds.[17]

The principal acknowledges that modeling is a "competitive field" but says that the "financial rewards" are great. And when pushed, the principal says the school is receiving a fee for its participation that will go to capital improvements—namely, bulletproof skylights for the swimming pool. This is only minorly hyperbolic; at the time, schools were increasingly turning to sponsorships to find funding.[18]

Throughout the show, there is a constant push between Daria being uncool yet unable to escape the social forces at play, even as Quinn embodies many of the undesirable superficial and consumerist ethos. While Quinn is excited to visit the Mall of the Millennium in the B plot of "Malled," Daria is forced to go for class. While Daria sees obvious problems in letting a modeling agency prey on the student body for money, she's unable to stop it and thus hopelessly mocks it; Quinn, instead, throws herself into the competition, convinced she could be a model. Even after their mother tries to talk her out of it by saying modeling is a career where "your value as a human being is decided entirely on the basis of how you look," Quinn asks, "When does the bad part come in?"

Superficial Rebellion

Some of *Daria's* critical sentiments can be traced onto Klein's *No Logo*, which was highly critical of the mall and corporate-controlled spaces, and Quart's *Branded*, which directly questioned the impact of consumerism on teens. In many ways, these critiques argued that there was a superficiality to all of this, and that was the problem—without the corporate world, teen culture would somehow be more "authentic"; Rushkoff's reporting in "The Merchants of Cool" especially plays into such mythic nostalgia of teen life.

Of course, it's not hard to see how the popular culture of the time could be understood as vapid and superficial: corporate sponsorships reigned while bands and recording artists were being assembled—at times live on television—for the sole purpose of making money. Yet, such cultural production was not new to the 1990s; the teen demographic was *created* as a marketing product. It seems only in hindsight that people believe there was "authenticity" in teen culture. And nowhere can this be felt more than in the valorization of rock music over pop music, the former treated as classic and the latter framed as inferior and unimportant. Such judgment reinforces a belief that art produced by and for marginalized groups—especially women and the LGBTQ+ community—is somehow less authentic and less valuable than music produced by straight white men.[19] Equally important here is the idea that artistic products—music especially, but other pop culture as well—have the potential to inspire rebellion and to say something meaningful and products that do not meet this requirement can be ridiculed.[20]

In "The Merchants of Cool," reporter Douglas Rushkoff was especially critical of the exploitation of teen life by marketers and television networks. Following teenagers and coolhunters—people paid to spot trends—Rushkoff noted that corporations were attempting to exploit youth to sell products in both a cynical and cyclical manner. Cynically speaking, brands and media companies nakedly stated they were in it for the money, which created a tongue-in-cheek way for capitalism and consumer culture to purport to be in on the joke. Sure, everyone's doing it for the money, but that's okay. Cyclically, MTV would hold a sponsored event, have teens appear at the event, and then use the footage of it on television—inspiring others to want to be there.[21] Such criticism essentially amounts to a nostalgic belief that teen culture was better in some mythic before-times and had only recently been bastardized by the pursuit of money and, at the time, sexualized to boot. Yet it's also naive to think this started in the 1990s, considering that *Seventeen* magazine had been advertising to teens since the 1940s and the entire teen demographic was a market construct.

One insightful piece of "The Merchants of Cool" examines Insane Clown Posse (ICP) and their hard-core fans, Juggalos and Juggalettes. The rap duo, known for its black-and-white face makeup and, at times, violent, sexist, and racist lyrics (some of which have purportedly been a joke), inspired a hard-core following and crossed over to professional wrestling. The documentary portrays ICP and their fans as an extremity in consumer culture—a musical group trying to resist consumerism through socially unacceptable imagery only to be subsumed by the consumer culture. Still, ICP's annual festival—the Gathering of the Juggalos—seemed to peak in cultural impact and attendance in 2009 and 2010, being lampooned by *Saturday Night Live* and getting written up in outlets like *SPIN* and the *Village Voice*.[22] While the Gathering largely operated under the radar for much of its existence, it received a boost of attention after MTV reality star Tila Tequila performed there and the crowd threw various objects at her. While ICP and their dedicated fans seem shocking and potentially offensive, they were (and are) still selling albums and concert tickets, and their fans are still attending while wearing face paint in styles similar to the band's and even getting tattoos of the band's logo; far from opposing consumer culture, ICP demonstrates that even the socially unacceptable can be commoditized.

Perhaps even more crucially, alternative lifestyles and identities need an appropriate mainstream from which to rebel.[23] This dynamic renders many critiques feckless, as was the case with Woodstock '99, a music festival that attempted to build on the legacy of the original 1969 event. After the original festival's success (and mythologization) and a successful follow-up on Woodstock's twenty-fifth anniversary in 1994, Woodstock '99 went down in infamy after the crowd rioted, destroying stands and starting massive fires. In 2021, "Woodstock 99: Peace, Love

Figure 6.3. Attacking the Boy Band: The Offspring's Dexter Holland attacks mannequins made to look like the Backstreet Boys at Woodstock '99.

and Rage," the first episode in the *Music Box* documentary series, revisited the riot and prompted a rash of articles from the likes of MTV VJ Dave Holmes and *Rolling Stone*'s Rob Sheffield (both of whom were at the festival), as well as pieces in the *New Yorker* and *Vulture*.[24]

Organizers and MTV positioned the festival as an alternative to the sleek pop music and related culture covered by much of this book. In a scene replayed in the documentary episode, Dexter Holland, lead singer for the punk band the Offspring, attacked mannequins dressed as the Backstreet Boys with a baseball bat to cheers from the crowd (figure 6.3). Holmes wrote that the festival consisted of "mostly" angry white guys who were upset by the conditions of the festival, including the summer heat and a lack of shade and water. But, he added, "they were also angry at MTV for leaning briefly away from rock music and toward boy bands and Britney Spears."[25] So while some people later suggested the rioting was the result of toxic masculinity, Woodstock '99 presented itself as an antithesis to the dominant popular culture of the time, even as the lineup consisted of acts like the Offspring, Korn, and Limp Bizkit—groups that frequently sat on the *Total Request Live* countdown alongside the boy bands and pop princesses.

MTV covered the concert extensively until it was determined to be unsafe. As a slightly younger teen at home, I remember watching the rioting on MTV as the VJs signed off for the last time, saying they felt unsafe. (Holmes noted that it was the only concert he had ever needed to be evacuated from.) The festival resulted in three deaths, hundreds of treatments at on-site medical facilities, dozens of arrests, and numerous sexual assaults; police in riot gear finally dispersed the unruly crowd.[26]

While there are minor differences between Woodstock '99 and the MTV-produced events criticized by "The Merchants of Cool," the event and the outcome underscore commodification and consumer culture. As a viewer of MTV and of Woodstock '99, it was the type of event I had *wanted* to be at (up until the rioting, of course); Woodstock, at the time, still maintained a mythologized ethos of young rebellion. But, as the documentary shows, a series of business decisions made the festival grounds inhospitable: the event was moved from grassy fields to a former air force base to better stop people from sneaking into the festival, and everyone remembers that the only water available was being sold for four dollars apiece—and ATMs were broken so people couldn't get cash. As such, it seems like the riot was as much about the conditions as the maleness of the crowd or the "toxic masculinity" to use the *New Yorker's* term.[27]

At the risk of trivializing a chaotic, traumatizing, and deadly moment in youth culture, the vapidness of such rebellion seems especially striking. Woodstock '99 was an event sanctioned, promoted, and reported on by MTV, trying to pass itself off as something more profound and countercultural than the dominant bubblegum pop music—*also played on MTV.* The counterculture might have had different sounds, lyrics, and clothes, but it played into the same consumerist ethos: packaged for money by concert promoters and then sold to audiences through MTV.

Conclusion

It is clear that the dominant culture and counterculture played into many of the same social structures. Yet, chalking one—or even both—up to vapidness misses the point. Regardless of how these texts were produced, these cultural products are what gave—and still give—life meaning. They are the information systems that teach people about the world and become the stories and differences we value. It might all be window dressing for the same consumer culture, but it does not *feel* that way. In other words, these differences—and the messages they provide to a consuming public—matter and should not be dismissed. Yet that's essentially not how critiques at the time or since have addressed the culture at hand—rather, they chose to believe it is lacking or unimportant because it had corporate backing.[28]

While not explicitly stated as such, *Daria* represents something of a dividing line between the overt cynicism that can be attributed to Gen X and the feel-good optimism and superficiality that has been attributed to millennials. Daria, the character, espoused jaded cynicism and individualism, while Quinn played into popularity and consumer culture. Although the two develop a begrudging respect for each other over the course of the series, it might seem like Quinn's worldview has won the day in the years since. Yet the binary choice of Daria or Quinn is too simplistic here. Other characters in the show—Jane and especially Jodie—provide a more nuanced view of the world. Sure, much of consumer culture is exploitive and ridiculous, but we didn't (or don't) have other options. In the scenes mentioned earlier, Jodie uses her knowledge to get a better deal—more free cash at the mall!—rather than hold out for an unreasonable ideal. That exchange brings to mind Josie in *Josie and the Pussycats*, whose dreams were warped by the consumerist system, but in the end she was able to use her newfound fame to the best of her ability by giving fans music she and her band were proud of. It might be small, but it's a way to work within the system. Regardless of how well-meaning any of these critiques were, it should also be no surprise that they could not shake consumer culture and its privileged frivolity; as we'll see in the next chapter, the ethos was even able to withstand a world-shaking terror attack to roll into the first decade of the 2000s.

SEVEN

SPRING BREAK '04

MEAN GIRLS AND
POST-9/11 HIGH SCHOOL

"They're teen royalty," Damian Leigh (Daniel Franzese) explains about the Plastics. "If North Shore was *Us Weekly*, they would always be on the cover." As viewers are introduced to the popular clique in *Mean Girls* (2004)—Karen Smith (Amanda Seyfried), Gretchen Wieners (Lacey Chabert), and Regina George (Rachel McAdams)—we learn not only who they are but also their consumption habits.

Karen Smith is "one of the dumbest girls you will ever meet," according to Janis (Lizzy Caplan); she asked Damian how to spell "orange." And Gretchen Wieners is "totally rich because her dad invented Toaster Strudel," Janis explains, adding that Gretchen knows everything that happens among the student body. But it's Regina who most people are interested in.

"Evil takes a human form in Regina George," Janis tells Cady (Lindsay Lohan). "Don't be fooled, because she may seem like your typical selfish, back-stabbing, slut-faced ho-bag, but in reality, she is so much more than that."

"She's the queen bee," Damian adds in a reference to the film's source material, the book *Queen Bees and Wannabes* by Rosalind Wiseman. "The star. Those other two are just her little workers."

"Regina George. How do I even begin to explain Regina George?" Janis asks, before the film cuts to a montage of other students describing Regina (figure 7.1).

"Regina George is flawless," an overweight student whose hair is pulled into two greasy pigtails says with an admiring grin.

"She has two Fendi purses and a silver Lexus," another student states matter-of-factly.

"I hear her hair's insured for $10,000," adds another.

"I hear she does car commercials," whispers a student in a trench coat, "in Japan."

"Her favorite movie is *Varsity Blues*," a different student tells us.

Figure 7.1. Queen Bees and Wannabes: In *Mean Girls*, the popular clique of Regina (*top left*), Gretchen (*middle left*), and Karen (*bottom left*) is shown as "teen royalty," while some of Regina's admirers (*right*) are shown in a less flattering light.

"One time, she met John Stamos on a plane . . ." begins a student with dwarfism.

" . . . and he told her she was pretty," finishes her friend, a wheelchair user.

"One time, she punched me in the face," a final student shares. "It was awesome."

"She always looks fierce. She always wins Spring Fling queen," Damian explains, before reiterating to Janis the importance of Spring Fling queen; the Spring Fling king and queen become the heads of the school's student activities committee.[1]

As the scene wraps up, Janis hands Cady a sheet of loose-leaf paper with a drawn map of the cafeteria, telling Cady that where she sits "is crucial." Janis then runs down a list of stereotypical high school archetypes, including first-year students, ROTC members, preps, junior varsity jocks, Asian nerds, cool Asians, varsity jocks, unfriendly Black hotties, girls who eat their feelings, girls who don't eat anything, desperate wannabes, burnouts, and sexually active band geeks. These tables are shown on-screen embodying the stereotypes, and some of these tables—like the girls that eat their feelings and the desperate wannabes—include the people who were gushing over Regina George.

Released nearly a decade after *Clueless* and a few years after the glut of teen films that followed it, *Mean Girls* continued to adhere to ideas of privileged frivolity: consumption, privilege, and issues of social life remain center stage. A focus remains on superficial concerns, including what people are wearing— "On Wednesdays we wear pink," Karen helpfully tells Cady in an oft-quoted line from the film. Yet, as I discuss in some of the coming pages, the movie's heightened seriousness raises the stakes and undergirds a moral ambiguity, although the privileged frivolity remains.

In the past two decades, it has become common thought that the September 11, 2001, terror attacks on New York City's World Trade Center and on the Pentagon in Washington, DC, marked a radical turning point in American culture and—along with the disputed and drawn out presidential election of 2000—brought an end to the "long 1990s."[2] After the deadliest attack on the US mainland, the American government invaded Iraq and Afghanistan, getting bogged down in a war in the latter for nearly twenty years. Moreover, the defining Gen X attitude of disinterest went out of style as the country became more politically engaged and eventually polarized.[3]

Yet the cultural impact of September 11 feels a bit overstated, at least when viewing it through a teen lens. Although references to the attack and its aftermath dotted popular culture, a good deal of life went on much like before; perhaps nowhere can this be seen better than in America's consumerism. In the days after the attack, President George W. Bush told the world, "Every nation . . . has a decision to make. Either you are with us, or you are with the terrorists," and he encouraged the American people not to be afraid to shop or to go on vacation to Disney World.[4] And while military families bore the brunt of the wars, the impact on the rest of society was remarkably muted.[5]

"Americans, by and large, didn't feel those sacrifices," journalist Emily Stewart wrote in *Vox* in 2021. "One of the phenomena of the past 20 years is that many Americans didn't feel them at all unless they were directly involved."[6]

Unlike in many previous wars, there was no draft and no rationing, and, if anything, Americans leaned into consumer patriotism—buying and spending as much (or more) than before the attacks. And perhaps this was to be expected; the United States has a long history of using consumerism as a stand-in for values and actions. The country was founded after a boycott of goods from Britain, after all, and throughout the twentieth century, consumerism represented a form of freedom against the repressive, socialist Soviet Union.[7] Shopping: it's the American way.

What seems striking here is that despite the geopolitical happenings, the cultural messages directed at teens that began in the 1990s seemingly continued largely unabated. Pretty teens continued to live their best high school lives; privileged frivolity largely survived intact. Still, the portrayed ideal did not survive wholly unscathed. Rather than feature solely good-willed protagonists in the vein of *Clueless*'s Cher Horowitz, teen films began to engage with moral gray areas—no one was good or bad per se, but everyone was a complex character with the potential to harm.

As such, this chapter makes two points. First, the cultural ethos of teenage privileged frivolity discussed in chapter 3 continued into the 2000s, despite the geopolitical earthquake of the September 11 attacks. Second, the discourse of war and the rise of the antihero—a morally complicated figure that gained prominence in adult fare directly before and after September 11—created more complex teen films. Although fewer teen films were being made than between 1998 and 2001, popular post-9/11 films such as *Mean Girls*, *John Tucker Must Die*, and even the indie teen film *Saved!* presented complex teen characters making morally ambiguous decisions and using more violent language and imagery—including animal attacks in *Mean Girls* and war metaphors in *John Tucker Must Die*. Here, teen social lives are life-and-death serious, but they're also absurd: nothing is permanent and everything is all right in the end.

Complicating Teen Films after 9/11

The September 11 terrorist attacks were a history-making event that set off other geopolitical and cultural actions; the attacks even reshaped how the United States understood historical events leading up to the attack.[8] In the aftermath, traditional gender roles were reasserted, including the glorification of masculine, paternalistic power demonstrated through father figures like John McClane (Bruce Willis) in *Live Free or Die Hard* and Jack Bauer (Kiefer Sutherland) on the TV show *24*. Often, this included "masculine" but morally gray actions, including torture, that were undertaken to protect families and, it was argued, were necessary to achieve a greater good (i.e., safety and security).[9]

The increasingly complex characters share qualities with the antihero, experiencing a rise at the time, embodied by Tony Soprano from *The Sopranos*, and "may have to do with the swaggering zeitgeist of the decade," according to journalist Brett Martin. "Under George W. Bush, matters of politics had a way of becoming referenda on the nation's masculinity: were we a nation of men (decisive, single-minded, unafraid to use force and to dominate) or girls (deliberative, empathetic, given to compromise)?" While Tony Soprano might be the most lauded archetype, such characters continued to appear on-screen in shows from the 2000s and 2010s like *Dexter*, *Mad Men*, and *Breaking Bad*. And while the dynamics of gender may certainly be at play, antihero couples like those in *House of Cards* and *The Americans* show that all genders and ages can assume the role. *Entertainment Weekly* went so far as to name Blair Waldorf (Leighton Meester), a high schooler in *Gossip Girl*, as an "ultimate antihero."[10]

Unlike other genres that could adapt to a traditional or patriarchal mold, the teen genre, which centers youthful and consumer-driven characters, seemingly stands in contrast to the patriarchy.[11] First, consumption and consumer culture are associated mainly with femininity and thus inherently at odds with masculine dominance; second, rebellion has long been painted as a facet of teen life.[12] Neither of these would easily adapt to centering masculinity and traditional masculine archetypes. Yet it's not that the terrorist attacks and subsequent wars had no impact on teen-oriented products; the themes were simply incorporated differently. Characters had moral ambiguity. In this way, the characters might have more shades of the "final girls" trope of horror films (think: Neve Campbell in *Scream*), where actions are predicated on survival even though they might be viewed immorally in a different situation.[13]

In many of the teen films discussed in chapter 3, the lines between good and bad were relatively neatly drawn: in *10 Things I Hate about You*, Kat was lied to and betrayed by Patrick, just as Zack hoodwinked Laney in *She's All That*. Sebastian and Kathryn from *Cruel Intentions* are the only characters who could be classified as antiheroes, but there's also not a *real* moral ambiguity; they are bad people with—wait for it—*cruel intentions* and are eventually punished for it.

Let's compare this to *A Cinderella Story* (2004), an updated fairy tale; the film broadly fits the post-*Clueless* mold but also involves more significant or life-altering situations. It tells the story of Sam (Hilary Duff), whose father passed away, leaving her to live with her stepmother, Fiona (Jennifer Coolidge), and stepsisters. Sam works at the diner Fiona inherited after Sam's father died and hopes to save enough money to go to Princeton. The diner staff, who worked there when her father was alive, watch over her, especially Rhonda (Regina King). Generally considered uncool because she has to work at the diner, Sam finds solace in an online romance with "Nomad," who turns out to be popular football player Austin (Chad Michael Murray). Austin cannot decide between attending the University of Southern California, where his father wants him to go, and Princeton, where he wants to go, after high school.

While Sam pieces together that her online beau is Austin, before she can reveal herself to him her stepsisters learn about the relationship and tell Austin's girlfriend. At a pep rally, the popular clique exposes Sam by reading her messages confessing her love to Austin and mock her as "diner girl." Elsewhere, Fiona intercepts Sam's acceptance to Princeton and replaces it with a rejection letter. Frustrated, Sam stands up to Fiona, quits her job at the diner, and moves in with Rhonda; the diner staff quits, saying they were only staying for Sam.

Ultimately, Austin and Sam reconcile, and he tells his father he wants to go to Princeton. And when Sam is cleaning out her room, she stumbles upon her father's will in a book of fairy tales and learns her father left *her* all of his inheritance—including the diner. Hoping to remain in Sam's good graces, her stepsisters retrieve Sam's actual acceptance letter to Princeton. In closing, Sam and Rhonda take over the diner, where Fiona and her daughters must work to replace the money they stole from Sam. Austin's father accepts him attending Princeton, and the happy couple leave for college together.

Like the teen films discussed in chapter 3, *A Cinderella Story* is based on a classic text cast in a high school setting. However, the content is more complicated than that of the films before it and a bit crueler. Sam is publicly humiliated for working at the diner and having an online relationship with the popular Austin.

While such humiliation is not unheard of in teen-focused films, even the closest example in *She's All That*—where Taylor dumps a drink on Laney—pales in comparison to Sam's broad mocking in front of the entire school. Moreover, Fiona's deception regarding Sam's college acceptance sets up a more serious situation because college represents an escape and promise of a better life (as discussed in chapter 5)—something Fiona is explicitly trying to impede. Even the film's resolution is harsher than that of previous films: Sam sells all of the family's possessions, and Fiona and her daughters are equally "degraded" and forced to work at the diner (more on that in chapter 8).

Everyone's a Mean Girl

A similar ethos exists in *Mean Girls*, perhaps the best-remembered high school movie from the 2000s. Based on a parenting book, the film was written by *Saturday Night Live* alum Tina Fey and produced by Lorne Michaels, also of *Saturday Night Live*. It was the top box office performer in its first week of release, making $24.4 million, ultimately netting $86 million domestically and $130 million worldwide. (It has been the basis for a television sequel, a Broadway musical, and a film version of the musical and is still referenced in bits of popular culture, like Ariana Grande's music video for "thank u, next.")[14]

Mean Girls tells the story of Cady Heron as she transitions from being homeschooled by her zoologist parents (Ana Gasteyer and Neil Flynn) in Africa to attending a typical US high school outside Chicago. Unsure of the school expectations and social hierarchies, Cady becomes friends with outcasts Janis and Damian but also catches the attention of Regina George and the Plastics. While Cady is conflicted about the two groups of new friends, Janis convinces her to spy on the Plastics. Eventually, Cady becomes obsessed with Regina as a rivalry develops between the two of them over Aaron Samuels (Jonathan Bennett). The film culminates when Regina releases the Plastics' "Burn Book"—a collection of insults and rumors about all the girls in the school that Regina and the group keep—to pin the book on Cady, Gretchen, and Karen. While none of the main characters come out of the film as blameless, Cady, Regina, and Janis are all complex characters with complicated motives driving their decision-making.

Cady is clueless about school, and Janis and Damian initially befriend her. They hoodwink her into skipping class by telling Cady her next class is in the "back building," which she later finds out burned down in 1987. Later, Regina invites Cady to sit with the Plastics at lunch; she reluctantly accepts the offer and is encouraged by Janis to gossip about the group behind their backs. Yet, Cady's villainous turn comes when she develops a crush on Aaron, Regina's ex, who sits in front of her in math class. Cady purposely fails math to get Aaron to tutor her and works to undermine Regina by tricking her into eating Kälteen bars that make her gain weight. Later, Cady hosts a party while her parents are out of town and lies to Janis to skip her art exhibit. Janis and Damian find out about the lie and drive past the house to confront Cady; in the verbal argument, Janis accuses Cady of becoming a Plastic, while Cady suggests Janis is just "in love with her"—an insinuation Regina has also made in the past. In the fight, Janis essentially sums up the point of the film: "At least me and Regina George know we're mean," she informs Cady, who has obviously become a mean girl.

When Regina finds out about Cady's sabotage, she makes copies of the Burn Book and passes them out to the entire school. Some of the rumors include that a coach was sleeping with a student (true) and that Ms. Norbury (Tina Fey) pushed drugs on students (false). The rumor gets Ms. Norbury suspended, but eventually Cady comes clean to save her teacher. When Cady attempts to reconcile with Regina, an angry Regina storms away only to get hit by a school bus. Despite (or possibly because of) rumors that Cady pushed Regina in front of the bus, Cady is elected Spring Fling queen, where she shares the crown with all the girls, demonstrating that she learned her lesson.

Morally speaking, the case against Cady is pretty solid. She betrayed the trust of her friends, Janis and Damian, in favor of Regina and the Plastics; betrayed the Plastics to Janis and Damian; and misconstrued a statement made by Ms. Norbury to the Plastics. Additionally, she lied to Janis and Damian, Aaron, and her parents and orchestrated a plot to cause fighting between Gretchen, Karen, and Regina. She also caused Regina to gain weight and attempted to expose the fact that Regina was cheating on Aaron—a fact she learned from an emotionally manipulated Gretchen. Despite these failings, though, Cady remains a somewhat sympathetic character. Not only is she trying to navigate high school social life after never being exposed to it, but she was also befriended under false pretenses by Regina and used as a pawn by Janis.

While Regina became Cady's main target and rival, she is hardly blameless herself. At the start of the film, not only is Regina considered to be the "queen bee" of the school, but she uses that power to intimidate people and forces her friends, Gretchen and Karen, to bend to her will—so much so that Regina controls how they dress. When she befriends Cady, she compliments Cady's bracelet by saying, "Oh my God, I love your bracelet! Where did you get it?" However, Cady later learns it was a backhanded compliment when Regina says the same thing to someone else—only to mock them to Cady privately. After Regina learns about Cady's crush on Aaron, she offers to talk to him but backstabs Cady by trash-talking her and reuniting with him herself. Regina also causes significant emotional damage to many at the school by copying and releasing her Burn Book. The release leads to the girls fighting, forcing the principal to convene an impromptu emotional retreat.

Among the characters in *Mean Girls*, Regina is perhaps the least redeemable: she treats people poorly throughout the film, and in events that occurred before the action of the film, she told people her then-friend Janis was a lesbian and didn't invite her to a sleepover. Yet Regina primarily accrues and uses power in the manners allotted to women—especially young women. In a deleted scene, after Regina is hit by the bus, Cady and Regina meet in the bathroom during the Spring Fling. When Cady attempts to apologize, Regina explains that women apologize too much for things that aren't their fault and they shouldn't feel the need.[15] Although much of the viewing public would not have known about the deleted scene, it underscores that Regina was neither a victim nor a saint but something in between.

And much the same can be said about Janis. In an initial read of *Mean Girls*, Janis might come across as the least morally questionable character; after all, she was wronged by Regina before the film's events and wronged by Cady throughout the film. Yet she freely admits she's "mean," implying that she mainly used Cady to hurt Regina. Janis remains a morally gray character because one can hardly fault her for wanting revenge after Regina's betrayal. Yet using the new girl as a weapon against a past tormenter is undoubtedly questionable.

Killing John Tucker

Using the new girl at school to achieve sinister ends is also the plot of *John Tucker Must Die* (2006).[16] Here, Kate (Brittany Snow) moves to town after her mother's (Jenny McCarthy) latest breakup. At her after-school job as a restaurant server, Kate sees that the popular basketball player from school, John Tucker (Jesse Metcalfe), is dating three women—each of whom he brings to the restaurant, where he alters his actions and personality to appeal to each of his dates. John is the high school heartthrob everyone falls for—even teachers—and he primarily gets away with this by dating people from different cliques so they don't talk to one another. However, after a teacher suffers an injury after seeing John, several gym classes are combined, and John's current girlfriends—head cheerleader Heather (Ashanti), vegan activist Beth (Sophia Bush), and school journalist Carrie (Arielle Kebbel)—realize they are all dating him. Inadvertently, Kate gets roped into a physical confrontation between the three girls, and soon the four of them realize John Tucker "must die."

Arguably, *John Tucker Must Die* may be the final film of the *Clueless*-inspired film cycle, but it also ups the seriousness and severity of *A Cinderella Story* and *Mean Girls*.[17] It is also a clear example of how popular "war" discourses reverberated in teen popular culture; not only do most of the characters have severe moral quandaries, but Kate, who is also the narrator of the film, uses war metaphors throughout.

After the girls unite under the premise that they "all want to kill John Tucker," they plot their first moves. In their first attempt, Beth gets John to model for a photographer friend, and they use his photos in an ad for herpes treatment. Although initially embarrassed and rejected by *another* girl he is on a date with when the ad appears, John ultimately uses the exposure to his advantage and receives an award for bringing the issue to light. As Kate tells the audience, "Rule number one in warfare? Never underestimate your opponent."

The girls' second revenge attempt starts when they see Heather taking her mom's estrogen pills. After some discussion over the ethics and usefulness of estrogen, Beth rants, "What we need is one major hit that's going to crush his whole macho thing, you know? We need him to understand what it's like to be us."

"Right. And what's more terrifying to a man than not being manly?" Kate asks as she holds up the bottle of estrogen.

Heather adds the estrogen to John's protein powder, and he begins to develop "feminine" qualities: his nipples hurt, he has an intense chocolate craving, and after missing a basket and getting yelled at by the coach, he breaks down crying in the middle of a basketball game. "It was a kill strike," Kate narrates, "and it landed with shock and awe."[18] Despite that war reference, the outburst of emotion makes John irresistible to women—stymieing the girls once again.

Their third effort is more sustained in the film's main story arc. Carrie, Heather, and Beth turn Kate, who thought of herself as invisible before the scheming, into a popular cheerleader to get John to fall for her—all so she can break his heart. While Kate is initially reluctant to go along with the plan, the girls coerce her participation, and she reluctantly agrees. Heather gets Kate onto the cheerleading squad, and the girls help Kate play hard to get. Eventually, they use undercover recording equipment to follow Kate's date with John, and Carrie even sneaks into the boys' locker room to record what John is saying about Kate. While in the locker room, Carrie whispers to the camera, "I'm reporting from behind enemy lines. A fortress, if you will, where the innermost workings of the male psyche reveal themselves like a slide under a microscope."

In another scene, the girls convince John to wear lace underwear, and he ends up exposed in front of a group of students, allowing them to take and share embarrassing photos of him. Still, he repairs his reputation, leading Beth to complain, "I'd hit him with my car if he wouldn't make a body cast a fashion statement."

Eventually, John confesses his love for Kate and gives her his watch. Although Carrie, Heather, and Beth are ecstatic because they can "crush him" and declare it "kill time," Kate reneges on the plan and doesn't want to do it. "You're either obsessed with destroying him or obsessed with dating him," Kate admonishes the girls. "Either way, it's all about him."

Even without Kate's help, the girls use a previously recorded video to splice together clips to show Kate harshly rejecting John's love. They scheme to play it during John's birthday party, which Heather explained is "like homecoming combined with prom combined with the MTV Music Awards." Indeed, John's birthday bash is over the top, complete with strippers popping out of a cake. After the video plays, Kate runs onstage to explain she didn't mean it, and a partygoer throws their drink at her for "ruining" the party. When the other girls rush to defend her, the crowd throws drinks at all of them, ignoring their defense of Kate. Even as John steps in to calm the group and take responsibility for lying to the girls, several of John's admirers reject his sentiment.

"There ain't nothing wrong with hookin' up with the finest girls at the school!" one yells to John as others cheer him on. After the crowd breaks into a chant of "Tucker!" and John relishes the attention, Kate realizes he hasn't changed at all. Reaching to grab a handful of the birthday cake, Kate throws it at John and starts a massive food fight.

In the resolution of the film, Kate and John make a truce. Kate goes on to date John's brother, Scott (Penn Badgley), who had been interested in Kate throughout the film and helped John court Kate. And John becomes more truthful—being up-front with girls that he wants to date more than one at a time. And of course, the foursome of girls—Kate, Carrie, Heather, and Beth—remain friends.

The moral quandaries within *John Tucker Must Die* are numerous. John is a morally compromised character; he consistently lies to the girls he is dating and uses his good looks, athletic abilities, and overall status as a popular person to escape the consequences. Likewise, the girls are not blameless. Carrie, Heather, and Beth are physically aggressive to one another when they realize John has been dating all of them, and they go to great lengths to "kill" him. While the phrasing is often used figuratively, not literally, the film shows potential for physical harm; giving John estrogen in secret and convincing him to "scale a building" (in his words) could easily result in serious injury but is played off for laughs. Moreover, as in *Mean Girls*, Carrie, Heather, and Beth take advantage of the lonely new girl in their revenge efforts. And of course, Kate helps conceive the various plots for revenge.

Satirically *Saved!*

While made on a smaller budget than the other films, independent "sleeper hit" *Saved!* (2004) provides some of the most biting commentary of the time while still fitting into the overall scheme of a teen film.[19] The film follows Mary (Jena Malone), a teenager at an evangelical school who starts out as part of the popular Christian Jewels clique with Hilary Faye (Mandy Moore) and Veronica (Elizabeth Thai). When Mary's boyfriend, Dean (Chad Faust), comes out as gay, Mary believes God is telling her to sleep with him to turn him straight. However, Dean's parents find out he's gay and send him to a Christian treatment center, and Mary becomes pregnant from their sexual encounter.

Mary begins to question her faith, which leads to a rift with Hilary Faye and to Mary's rejection by the Christian Jewels to the extent that Hilary Faye and Veronica try to perform an exorcism on Mary, which she rejects.

"Why won't you accept Christ's love?" Hilary Faye demands.

"You don't know the first thing about love," Mary tells her.

"I am filled with Christ's love!" Hilary Faye yells as she throws a Bible at Mary. "You are just jealous of my success in the Lord." Mary scolds Hilary Faye, saying that the Bible isn't a weapon, and leaves.

Cassandra (Eva Amurri), Hilary Faye's nemesis and the only Jewish student at the school, and Roland (Macaulay Culkin), Hilary Faye's paraplegic brother, see Mary leaving Planned Parenthood, and throughout the course of the film the three become friends. Cassandra realizes Mary is pregnant and helps Mary hide her pregnant stomach with new clothes. However, when Patrick (Patrick Fugit), the principal's son, returns to school, a rivalry develops between Hilary Faye, who is interested in him, and Mary, whom Patrick is interested in.

After Roland tells Cassandra and Mary that Hilary Faye used to be overweight and unattractive, Cassandra uploads a picture of a younger, unattractive Hilary Faye to all of the school computers with the phrase "Jesus Hates You." Although Hilary Faye blames Cassandra and Mary for the photo, the principal refuses to do anything because there is no proof, saying only that God knows. The next day, the school is vandalized with spray paint, which is then found in Cassandra's and Mary's lockers—along with Mary's ultrasound. Eventually, Roland learns from a credit card statement that Hilary Faye bought the spray paint, and Roland, Cassandra, and Mary present the evidence at the prom with the support of Veronica and Tia (Heather Matarazzo), who replaced Mary in the Christian Jewels; Tia and Veronica say they found spray paint in Hilary Faye's van. As Hilary Faye flees the prom, she crashes her van into a statue of Jesus, and Mary goes into labor. The film ends with Mary happily giving birth, with Dean, Patrick, and her mother by her side.

Because *Saved!* is lampooning evangelical Christian culture, the moral issues in the film are multilayered. Hilary Faye represents the most righteous character, and she expresses a desire to do right and care for Roland; however, she also uses religion as an excuse to be exclusive and divisive and treats Roland as a burden. She also vandalizes the school and frames Cassandra and Mary for it. At the same time, Cassandra had been expelled from other schools and openly derides students' beliefs; at one point, she mockingly speaks in tongues and rips open her shirt during a school assembly. Yet she is the character most accepting and supportive of Mary throughout the film. Mary is perhaps the most moral character: she attempts to "save" Dean from being gay and begins questioning her religion when he is sent away and she gets pregnant. She's even the voice of reason, telling Hilary Faye she's not living her espoused beliefs.

Depictions of Privileged Frivolity

Even though these films had more complex characters and interrogated the gray areas of human action, all continued to present a teen life of privilege (or proximity to privilege), filled with consumer culture and lack of consequences. These students do not attend inner-city schools; the characters are primarily white (although Ashanti, who is Black, plays one of the main characters in *John Tucker Must Die*); and shopping and self-presentation are understood to be key to popularity. Like in earlier films, themes of consumer culture, self-objectification, and lack of consequences continue to underscore a hopeful naiveté about what is possible—and how.

Throughout *A Cinderella Story*, Sam is treated poorly by her stepmother and stepsisters; however, the family has enough money to survive. This fact does not afford Sam (or her stepsisters) the ability to become popular—and her high school peers largely mock her for having to work in the diner—but she is not in danger of going hungry or becoming homeless. Yet the focus on consumer culture permeates the film: Sam and Austin see the consumption of college as a way out of their current situation, like characters in the earlier high school films discussed in chapter 3 and college films examined in chapter 5. Although money (and greed) drives Fiona's scheming, it is also understood to be the key to success and popularity. While Fiona and her daughters get a comeuppance, there is little consequence for popular students who mocked and denigrated Sam.

Mean Girls is much the same. The high school, again, is mainly white and affluent. However, there are students of color, though some are classified negatively, especially the Asian girls who are preyed upon by a coach and depicted as oversexualized.[20] Cady's parents had homeschooled her and only moved to Evanston, Illinois, from Africa because her mother received tenure at Northwestern University. While Cady's family is not hurting, their wealth pales in comparison to Gretchen's and Regina's. The insight into Regina's life best illustrates privilege; not only is Regina conventionally attractive, but she drives a convertible and commandeered her parents' bedroom. Consumer culture looms large in the film. The various cliques within the high school are distinguished by what they wear and where they sit in the lunchroom. Likewise, the Plastics have a strict code about what they wear, and they take Cady shopping so she fits in. As Cady becomes popular, her clothing transforms from her usual attire—including a pink shirt she has to borrow from Damian—to sexy outfits like those Regina wears. And even though there are some significant issues with the plot, there are few consequences. Regina has a very permissive mother (Amy Poehler), who is more interested in being liked than being an authoritarian, and Cady's parents don't know how to discipline her. Even after the Burn Book is released, causing mass hysteria at the school, there is an assembly centered on trust exercises rather than punishment. And all is resolved by the end of the film: the girls advance to the next grade while trying to keep peace among the younger students.

John Tucker Must Die similarly repeated these themes. Although Kate's character frequently moves towns and has something of an unstable home life, it's due to her mom's relationships, not poverty or other problems. All the girls seem privileged and affluent, but none compare to John Tucker: popular and attractive, he drives a Range Rover and can host massive annual birthday parties. While

Figure 7.2. Product Placements: In *John Tucker Must Die*, Carrie is wearing a Hollister polo (*top*), and the girls conspicuously drink Diet Coke (*bottom*).

consumer culture is less prominent in this film's plot, John can take girls out for fancy dinners and even romances Kate on a private boat. Personal appearance remains essential throughout, and the idea that being a cheerleader is enough to catch John's attention underscores the superficiality. The girls also drink a lot of Diet Coke and are frequently seen wearing Hollister brand clothing (figure 7.2). And again there are no authoritarians or punishments; John continually rehabs his reputation, and the great lengths the girls go to to harm him are generally laughed off by all involved.

Finally, *Saved!* is the most conflicted here but still leans into many of the same ideals. Throughout, privilege remains a prominent backdrop: the characters are largely white and financially well off enough to attend a private school. Privilege often comes into conflict around Roland; as a person with paraplegia, he uses a wheelchair, leading Hilary Faye to drive a specially equipped van—rather than a Lexus Gold Edition. Moreover, Hilary Faye underscores all she does for Roland without actually empowering him, a fact made clear through his relationship with Cassandra; Cassandra has her car adapted so Roland can drive it. The film also pokes holes in the concept of privilege and what it means to be a moral Christian, as people who deviate from the norm are pushed aside or sent away (as Dean was). Consumer culture is also present in various forms, from the cars the characters drive to the clothes Mary buys to hide her baby bump. Yet appearances are key to the film. Cassandra's messy style clashes with the dour demeanor of Hilary Faye and the rest of the school. And when Roland tells Cassandra and Mary about Hilary Faye's glow-up, he jokes, "My parents didn't want two handicapped kids, and she was the easy fix." And, even here, there is a relative lack of consequences. That's not to say there are *no* consequences—Dean gets sent away for being gay; the school expels Cassandra for a time; and Mary does have a baby—but the film ends on a positive note, suggesting that everything will be okay.

As discussed in chapter 3, once a pivotal film comes to define a genre, elements of the film will continue to define the genre—until another film redefines it. We can see here that *Clueless*'s long shadow persisted in teen films through at least 2006. Although such films began to taper off after 2001, they still relied on similar tropes, even as US culture overall was dealing with an ongoing threat of terrorism and war. Instead of disappearing, these films adapted to include antiheroes and military discourse; characters' actions were more serious and morally ambiguous, and the language films used was that of life-and-death struggle.

Moreover, these films more fully examined the ideas of cliques, especially the negative impact of the popular clique. As critics like Alissa Quart have noted, the earlier teen films primarily centered on the social lives of popular students—a trend that largely continued in the four films discussed here.[21] Even if these films shy away from purely valorizing the popular students, the films continue to highlight appearance and consumption as the means to popularity. *Mean Girls'* Plastics are feared, while Hilary Faye weaponizes her popularity against other students, and John Tucker is given pass after pass because of his inherent popularity. Additionally, these films focus on the social work of cliques, constructing an us-versus-them mentality, and the films play into the broader cultural discourses about war: you're either with us or against us, as George W. Bush said at the time. In these teen films, you're in either one clique or another.

Conclusion

This chapter showed that teen films' dominant messages of privileged frivolity did not end with the September 11 terrorist attacks, and even though the teen genre incorporated some of the more militaristic language and moral ambiguity of the time, the focus on privileged consumer culture rolled on more or less unabated. As discussed in chapter 3, there were still stark differences between the high school life presented on-screen and the one that everyday teens were living. But the fact that those representations still resonated more than ten years after *Clueless*'s release speaks to the centrality and longevity of the idea of privileged frivolity and underscores the promises that were made to nearly the entire millennial generation. Although I—and other elder millennials—were close to or in our twenties when the films discussed in this chapter were released, the movies continued to exemplify the same optimistic messaging. Further, as the next chapter shows, this messaging even extended into movies about adulthood—even though differences between fictional portrayals and lived experiences were becoming increasingly stark.

EIGHT

SUMMER '06

THE DEVIL WEARS PRADA
AND EXPECTATIONS OF
MILLENNIAL ADULTHOOD

Perhaps the lowest point of Andy Sachs's (Anne Hathaway) tenure at *Runway* magazine was when an impending hurricane prevented her from getting her boss, editor Miranda Priestly (Meryl Streep), home from Miami for her daughters' recital.

"Do you know why I hired you?" Miranda begins scolding Andy. "I always hire the same girl—stylish, slender, of course, worships the magazine. But so often they turn out to be—disappointing and, um, stupid. So you, with that impressive résumé and the big speech about your so-called work ethic, I, um, thought you would be different. I said to myself, 'Go ahead. Take a chance. Hire the smart, fat girl.' I had hope. . . . Anyway, you ended up disappointing me more than any of the other silly girls."

After being dismissed, Andy seeks solace in Nigel (Stanley Tucci), announcing that Miranda "hates her." Nigel initially mocks Andy before explaining that Miranda is committed to publishing the best magazine possible. Andy's distaste for fashion has shown through in her work ethic—and her style.

"Wake up, six," Nigel says, referring to Andy's (obviously unacceptable) dress size. "She's just doing her job. Don't you know that you are working at the place that published some of the greatest artists of the century? Halston, Lagerfeld, de la Renta. And what they did, what they created, was greater than art because you live your life in it." Nigel tells Andy that the magazine was a beacon of hope for him as he pretended to go to soccer practice but secretly loved sewing.

And after that tough love, Andy gets it.

"Okay, so I'm screwing it up," she admits to Nigel. "I don't want to. I just wish that I knew what I could do—" Andy stops short and realizes the answer: she needs a makeover. And for that she needs Nigel's help.

Based on the book of the same name, *The Devil Wears Prada* is widely understood as a fictionalized depiction of author Lauren Weisberger's time working for Anna Wintour at *Vogue*. The book was published in 2003 and adapted into a feature film released in 2006, making $27.5 million on its opening weekend with an overall sum of $124.7 domestically and $326.7 million worldwide.[1] While the book told of Andy's multiple humiliations until she finally quit her thankless job, the film adaptation turned Priestly into something of a sympathetic girlboss—one who had to be demanding to get the most out of people while she threw herself into her work at great personal expense. Andy's makeover in the film drives a change in attitude, showing she takes the job seriously, and ultimately wins Miranda's respect.

This chapter examines a set of young adult films from the early 2000s that deal specifically with workplaces and career expectations. *The Devil Wears Prada* and several other films in this vein—*Sweet Home Alabama*, *How to Lose a Guy in 10 Days*, and *13 Going on 30*—set career expectations in a way similar to what teen and college films had been selling since the mid-1990s. In other words, privilege and the right type of consumption could help you go far in the adult world. In comparison, films like *Waiting . . .* and *Employee of the Month* showed that people would become a tragic laughingstock if they lacked cultural capital and had unsuccessful consumption habits. This aspirational ethos maintained that something better could or would be possible, even as social stratification continued to grow and a global reckoning would soon strike the world economy.

Privileged Frivolity Grows Up

Unlike the previous chapters, which focused explicitly on pop culture products that easily fit into the teen genre, this chapter extends the view toward career films. While this may seem incongruous, there are a few reasons to include these films in the same general trajectory. First, the age cohort most impacted by the *Clueless*-inspired film cycle of 1999 and 2000 was entering adulthood by the mid-2000s, when these movies were coming out. For example, although I was a tween when *Clueless* came out and in my mid-teens between 1998 and 2001, I was in my early twenties when *The Devil Wears Prada* was released and gearing up for postcollegiate life. These films continued to convey similar messages as my age cohort entered adulthood.

Second, some of the actors in these films were already familiar to audiences from their earlier work. For example, *The Devil Wears Prada* starred Hathaway, known for her teen-focused *Princess Diaries* films in 2001 and 2004; Adrian Grenier, who had starred in *Drive Me Crazy*, played Andy's boyfriend, Nate.

Likewise, *Sweet Home Alabama* starred Reese Witherspoon, known for *Cruel Intentions* and *Legally Blonde*; *Waiting...* starred Ryan Reynolds of *Van Wilder* fame and Anna Faris (who was in the *Scary Movie* franchise); and *Employee of the Month* featured pop singer Jessica Simpson.

Finally, these films still largely fit into the teen genre even though they don't feature teens and invite an audience well beyond the teen market. To recap arguments from earlier chapters, the teen genre developed into more of a lifestyle category than a focus on a particular age group.[2] For proof of this, we don't have to look any further than the Teen Choice Awards, which nominated many of the above films, including *Sweet Home Alabama*, *The Devil Wears Prada*, and *Employee of the Month*, for awards even though they were ostensibly "adult" films.[3] Moreover, these films still focused on questions of identity, personal growth, and personal relationships and were told lightheartedly, reflecting the themes and techniques of teen fare.

While the tenets of privileged frivolity—an embodiment of privilege, objectification through consumer culture, and overall lack of consequences—look a bit different in early adulthood, they are present nonetheless. Overall, these films continue to highlight the eternal optimism of the time, reinforcing the belief that everything will be all right, even as opportunities in aspirational professions shrank and less desirable career paths grew.

A Change Will Do You Good

While we've touched upon the idea of transformation in teen films, trying on new identities and figuring out who one wants to be is expected of teens and seen in many teen narratives. Likewise, transformation is key to both the Hollywood movie structure and society at large. Most importantly, the ideals of self-transformation—which often focus on aesthetics and consumption habits—generally gain traction and prominence during "times of despair" and "enormous social, political and economic changes," according to sociologist Mickie McGee. Similarly (and usurpingly as a visual medium), on-screen transformations generally reflect changes in costuming and appearance but denote more profound changes in the individual—and indicate that change is possible for audience members, too. While the need for transformational narratives has waxed and waned, they returned to the zeitgeist in the late 1990s and early 2000s.[4]

Transformational narratives on-screen often rely on the idea that a makeover and subsequent changes represent the "true self" coming out. However, the idea of an authentic or "true" self is certainly socially constructed.[5] In the previous chapters, I argued that consumption changes were the path to success rather than the exposure of some "true self"; as such, it is also an acknowledgment of a *constructed* self. Tai's change in *Clueless* was not to demonstrate her inner self but to make her more desirable to a subset of men. Much the same can be said of Cady in *Mean Girls*; the transformation did not expose her true self but a new version of herself (and one that she did not recognize or like). Regardless, the films in this chapter support consumption—not just of fashion but of activities, locations, and even education—as a means for people to become a new, more desirable and perhaps even ideal self.

In the case of *Sweet Home Alabama* (2002), the film tells a transformation story nearly in reverse.[6] It opens with Melanie Smooter (Reese Witherspoon) and Jake Perry (Josh Lucas) as children sharing their first kiss on the beach, but viewers quickly learn that now Melanie *Carmichael* is a budding fashion designer getting ready for her first runway show at New York Fashion Week. Melanie gets engaged to Andrew Hennings (Patrick Dempsey), the son of New York City mayor Kate Hennings (Candice Bergen). Although Melanie tries to keep the engagement a secret, Kate feels Melanie's engagement ring during a public charity event, and the tabloid press jumps on the story with headlines like "Mayor's Son to Wed Fashion Princess."

Melanie returns to her hometown of Greenville, Alabama, to get her estranged husband, Jake, to sign divorce papers. Melanie is now a fish out of water—her silver convertible Saab, high-heeled boots, and feathered hair stand in contrast to the people she left behind, who look provincial and unfashionable in comparison (figure 8.1). This chasm crystallizes after Jake refuses to sign the divorce papers.

"Jake! You dumb stubborn redneck hick!" Melanie yells through Jake's screen door in a heavy southern accent. "The only reason you won't sign these papers is 'cause I want you to!"

"Wrong!" Jake retorts. "The only reason I ain't signin' is 'cause you've turned into some hoity-toity Yankee *bitch*, and I'd like nothing better right now than to piss you off!"

Viewers learn that Melanie has a complicated relationship with her parents, whom she doesn't see often and who are unwilling to visit her in New York. Melanie also sees her "new self" as better than the friends and relations she left behind in Alabama. Yet her old friends are still kind to her, even if they seem a bit provincial. In one exchange, Lurlynn (Melanie Lynskey) tells Melanie "You look like you just stepped out of a magazine" and compliments her sweater. However, there

Figure 8.1. Going Home Again: After moving to New York City, Melanie looks out of place when she returns to her hometown in *Sweet Home Alabama*.

is a notable disconnect when Melanie explains that it is a look she designed—and has just been picked up by luxury department store Bergdorf Goodman—while Lurlynn treats Kmart's Jaclyn Smith line as the height of fashion.

Eventually, viewers learn that Melanie had not taken just any last name but adopted "Carmichael" because it was the name of a prominent family in town, and Melanie confesses her humble upbringing to Andrew. While his mother is livid at the betrayal, an exchange between her and Andrew demonstrates the desirability—if not necessity—of transformation. "What would you suggest I do, Mom," Andrew asks Kate, "dump her for being poor? You're supposed to be a Democrat, remember?"

"There is nothing wrong with being poor. I get elected by poor people," Kate tells him. "And I'm a big enough person to commend her for making something of herself. What upsets me is that she lied to you." Yet both viewers and Andrew know this to be fake sincerity, as Kate's dislike for Melanie was made clear; as Andrew recounted to a friend, Kate had told him he "should date women like Melanie, not marry them."

Moreover, it is revealed that Melanie moved to New York City and adopted a different name after having a miscarriage. "All of a sudden, I just needed a different life," Melanie explains to Jake about her decision to leave. Yet the Jake she is now trying to divorce is a different person than the one she had left; in an attempt to win Melanie back, he started a thriving glass business. While Melanie and

Andrew still gather for their wedding, Melanie ultimately leaves him at the altar (so to speak), realizing she's still in love with Jake.

Although the story is told as one that uncovers a hidden—or even sordid—past that Melanie would rather forget, *Sweet Home Alabama* supports the tenets of privileged frivolity. Melanie embodies privilege; even though her family is what someone might derogatorily refer to as trailer trash, she was able to build a successful fashion career in a few short years and reach the upper echelons of New York society. Compared to those who stayed in Alabama, she is at the forefront of fashion, while they remain in the past, have kids, and continue to make "poor" life choices (exemplified by bringing a child to a bar). Moreover, comments reinforce Melanie's attractiveness and underscore the fact that she is making a name for herself in fashion—the vanguard of consumer culture. Finally, Melanie constructed an entire history for herself, complete with a lie that her family was one of the richest in Greenville, and usurped a new last name when she left for New York. This narrative highlights that transformation *is* possible, even if the truth might eventually come out, and ultimately little is made of the fact that Melanie lied about her last name and took on a new identity. Even her fiancé is understanding, and there's little to no consideration that staying married to Jake might harm her budding fashion career.

Success in the Creative Industries

The Devil Wears Prada has received its share of academic attention, although it was not the only film to position successful and desirable adulthood within the creative industries or media fields (e.g., advertising, journalism, and entertainment).[7] Take *How to Lose a Guy in 10 Days* (2003). The romantic comedy starred Kate Hudson as Andie Anderson, a budding magazine writer trying to flex her writing muscles. Inspired by a friend's recent breakup, she pitches a story where she does everything "wrong" in a relationship to push away a beau, which her editor (Bebe Neuwirth) eagerly accepts. Separately, advertising executive Ben Barry (Matthew McConaughey) has his eye on the account for a diamond firm; to prove he can sell diamonds, he bets his colleagues that he can get any woman to fall in love with him in ten days. However, Ben's coworkers overhear Andie's story pitch and select her as Ben's unwitting target. Throughout the film, Ben willingly puts up with Andie's abuse in an attempt to win the account, and—although both Andie's intended article and Ben's wager are uncovered at an elegant gala for the diamond brand—they realize they developed feelings for each other and end up together.

For the purposes of this chapter, the characters and their careers are more important than the specifics of the plot. Andie is a writer at a women's magazine; although she is unhappy with the range of topics her editor will approve, she's shown as living a good life in New York City. Ditto for Ben. They both have their own apartments and can attend events like NBA games and Celine Dion concerts at the drop of a hat. The film culminates at a high-status advertising gala that underscores the desirability of their lifestyles. The fact that Andie's article was a hit, Ben got his account (and his colleagues got their comeuppance), and all is forgiven so Andie and Ben can get together at the end, is just icing on the cake.

Likewise, *13 Going on 30* (2004) tells the story of thirteen-year-old Jenna Rink (Jennifer Garner), who wishes to be thirty after she's humiliated by the popular clique she desperately wants to befriend. When she wakes up the next day, she is a successful thirty-year-old magazine editor with no memory of the intervening years. Jenna is now best friends with her teenage tormenter, Lucy (Judy Greer), and they are coeditors of *Poise*, a struggling women's publication that is frequently scooped by its rival. Jenna lives a luxurious life, but as she pieces together the intervening seventeen years, she learns her life took a different turn than anticipated: she has become a cutthroat editor who steals ideas and has slept with a coworker's husband. Most shockingly, Jenna discovers she is conspiring with the rival publication to undermine *Poise*, hoping to get a job there.

In the denouement, Jenna returns to her thirteen-year-old self and makes different choices—rather than become friends with the popular clique and a successful magazine editor, she dates and marries her best friend and neighbor, Matt (Mark Ruffalo). Yet the film still portrays a successful and desirable life for a magazine editor, even if it might be challenging to untangle Jenna's morally questionable decisions from her success. And, let's be honest, Jenna would have been heralded as a girlboss a few years later rather than admonished for her take-no-prisoners ethos.

But perhaps nowhere are such dynamics more at play than in *The Devil Wears Prada*. As mentioned earlier, the film follows Andy Sachs as she works for Miranda Priestly at *Runway* magazine. Andy has just graduated from Northwestern (a "good" school—see chapter 5) and moved to New York City with the desire to be a journalist. She lives with her chef boyfriend, Nate, whom she becomes increasingly estranged from as she enters the fashion world. After her growing pains, she's welcomed into fashion's inner circle of fantastic parties and international travel. Andy can now not only outfit herself with the samples from *Runway*'s closet but give her friends lavish gifts that Miranda doesn't want. At a party thrown by designer James Holt (Daniel Sunjata), she meets writer Christian Thompson (Simon Baker), whose work she admires and wrote about for her undergraduate thesis. Eventually, Andy has a fling with Christian and stumbles upon a plot to oust Miranda from *Runway*. Andy tries to warn Miranda, who rebuffs her but manages to sideline her replacement nonetheless—saving her editorship of *Runway*.

Afterward, Miranda lauds Andy's tenacity in trying to warn her about her impending ouster.

"You thought I didn't know," Miranda says as they ride through the streets of Paris. Miranda explains that it took time to save her job and she saw herself in Andy's determination to warn her of the potential ouster. "You can see beyond what people want and what they need, and you can choose for yourself," Miranda explains. Andy blanches at the suggestion that she could put herself above others, and Miranda points out that she already has.

"You choose," Miranda tells Andy. "You chose to get ahead. You want this life; those choices are necessary."

"But what if this isn't what I want?" Andy asks. "I mean, what if I don't wanna live the way you live?"

"Don't be ridiculous, Andrea," Miranda admonishes. "Everybody wants this. Everybody wants to be us."

Andy decides she does not want that to be her life; she quits her job by walking away from Miranda and throwing her phone in a fountain. When she returns to New York, Andy reconciles with coworker Emily and beau Nate, who plans to move to Boston to further his career. And Andy interviews for a job at the *New York Mirror*, whose editor lauds her college news reporting. Although the editor is skeptical of her time at *Runway*, he says that Miranda herself sent a fax calling Andy her "biggest disappointment" and that he would be an idiot if he didn't hire her.

All of the films above demonstrate what consumer culture makes possible. Not only are these characters—Andie Anderson, Jenna Rink, and Andy Sachs—successful at consumer-focused publications, but some of them, Jenna and Andy especially, can transform themselves through their work, habits, and personal appearance. While both *13 Going on 30* and *The Devil Wears Prada* are framed as cautionary tales of losing oneself, the transformative message is there: transformation *is* possible and even desirable. After all, as Miranda explained, "everyone wants to be us."

Failure to Launch

Not all of the films of this era, however, show characters growing up—or growing old—successfully. Those who do not consume properly find themselves in undesirable situations. Take two movies showing people working in the service industry: at a restaurant in *Waiting . . .* and a big-box retail store in *Employee of the Month*. What underlies the premises of both films is the idea that such work is low-status and even downright degrading, something people should be trying to escape from.

The independent film *Waiting . . .* (2005) mostly takes place over a single shift at the restaurant Shenaniganz, an amalgamation of real-life chains like TGI Fridays, Ruby Tuesday, and Applebee's.[8] The decor is familiar to anyone who visited chain restaurants in the 2000s: a mishmash of items tacked onto walls that look vaguely "vintage" while also nodding to celebratory times (figure 8.2). Before the start of his shift, Dean (Justin Long) has lunch with his mother, who talks about the success of Chet, a high school classmate who now works as an electrical engineer. At work, Dean complains about Chet's success to friend and fellow server Monty (Ryan Reynolds), a "cool" ladies' man, who encourages Dean to forget it. (As an aside: the characters played by Long and Reynolds seem to mirror those in *Accepted* and *Van Wilder*, discussed in chapter 5; *Waiting . . .* was released after *Van Wilder* but the year before *Accepted*.)

"Yeah, but come on man," Dean continues. "We haven't even graduated from community college. We haven't even got our AA [associate's] degree. Then, when we do, what? What the hell can you do with an AA degree anyway?"

During the shift, hapless manager Dan (David Koechner) offers Dean the chance to become an assistant manager of the restaurant, and, noticing Dan's framed associate's degree on the wall, Dean wrestles with the question of whether or not he wants to end up like Dan. Dean takes his existential crisis out on customers and coworkers alike, asking another server, "Did you ever just wake up and realize, 'Holy shit, I'm a fucking loser'?" and explaining, "God, I just wanna be able to say 'I wanna be a teacher,' you know, or a podiatrist or a fucking electrical engineer. Anything, just have a fucking clue."

Figure 8.2. The Millennial Chain Restaurant: The restaurant in *Waiting . . .* is decorated with assorted tchotchkes, as seen behind Dean (*top*) and Mitch and Monty (*bottom*).

The night doesn't get much better for Dean: After customers at one of his tables heavily compliment him, they offer him a job—which he is initially excited about until he finds out it's at a rival restaurant. And, just as the restaurant is about to close, Chet comes in and is seated in Dean's section. The two make small talk about their lives. We find out that Chet graduated and began his "new career," where he started earning $48,000 a year. The exchange between the two is stilted as Dean meekly explains he's been considering becoming an assistant manager, only to be interrupted by Chet asking for more iced tea. The final humiliation occurs when Chet leaves Dean a nearly seventy-dollar tip. Thinking it's a mistake, Dean gives Chet the change but is rebuffed.

"Look," Chet explains with a look of pity, "I just thought maybe you needed it more than I do."

Realizing he doesn't want this to be his life, Dean goes to the office, tells Dan he doesn't want the promotion, and quits Shenaniganz completely.

"You know, I thought about it," Dean tells Monty afterward. "I thought a lot about it. And I know I don't wanna wait tables anymore. Ya know, I know that. And this is all temporary. This is supposed to be the in-between time."

A more forceful condemnation of the restaurant industry and those who work in it comes from Mitch (John Francis Daley), who was training with Monty and was generally ignored and demeaned throughout the shift.

"You're all fucked in the head! All of you!" Mitch yells as he begins to insult each member of the staff. Pointing at Dean, he yells, "'Waa! I don't know what to be when I grow up!' Join the fucking army or something!"

When he eventually gets to Monty, Mitch articulates the film's theme. "Fuck you, Monty!" he begins by flipping him off with both hands. "You always gotta be right with your little quips! We get it, man. You're fucking edgy and cool. Yeah! You're the coolest fucking guy at Shenaniganz! Woo! That's like being the smartest kid with Down syndrome!"

The force of Mitch's ableist condemnation highlights everyone's struggles at the restaurant and the "questionable" views and activities of all involved.[9] More to the point, his insult of Monty underscores society's low esteem for restaurant work and, by and large, the service industry as a whole. *Waiting . . .* only makes sense if we understand service industry work as low-value and meaningless: even though Dean had the chance to move into management, becoming like Dan is considered a terrible fate. *Waiting . . .* shows us that service work is considered directionless and that, by extension, those who perform it are considered devoid of aspiration.

While not nearly as aggressive in its denunciation, *Employee of the Month* (2006) has a similar premise: that retail work is of low value and otherwise dehumanizing. Set in a big-box store named Super Club—understood to be Costco but with employees wearing blue vests similar to those used by Walmart—the film follows the rivalry between "box boy" Zack (Dane Cook) and cashier and seventeen-time employee of the month Vince (Dax Shepard) as they vie for the attention of new girl Amy (Jessica Simpson). Amy has transferred from another location, where she had a relationship with the employee of the month that ended badly. Zack determines that winning employee of the month is the path to winning Amy's heart, while Vince is trying to become the first person in the history of Super Club to win employee of the month for eighteen straight months and win a "brand-newish" 2005 Chevy Malibu.

At the start of the film, Zack is a box boy and general slacker at the store, even setting up an unofficial poker room with coworkers Lon (Andy Dick), Iqbal (Brian George), and Russell (Harland Williams). Comparatively, Vince, who recently was named the fastest cashier in the Southwest, takes his job too seriously and has an inflated sense of self-importance. However, Super Club has a definitive hierarchy of positions, as cashiers have their own break room, and Vince is portrayed as a "celebrity" thanks to his fast and performative checkouts.

The premise that working at Super Club is low-status becomes apparent early on. Even as management lauds Vince for being "employee of the month" for the seventeenth consecutive time, other employees at a store meeting seem bored and are only excited when they're told that the store will close early. Unfortunately for the workers, the store is closing early for a corporate banquet awards show that they must attend, and the manager (Tim Bagley) instructs the employees to dress nicely in "church clothes."

Later, there's an exchange between Iqbal and Lon that sheds light on their feelings about working at Super Club. While consoling Zack, Iqbal says, "I think there's honor in a good day's work."

Lon replies, "There's no honor working in that black hole." While Russell jumps in to say they could be working at Maxi Mart, a worse place, it comes through that working at Super Club is degrading or, at the very least, undesirable.

After her transfer, Amy initially goes on a bad date with Vince, and Zack continues to pursue her and the title of employee of the month, going above and beyond to help customers. Later, when Zack takes Amy on a date through the closed aisles of Super Club—set up for movie watching and minigolf on the roof—they each share why they are working at Super Club. When discussing how they naturally seem to relate to each other, Zack asks how Amy became so normal since she treats everyone well despite being a "nine or ten" (on an attractiveness scale). In response, Amy reveals a secret hidden by her long blonde hair: she has giant ears that got her made fun of when she was young! While Amy is skeptical that Zack is still a box boy, believing it shows a lack of drive, he explains that he borrowed money for a dot-com company that went bust and ended up living with his grandmother and working at Super Club after the failure.

Yet throughout the film, what remains consistent is the idea that working at Super Club is ridiculous and that Vince, especially, is pathetic for taking the job so seriously. When the store needs a cashier and Zack offers to do it, Vince scoffs and says Zack will never be ready for the shift. "I mean, you can't just walk in off the street and do what we do. It takes years and years of training," Vince protests. "I mean, let's just let him perform a tracheotomy. This is ridiculous." The inherent joke is that it doesn't take much training to be a cashier—certainly not as much as becoming a doctor—and the humor mocks Vince's earnestness and egotism while holding such a low-status job.

Taken together, both *Waiting...* and *Employee of the Month* provide cautionary tales of the life people don't want to live and what happens if they do not act purposefully to consume in the right ways. These are people who do not embody privilege (though it should be noted that these individuals are white and at least have jobs, so there is *some* privilege) and have limited options for getting themselves out of their current situations. As such, they end up as service industry workers: the people forced to degrade themselves by serving others. Worse yet, some characters are too naive or too dense (Dan in *Waiting...* and Vince in *Employee of the Month*) to truly understand their lot in life.

Consumable Aspiration and Successful Adulthood

Collectively, these films embody contradictions from the popular culture of the time and US culture writ large. Yet the types of jobs one performs in contemporary consumer society vary and are held in different regards. As discussed in the previous pages, retail and service industry work is generally looked down upon—something embarrassing to perform and not something a person strives for—while publishing and creative industries can lead to "the good life."

This is not totally surprising; those who work in the film industry have been understood as cultural intermediaries and "petite bourgeoisie," an upwardly mobile group, and can translate upper-class tastes for the masses.[10] As noted in chapter 4, even though the US mythology holds that hard work allows you to transcend class boundaries, that is not always the case.

As conveyed in the above films, there are desirable career paths (publishing and fashion design) and undesirable jobs (food service and retail). Yet to look at statistics, more people worked, and continue to work, in low-status jobs than in high-status positions. To bookend the films, TV shows, and other texts discussed throughout this book, in July 1995, the month *Clueless* hit theaters, roughly 13,814,100 people worked in retail, according to the US Bureau of Labor Statistics (figure 8.3). That number rose through the dot-com bubble of 2000 and 2001 and peaked at 15,577,400 in December 2007. After sliding during the Great Recession, retail work reached an all-time high of 15,917,800 in January 2017, and even after the COVID recession, roughly 15.8 million Americans work in retail.[11]

Or consider restaurants, bars, and the hospitality industry at large (figure 8.4). In July 1995, 7,412,400 people worked in the industry, according to the US Bureau of Labor Statistics. But this steadily increased, even during the 2000

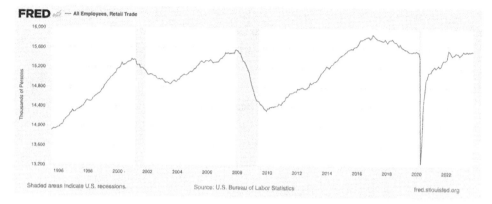

Figure 8.3. Retail Workers: The number of people working in retail in the United States since 1995, according to the US Bureau of Labor Statistics. Source: Federal Reserve Economic Data/Federal Reserve Bank of St. Louis.

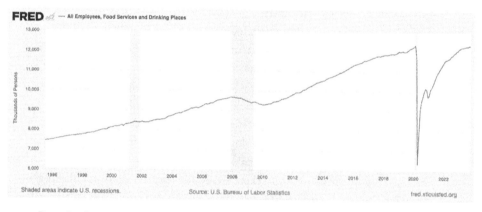

Figure 8.4. Restaurant and Bar Workers: The number of people working in food service and bars in the United States since 1995, according to the US Bureau of Labor Statistics. Source: Federal Reserve Economic Data/Federal Reserve Bank of St. Louis.

recession. By December 2007, 9,673,000 people worked in food service, with a slight downtick during the 2008 recession: 9,514,200 worked in food service in November 2008, and that bottomed out at 9,387,700 in April 2009. Before COVID, that number had grown to 12,306,600 in February 2020, and even after COVID, the number had rebounded to 11,609,900 in May 2022. That's roughly 4.2 million more people working in food service since July 1995, or 56.6 percent growth. The closely related leisure and hospitality industries also saw substantial

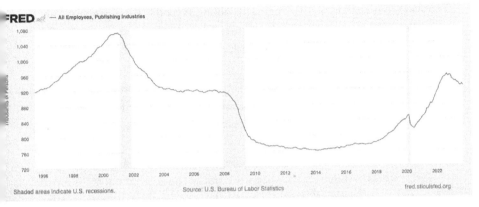

Figure 8.5. Publishing Field: The number of people working in publishing in the United States since 1995, according to the US Bureau of Labor Statistics. Source: Federal Reserve Economic Data/ Federal Reserve Bank of St. Louis.

growth: from 10,535,000 people in July 1995 to 13,550,000 in December 2007 and 16,983,000 in February 2020.[12]

Both of these numbers swamp the number of employees working in the publishing industry (figure 8.5). Roughly 912,200 worked in publishing in July 1995, according to the Federal Reserve of St. Louis. That number would rise through the 1990s and peak at 1,045,700 in January 2001. It then fell during the early 2000s and settled at about 900,000 for much of the decade. But the 2008 recession saw the numbers crater: from 895,400 in December 2007 to 859,300 in November 2008 and 794,700 by June 2009. The bottom would finally come in September 2014, when only 726,000 people worked in publishing.[13] Even if we're generous and include *everyone* working in the "information industry" as classified by the Federal Reserve—publishing, broadcasting, motion pictures and recording, telecommunications, and data processing—those industries employed 2,843,700 in 1995 and 2,983,200 in 2008 before falling back to 2,720,600 in 2020.[14] In short, roughly 3 million people work in publishing and production, but about 10 million more people work in retail and 14 million more work in hospitality than in the total of the publishing and information-related industries.

What's most relevant here is the break between "desirable" and "undesirable" careers within the consumer economy. The films discussed above focused on various aspects of the creative industries—fashion design, publishing, and advertising, or those who produce or mediate popular and consumer culture. These jobs are seen as desirable, if cutthroat, enabling a "good life" for people in those positions. While the desirability of these positions is left unstated in some of the films, such as *How to Lose a Guy in 10 Days* or *Sweet Home Alabama*, it's more explicit in others. In *13 Going on 30*, this is literally the life Jenna wished for, and in *The Devil Wears Prada*, Miranda states that everyone wants to be the people who work at *Runway*. Although these films also highlight the downsides of these positions, they maintain that achieving such success is possible and, by and large, desirable.

This narrative contrasts with the message in *Waiting . . .* and *Employee of the Month*, which assumes that service work in the consumer economy is for the lazy and unmotivated. *Waiting . . .* especially sets it up as a matter of consumption; servers are the people others look down upon and treat badly, and those working at chain restaurants do so because they have not set themselves up for better options. The through line is that having a bachelor's degree is better than having an associate's degree, with the former setting one up for "success" while the latter can—at best—get you to be a manager at a restaurant. Similar to the case made in chapter 5, here, better educational consumption makes a bachelor's degree attainable and a better life possible. *Employee of the Month* does not make academic attainment key to its degradation of retail work, but the film makes it clear that service work is not a serious or respectable profession. Even when Vince ostensibly "succeeds" in a retail career, he is driving a beat-up car and competing to win a used car.

Beyond the divergent storylines, which position the creative-industry careers as desirable and service careers as loathsome, it is important to remember that the service and retail industries saw substantial growth over this period. While it may be that the creative-industry professions are desirable primarily *because* of their limited availability and exclusivity, that does not change the dynamic that the more exclusive industries are being lauded and promoted while the much more available and growing career paths are mocked and degraded.

Finally, even if someone grabbed the brass ring and made it in the creative industries, the lifestyles portrayed on-screen did not reflect most lived experiences. Journalists' annual salaries ranged from $25,000 to $37,400 in 2007, according to a survey from the University of Georgia's James M. Cox Jr. Center for International Mass Communication Training and Research.[15] That was slightly below the median US salary in 2008, estimated to have been between $32,390, according to the US Bureau of Labor Statistics, and $39,653, according to the Social Security Administration.[16] The average salary for the entire information jobs industry was roughly $58,593 in December 2007, according to the US Bureau of Labor Statistics.[17] Of course, the characters in the aspirational films might be considered the elite of the elite. Still, the lived experience of the vast majority would not be in line with these representations.

Conclusion

As I wrote in the introduction of this book, there's nothing wrong with producing films or other elements of pop culture that are not true to real life; arguably, that is the heart of most fiction. The movies discussed in this chapter described aspirational transformations through consumer culture: one could leave their backwoods Alabama town to become a successful fashion designer and member of the New York City elite; one could raid the closet of a high-end magazine to become a successful publishing assistant; and just completing a bachelor's degree could get one out of the service industry. Regardless of the impetus for portraying self-transformation in these films, each one supports aspiration through specific uses of consumer culture and the idea that things should, could, or would get better. Jenna Rink in *13 Going on 30* might not have liked the adult she became after her wish came true, but she could very well have made the decisions that got her there. Comparatively, in *Waiting . . .* Dean believed that future career success would come from consuming the proper education.

At the same time, while these films individually promote the idea that transformation is possible, the narratives agree that some careers are better than others and thus provide a more desirable life. Yet it was the "nondesirable" professions that were growing at the turn of the millennium and continue to do so. This is yet another schism between what was presented as possible and desirable in popular culture, even as the ability to achieve such heights was growing increasingly less probable. As such, the feelings of optimism and possibility present at the time have given way to a jaded cynicism that currently dominates the cultural landscape. In the concluding chapter, we'll look at the end of the privileged frivolity narrative and how cultural products have constructed a different vibe since.

NINE

CHRISTMAS '08

GOODBYE TO *TRL*,

AND THE LEGACY OF

THE ABERCROMBIE TEEN

On November 16, 2008, MTV pulled the plug on its once flagship show, *Total Request Live*. Dubbed "Total Finale Live," the last, special episode of the show amounted to what journalist Ben Sisario called "MTV's version of a New Orleans funeral."[1] In its famed Times Square studios, the show welcomed back original host Carson Daly, a raft of celebrities, and of course, a crush of fans. Artists like the Backstreet Boys, Justin Timberlake, JC Chasez, Diddy, and Beyoncé made appearances, although Britney Spears, whose music video for "...Baby One More Time" was ranked as the top song of *TRL*, wasn't in attendance.[2]

Even though obituaries for *TRL* blanketed the media, as the *New York Times* noted, the show's peak influence was already well in the rearview mirror. By 2008, its viewership and cultural cachet had waned as the network's reality television shows, such as *The Hills*, eclipsed *TRL*. Ultimately, the show had grown old, as Daly and other guests acknowledged during the finale. "The 'American Bandstand' (and also the 'Today' show) of Gen Millennium," journalist Robert Lloyd wrote of *TRL*, noting that by its final show, the studio audience looked like they had been "still in elementary school when the show went on the air in 1998."[3]

It's challenging to overstate the changes that occurred in the pop culture landscape between the premiere of *TRL* and its ending. In 1998, there were no smartphones; CDs were the dominant way people purchased and listened to music. There was no Facebook, Twitter, or YouTube. Even though the show aired on MTV, which pioneered reality television with *The Real World*, the massive influence of reality competition shows like *Survivor* and *American Idol* would come after *TRL* premiered. Original *TRL* host Daly moved to a late-night show, *Last Call with Carson Daly* on NBC. Musically, by 2008, Spears was on her sixth studio album (*Circus*, which was released a few weeks after *TRL* ended), 'N Sync had been "on hiatus" for six years, and *Destiny's Child* had cycled through three members and disbanded, giving way to Beyoncé's solo career. Taylor Swift, who was at the *TRL* finale asking people to sign a yearbook, had just released her second album, *Fearless*.[4]

When *TRL* debuted, Swift was nine.

But it wasn't just teen pop culture that had changed. *TRL* had launched before the Columbine school massacre and the September 11 attacks. The show survived the dot-com bubble and was still airing amid the 2008 financial crisis. And the United States elected its first Black president days before *TRL*'s final airing. In short, the world had changed.

Roughly two years later, Aéropostale, a teen retailer that offered cheaper versions of the preppy Abercrombie & Fitch aesthetic, would open a flagship store in the space that had been the *TRL* studios.[5] Gone were the hosts and the screaming crowds, but shoppers in the know could still stand at the corner window where Daly once counted down the day's top videos. Outside its windows, though, there had been more changes. Virgin Megastore, a massive music store across the square from the *TRL* studios, closed in early 2009.[6] And by May 2009, New York City had "de-mapped" the stretch of Broadway outside the studios to make pedestrian plazas; the city made these plazas permanent in 2010.[7]

This concluding chapter argues that popular culture—especially teen popular culture—took a turn after 2008 and the demise of *TRL*. Encapsulated by the popular *Twilight* series, the TV show *Glee*, and the rise of pop stars like Lady Gaga, Kesha, and Katy Perry, the mood shifted to an acceptance of individuality and uniqueness, moving away from attempts to fit within cultural expectations. While the typical teen fare didn't completely disappear—for example, *Easy A* was released in 2010—it came with more baggage, less privilege, and less frivolity than before.[8]

Second, as elder millennials—the cohort whose pop culture most fully embodied privileged frivolity—grew into adulthood, we have been confronted with an ever-increasing disparity between a promised and a lived future. Ultimately, we seem to be on a downward trajectory, as either Gen Xers or millennials are likely to be the first generation poorer than their parents, and both generations already control less wealth than previous generations did at comparable ages.[9] At the same time, millennials have been criticized for several perceived social transgressions (spending too much on avocado toast, anyone?) when broader economic and sociocultural forces are at play, making it more difficult—or at least making it feel more difficult—to meet adult hallmarks like buying a home and raising children. These sentiments have taken root across social media, and several works have rejected the previous social structures and reconsidered the culture in which elder millennials grew up.

When taken together, these factors speak to how the vibe of teen popular culture changed and how the privileged frivolity portrayed on-screen had a lasting impact on teens at the turn of the millennium and continues to have repercussions today. As mentioned in chapter 1, this is not to say that everyone had the same experience with pop culture or internalized it in the same way; thus, not everyone has the same feelings of disillusionment today. I'm even positive some people are living their best lives as pop culture told them they would. Yet it seems indisputable that the cultural mood shifted, as the once widely felt optimism now manifests as consternation, if not outright dread of the future.

Pop Culture after *TRL*

The day after "Total Finale Live" brought down the curtain on the show, a different teen pop culture product was gearing up to take the world by storm. The teen vampire film *Twilight* (2008) premiered in Los Angeles on November 17 and then across the United States four days later.[10] Based on the book series of the same name, the film starred Kristen Stewart as Bella Swan, the new girl at school who falls in love with Edward Cullen (Robert Pattinson), a vampire. Unlike the fun-filled high school films discussed in chapter 3 or even the later teen films in chapter 7, this was a brooding romance set in the woods of Washington rather than on the beaches of California (figure 9.1). Bella didn't need a makeover but was lusting after a classmate and dealing with the repercussions of this attraction.

That's not to say *Twilight* was without precedent; there had been some supernatural elements in 1990s and early 2000s teen fare, too. Perhaps the most direct influence came from the TV show *Buffy the Vampire Slayer*, but there was also the series *Charmed*, about three witch sisters who fight the forces of evil, and *Smallville*, a teen take on Superman. And of course, there was the massive success of the *Harry Potter* book and film series, which began in 1997 and 2001, respectively. However, these earlier shows and films that used fantasy and supernatural elements often played with—or at least examined—the interplay between good and evil. That is generally not the thrust of *Twilight*, which focuses more on Bella's desire to be with and like Edward (i.e., a vampire) and on the in-fighting between supernatural parties rather than on a "good" human or party fighting the supernatural forces of evil.

Figure 9.1. Dark and Stormy: Unlike *Clueless* and similar films, with their picturesque high school scenes, *Twilight* is set in Washington and has a darker, brooding tone. Bella drives an old, rebuilt truck to school, and even the cafeteria is more realistic as a somewhat confined eating space.

Regardless of the dynamics within the fantasy teen genre, other intricacies underscore the shift. First, Bella is a social outsider in *Twilight* and removes herself from general "teen life" to instead become part of an outsider family—the Cullens. In this way, Bella is *vastly* different from the teen protagonists previously discussed; characters like Cher and Dionne in *Clueless* were the popular teens, and others like Cady (*Mean Girls*), Kat (*10 Things I Hate about You*), Laney (*She's All That*), and Sam (*A Cinderella Story*) interacted with "popularity" in various ways. Even where there was a relative rejection of the teen social hierarchy (e.g., Kat), it occurred because one had been previously hurt; more often, characters were just waiting for their chance to become part of the "popular" clique (e.g., Laney, Cady). Bella's outright rejection of and disinterest in popularity were seemingly new in a protagonist.

Yet this recentering of the teen story—from the popular or could-be-popular to the not popular/never will be popular/doesn't want to be popular—would come to dominate other parts of popular culture as well. Beginning in May 2009, the television show *Glee* focused on the outcasts in a high school ~~show choir~~ glee club. While the show highlighted conflicts between the "popular" cheerleaders and the "unpopular" glee club, the show foregrounded those who were different—willingly or unwillingly—and leaned into characters embracing themselves.

Similarly, popular music came to be dominated by a trio of pop artists—Katy Perry, Lady Gaga, and Kesha—who conveyed similar messages. All three had catchy dance-inspired pop hits but played these off to various quirky, nontraditional ends. Perry's "I Kissed a Girl," released in April 2008, was the first song in this vein and played with ideas about sexuality, as did her album *Teenage Dream* (2010), which became the second album in history to garner five number one singles on the *Billboard* Hot 100. Even though Perry's songs and music videos looked and sounded like earlier pop, her songs leaned into a candy-coated feminism. In the video for "California Gurls," the first single from *Teenage Dream*, Perry parades around in cupcake bras and, toward the end of the video, takes down a gummy bear army (led by Snoop Dogg) using her whipped-cream-dispensing bra. (The next scene shows Snoop buried to his neck in sand while Perry and several other candy-clad women celebrate on the beach.) While some of her videos were more "traditional" in their aesthetic and representation (the title track wouldn't be totally out of place in the *TRL* era), Perry dedicated her third single from that album, "Firework," to the LGBT community and the It Gets Better campaign. This time, Perry was shooting fireworks from her bra. *Billboard* noted that the song and video preached "personal acceptance" (figure 9.2).[11]

Personal acceptance was also the rallying cry for Lady Gaga. While her first song, "Just Dance," was released a few weeks before Perry's "I Kissed a Girl" and built attention slowly, Gaga became a more lauded artist than Perry thanks to her red-carpet looks and general sheen of artistry (figure 9.3). After her debut album, *The Fame* (2008), was rereleased as *The Fame Monster* (with eight new songs), the singer embarked on the Monster Ball Tour and began referring to her fans as "Little Monsters." Lady Gaga embraced the LGBT community and rallied for gay rights politically and financially; 2011's "Born This Way" became shorthand for acceptance and became a *Billboard* number one hit.[12] Broadly speaking, Lady Gaga was cast as a more avant-garde and artistic singer than Perry and was more challenging to the status quo, but both singers played into (and up) personal acceptance and a willingness to step away from the in crowd.

Figure 9.2. Sugar and Lights: In the music video for "California Gurls" (*top two images*), Katy Perry plays with the idea of sweetness and female sexuality, while the video for "Firework" (*bottom two images*) shows people overcoming insecurities surrounding body image and homosexuality.

Figure 9.3. Messy Individualism: Starting with "Just Dance" (*top left, right*), Lady Gaga showed a penchant for individuality, a theme later reinforced in "Born This Way" (*bottom*), which featured a variety of dancers in an outer-space-themed video.

Figure 9.4. Messy Fun: Like Lady Gaga's music video for "Just Dance," which showed a messy party scene, "TiK ToK" featured a disheveled Kesha, after a night of partying, waking up in the bathtub of a picture-perfect family.

The same can be said for the third singer of this set, Kesha (sometimes styled as Ke$ha). Her first single, "TiK ToK," was released in August 2009, and her album *Animal* followed in January 2010 (figure 9.4). She, too, had an offbeat persona, perhaps best illustrated by a scene in the 2013 documentary television series *Ke$ha: My Crazy Beautiful Life* where the singer drinks her own urine.[13] Kesha had seven top-ten hits between 2009 and 2012, but a protracted legal battle with producer Dr. Luke, whom she accused of being abusive, slowed her career. Still, her early music and persona played into much of the same themes found in Perry's and Lady Gaga's music.

It was not only about outsider status—as the musicians and *Twilight* played—but the pop culture industries moved toward science fiction and fantasy elements and away from the realistic, picturesque portrayals of teen life. Much of this was not just a teen phenomenon, but it does speak to mid-2010s teen-oriented film series like *The Hunger Games* and *Divergent*, which prioritized creating a space for multiple films rather than one-offs. The happy-go-lucky sun-kissed and privileged teens of the 1990s and early 2000s had been replaced by thoughtful, unique, and powerful individuals, some even trying to survive in magical or dystopian futures.

Easy A and the Turning of Teen Narratives

To make a more direct comparison to the earlier *Clueless*-inspired teen films, we can see some of the changes pervading pop culture at the time by taking a look at *Easy A* (2010). The film is similar to those discussed earlier in this book: it is a high school retelling of *The Scarlet Letter* centering Olive Penderghast (Emma Stone) as a kindhearted teen who allows guys—first her gay friend, but later other "uncool" kids—to say they slept together in exchange for money, gift cards, and coupons. Despite not actually sleeping with anyone, Olive develops a reputation as a slut and gets into more aggressive confrontations with the Christian student group led by Marianne (Amanda Bynes) and Olive's former best friend, Rhiannon (Aly Michalka). Two things bring the story to a head. First, Olive goes on a date with Anson (Jake Sandvig), who wrongly believes Olive is actually prostituting herself (not just pretending to), leading him to accost her when she refuses to sleep with him. Second, Marianne's boyfriend catches chlamydia from sleeping with the school guidance counselor, Mrs. Griffith (Lisa Kudrow), and instead of coming clean about the affair, he blames Olive. When Olive threatens to expose the situation, Mrs. Griffith tells her no one would believe her, so Olive tells Mr. Griffith (Thomas Haden Church), her English teacher, about the affair, thus breaking up the Griffiths' marriage. Ultimately, Olive reconnects with an old friend, Todd (Penn Badgley), performs a sexy cabaret-style dance at a school pep rally, and gets everyone to log on to a YouTube-like channel, where she comes clean about the situation. As she's wrapping up the video, Todd comes to her house on a riding lawn mower, playing "Don't You (Forget about Me)." Olive logs off and rides off with him in a callback to the 1987 movie *Can't Buy Me Love*.

Film scholar Frances Smith has argued that *Easy A* is a nostalgia piece that looks back at the peaks of the teen film genre. Elements of the film—like the closing scene with Todd and the lawn mower—channel the golden age of 1980s teen films, and the film is frequently in conversation with classic works (namely *The Scarlet Letter*) and a host of other cultural reference points (figure 9.5). In many ways, *Easy A* was out of place when it was released, although through its references and reflexivity, it feels nostalgic for an earlier cultural moment.[14]

The film also seems to have a different relationship with the tenets of privileged frivolity. First, in *Easy A*, Olive has a close relationship with her middle-class family. While her parents (Stanley Tucci and Patricia Clarkson) are more friends than authority figures, they are seen throughout the film taking more than a passing interest in Olive's life. Further, Olive and her family are decidedly

Figure 9.5. Channeling the Good Times: In *Easy A*, the sun-kissed, airy high school returned, along with house parties, pep rallies, and references to past teen movies.

upper-middle class but not particularly wealthy. Nor is she particularly popular; she kept a relatively low profile until rumors of her sexual escapades began.

Olive's interaction with consumer culture is markedly different than in the films discussed in earlier chapters. *Easy A* suggests we are shaped more by outside culture than by our inner desires and transformational consumption. An early example of this in the movie occurs when Olive receives a birthday card that plays Natasha Bedingfield's "Pocketful of Sunshine" when opened. Olive initially expresses disgust at the song but eventually comes to enjoy it while spending the weekend at home alone, opening the card so much that it wears out. This was not something Olive chose to like (nor did the film ingrain the song through a fanciful school dance); rather, the earworm comes from a piece of (essentially) throwaway culture that Olive can't seem to ignore.

Moreover, once rumors of Olive's promiscuity begin to circulate, she undergoes a self-stylized makeover, where she begins to wear "sexier" clothing, including bustiers and corset tops adorned with a red "A." This makeover is a notable reworking of consumer culture: Olive is not trying to change her appearance to become popular, as characters did in *Clueless*, *She's All That*, and *Mean Girls*, but is actively changing her clothing to *conform* to what others are saying about her. While she intends to do it tongue-in-cheekily, the dynamics imply that social pressure alters our lives. Moreover, Olive's invocation of *The Scarlet Letter*—a novel she is reading in English class—follows some of the intertextuality of earlier teen films, allowing it to evoke the appropriate nostalgia.[15]

Finally, unlike the earlier teen films where everything worked out, *Easy A* portrays significant consequences. After a member of the Christian group insults Olive in class, Olive calls her an "abominable twat," for which Olive is sent to the principal's office and receives after-school detention. However, even beyond this minor infraction, the entire film shows repercussions for lying—even when well-intended. And even minor characters get a comeuppance. Micah, Marianne's boyfriend who is sleeping with the guidance counselor, first gets a sexually transmitted infection and is then sent to live with his grandparents. And after Olive exposes the affair, she helps end the Griffiths' marriage. (Unlike previous teen fare from *American Pie* to *Dawson's Creek*, *Easy A* explains that Micah is legally an adult; he failed several years of school.) Granted, there are still some instances where there are no consequences: the teen drinking party remains; Olive doesn't get in trouble for disrupting the pep rally; and, all told, Olive personally seems to come out of the entire episode pretty well after publicly "coming clean"—even if others did not.

Although some writers have gone so far as to see *Easy A* as marking the "end" of high school comedy films because few have been as commercially or critically successful in the years since, the teen film is hardly dead, even if it is taking on different forms.[16] More recent teen films have centered those excluded rather than popular cliques. For example, the animating feature of *The Duff* (2015) is the realization that one friend in every group is the "dumb, ugly, fat friend" and is more approachable than the better-looking, brighter, and "more desirable" members. *Love, Simon* (2018) deals with the friction of being gay in high school, calling out the dominant heteronormative narratives and interrogating how far people are willing to go to "save face." And in *Booksmart* (2019), class president

Molly (Beanie Feldstein) has been singularly focused on going to Yale, only for her and her best friend, Amy, to realize that all of their classmates also got into "good" schools while still enjoying the usual trappings of teen life (e.g., partying, sports, relationships) that Molly had been sacrificing. Rather than playing with these various consumable identities, these films call out the social pressures and expectations imposed upon teenagers.

Revamping the Cultural Narratives

It's not just the narratives of teen films that have changed but the very idea that consumer culture, and aspirational consumption, is a worthwhile endeavor. Teen narratives are no longer rooted in the idea that new clothes, makeovers, and (essentially) money will make things better. The use of clothing and personal adornment to identify and transform yourself and others, if not explicitly denounced, is largely ignored in recent films. Although these changes have taken some time to take hold across the pop culture landscape, they started around 2008, near the end of *TRL* and during the economic tumult of the Great Recession.

For example, consider *Confessions of a Shopaholic* (2009). Based on the book series by Sophie Kinsella, the film tells the story of financial journalist Becky Bloomwood (Isla Fisher), who helps others save money by day but is secretly a "shopaholic" who has accrued massive debt due to her inability to pass up purchases. Because of her shopping habit, Becky loses her job and alienates her close friend. She declines her parents' offer to bail her out and instead sells most of her closet to pay off her debt. In the film's closing scene, Becky walks away from an Yves Saint Laurent window, implying she has overcome her predilection for overshopping. It is worth noting that Kinsella's book series, which was UK-based and debuted in 2001, is still going strong, although the film was based on just the first two books. Moreover, the film's invocation that aspirational shopping is something that one needs to overcome seemed poignantly geared at the United States in the months after the Great Recession. Although critics generally panned *Confessions of a Shopaholic*, it still made $44.2 million domestically and $108.3 million worldwide during its release.[17]

A more successful film that retooled consumption-based narratives was *Bridesmaids* (2011), which made $169.1 million domestically and $288.3 million worldwide.[18] In the film, down-on-her-luck Annie (Kristen Wiig) is going to be the maid of honor for her best friend, Lillian (Maya Rudolph).[19] Annie is both single and out of money after her bakery closed, yet throughout the prewedding activities, she feels threatened by Helen (Rose Byrne), a more recent and wealthier friend of Lillian. High jinks ensue, but in the end, Annie and Helen become friends and help get Lillian down the aisle. While Annie reconciles with her friend and the wedding ultimately goes off with only a few minor hitches, Annie is not in a much better situation at the end of the film than she was at the beginning. Sure, she rediscovered her love of baking, started dating someone, and purportedly has some new friends, but her actual station in life hasn't changed.

Ultimately, though, the moral of *Bridesmaids* also involves individuality. First, *Bridesmaids* makes it clear that not everyone can be Helen. While the film suggests Helen has flaws, too, it doesn't indicate that a good makeover will put Annie on par with her. Second, the film relies on finding one's passion and sociality rather than popularity. Annie's connection to the other bridesmaids pulls her out of her funk and inspires her to start baking again. While there is no guarantee this will be successful, there's a reliance on personal connections over consumption practices.

In many ways, this mirrors the story arc of *Pitch Perfect* (2012), a college film that shares commonalities with the teen and college films discussed in earlier chapters.[20] In *Pitch Perfect*, Beca (Anna Kendrick) is a reluctant college student at Barden University, where her father is a professor. Beca wants to move to Los Angeles to embark on a music producing career, but her father insists she attend college. After her father demands she gets involved in college life—and that he'll support a move later if she still wants to—Beca joins the college radio station and the Barden Bellas, the all-female a cappella troupe that famously flamed out at the previous year's national competition. Headed by Aubrey (Anna Camp) and Chloe (Brittany Snow), the Bellas seek to rebuild the group's membership and reputation to get to nationals again while being tormented by the all-male a cappella group on campus. There is friction between Beca's sense of individuality and the need for group conformity. Still, Beca ultimately realizes the error of her ways and asks forgiveness, and the group wins nationals.

Pitch Perfect also centers individuality and female friendships over widespread popularity and appearances. While Beca is the cool, alternative outsider, the current Bellas group is deeply uncool. Part of this is because of their disastrous national performance and (now) inability to attract ideal members, but also, in the eyes of the rest of campus, the a cappella world is uncool. Even as *Pitch Perfect* leans a bit more into consumer culture than other movies of its time, there is a clear focus on individuality; the Bellas are trying to reproduce their performance from the previous year, which featured outfits reminiscent of flight attendant uniforms, but it's not until each member dresses in ways that feel "authentic" to them that they can genuinely connect and succeed. The success here is a tale of the misfit toys coming into their own and winning the day rather than of the misfits learning to "fit in."

And perhaps nowhere is the revamping of the cultural narratives more evident than in *He's All That* (2021), an update to *She's All That*. The film centers Padgett Sawyer (Addison Rae), a well-known influencer, who makes a bet that she can turn an unpopular guy into the prom king. Yet rather than focusing on her popularity, viewers see that Padgett's fabulous life is mostly a sham: her single mother (Rachael Leigh Cook) is struggling to provide, and Padgett goes so far as to lie to her friends about where she lives. Although the story's contours are essentially the same—in the end, the couple gets together, and Padgett loses the bet—*He's All That* tells a story about the superficiality of consumer and media culture rather than positioning it as a means to success.

Notably, these films—and other teen-centered films and television shows after 2008—were far more diverse in casting. For example, plus-sized Rebel Wilson became a household name thanks to her roles in *Bridesmaids* and *Pitch Perfect*, and the TV show *Glee* featured characters of color and a wheelchair user, along with various LGBTQ+ storylines. An even more comprehensive representation of teens has appeared in more recent productions, such as the films *He's All That* and *To All the Boys I've Loved Before* and its various sequels, and the TV shows *Euphoria, Never Have I Ever, The Sex Lives of College Girls, The Summer I Turned Pretty*, and *Love, Victor*, all released in 2018 or later. The diversity among the cast and crew speaks to a more open and inclusive cultural moment than was offered to millennials.

Disillusionment and an Uncertain Future

It's unsurprising that the Great Recession spurred a revision of our cultural narratives, especially as the United States transitioned into a different stage of the New Gilded Age. We may be living out our stated goals of being inclusive, nonjudgmental, and less materialistic, but it also feels like the vibe shifted from one that promised hope and aspiration (whether realistic or not) toward one of stasis or even acceptance of impending decline. And perhaps more importantly, the elder millennials who were most prominently sold this aspirational consumer culture through all elements of popular culture are becoming disillusioned as they enter their forties.

To start, the "New Gilded Age" has been the subject of books since at least 2001 and reached the pages of the *New York Times* in 2007.[21] As noted then, the concentration of wealth had reached levels not seen since the 1920s; relying on analyses by Thomas Piketty and Emmanuel Saez, the newspaper wrote that nearly 5 percent of the national income went to the wealthiest 0.01 percent of the population.[22] Moreover, in the wake of the Great Recession, Pew Research Center found that the median household income and net worth fell from 2001 to 2010 and that by 2011, only 51 percent of the population was classified as "middle class" (down from 61 percent in 1971), with more people classified in the upper and lower classes. Yet it was only the upper-class tier who saw their income going up, as they took home 46 percent of all income, compared to 29 percent in 1971. The middle class took home 45 percent of income (down from 62 percent), and the lower tier took home 9 percent (down from 10 percent).

Perhaps equally important, Pew found that people generally weren't as optimistic about the future.[23] In 2012, only 63 percent of people felt hard work pays off, which was lower than when Pew initially asked the question in 1994 and 12 percentage points below peak agreement with the statement in 1999. In 2008, 51 percent of the middle class felt their children would have a better standard of living than they did; by 2012, that number had fallen to 43 percent. Equally important, the number of people who believed their children would have a worse standard of living rose from 19 percent in 2008 to 26 percent in 2012.

And middle-class families had (and have) reason to be concerned. Later, analyses found that in 2019, millennials had less wealth than both the baby boomers and Gen Xers did at comparable ages.[24] And millennials are only 80 percent as wealthy as their parents were at the same age.[25] The *Washington Post* called millennials "the unluckiest generation" because there has been slower growth during their adult lifetime than for any other American generation. The newspaper blamed the Great Recession and the pandemic recession for impeding millennials' earnings.[26]

But ultimately, this is hardly bad luck. The economic revolution of the 1980s saw the implementation of tax cuts for the wealthy in 1982 and 1987; yet as economists have found, tax cuts do little to boost the economy and instead grow inequality.[27] Essentially, trickle-down economics tends not to trickle down. Moreover, after adjusting for inflation, wages for typical workers increased by only 0.02 percent between the 1970s and mid 2010s, with productivity outpacing pay.[28] Further, housing, health care, and college costs have far outpaced wage growth since 2000.[29] Ultimately, people have been working harder, get paid the same, and have less purchasing power.

Through the 1990s, life *seemed* to be getting better. It was a period of "irrational exuberance" in the stock market, in the words of Federal Reserve chairman Alan Greenspan, that ultimately led to the dot-com bubble of 2000.[30] But, as the chapters of this book have shown, for teens it wasn't just the stock market; much of popular culture sold a narrative where money was no object and consumerism would lead to a good life. This feeling even survived one market downturn and a major terror attack. Ultimately, though, by 2007 and 2008 the chasm between the lives people were promised and the lives they were living was too big to be ignored.

Had the outcome of the Great Recession been different, the belief in consumer culture might have survived. However, the government bailed out a series of corporations while many people lost what has traditionally been the best way to accumulate wealth: their homes. Moreover, as noted above, millennials especially bore the brunt of these economic tides, and as of 2012, more than half reportedly moved back in with their parents because of the weak economy—giving them the moniker "the boomerang generation."[31] Again it was the oldest millennials who were hit the hardest; they were "the poor suckers in the middle—first given a sweet taste of the good life, then kicked in the face," as noted in the introduction to this book.

It is perhaps not a surprise, then, that tensions between older generations—specifically baby boomers—and millennials have risen as the younger generation has been blamed for "killing" things as diverse as Applebee's, breakfast cereal, and diamonds. As millennials have become adults, a variety of works have questioned the dominant cultural narratives. Not only has this been prominent on social media with the prevalent "okay, boomer" sentiment (and more recently with the rise of "quiet quitting"), but it has been addressed more substantially in the book *OK Boomer, Let's Talk: How My Generation Got Left Behind* by journalist Jill Filipovic. The book shows how previous generations set the stage for the baby boomers' financial success and how boomer leaders pulled the economic ladder up behind them.[32]

Moreover, Malcolm Harris's *Kids These Days: The Making of Millennials* is a substantive takedown of how the culture put in place by millennials' parents and grandparents has heavily influenced how millennials understand and interact in the world. Harris denounces everything from the pressure put on kids at school to the increasing expense of college and changes in work, social media, and habits. While he, too, sees signs of a dismal future, he also sees the potential for millennials to change it, however daunting that might seem.[33] Many other books have called various systemic issues into question, including *The Twilight of the Elites: America after Meritocracy* by Chris Hayes and *After the Ivory Tower Falls* by Will Bunch. Moreover, books like *The Ones We've Been Waiting For* by Charlotte Alter and *How to Start a Revolution* by Lauren Duca have urged young people to be politically engaged.[34]

My goal with this book is not to say that millennials are worse off than other generations. However, I believe the statistics above convincingly demonstrate that. Other research suggests millennials have more debt than previous generations but otherwise reflect the same consumption patterns.[35] And as Filipovic notes, millennials overall are more diverse than previous generations, which can also speak to some of the financial differences.[36] Regardless, the popular culture analysis of this book cannot begin to make such an argument about economic specifics.

Instead, I want to emphasize that the cultural *feeling*—what I've described elsewhere as affect or vibe—has changed, and what was once optimism is now resignation, disillusionment, and even fear. For example, in response to an article in the *Atlantic* arguing against a recent narrative that people don't want to work, *New York Times* journalist Stuart A. Thompson commented, "The story ignores the central part of anti-work which is that the supposed rewards for hard work have disappeared or are disappearing, such as decent housing and rising quality of life, as those markers of success are reserved for older generations."[37]

Similarly, Sunny Moraine, a sociologist and author, argued on Twitter that millennials "don't actually know how old we are because all the benchmarks for maturity we were promised by our parents have been destroyed by our parents."[38] Their point follows an earlier thread they wrote arguing that hallmarks like getting married, having kids, and even starting a career have been undermined and that a sense of time and progression has ended.[39] And other Twitter users such as reporter Jack Jenkins have also noted that elder millennials have seen several social shifts, from the 1990s tech boom through September 11, the rise of social media, the successive presidential elections of Barack Obama and Donald Trump, and, most recently, a global pandemic.[40]

I could go on with anecdotal evidence here, and I have been collecting such examples since I began writing this book, but even the *New York Times* has picked up on the "economic anxiety" millennials feel.[41] Moreover, the fact that people are giving voice to these concerns proves my point: the cultural feeling has shifted. It seemed slow at first—as my examples from *Easy A*, *Confessions of a Shopaholic*, and *Pitch Perfect* suggested—then seemingly all at once. And who can blame anyone—Gen X, (elder) millennials, Gen Z, or younger—who is feeling despair in the 2020s? Not only is the economy stacked against progress, but the United States faced an attempted overthrow of the government, the economy feels lackluster after the global community failed to rise to the challenge of the COVID pandemic, and climate change is wreaking havoc around the globe.

Conclusion

"Nostalgia is partly a response to disappointment with the present," journalist Kyle Chayka wrote in an examination of pixelated digital images from the early days of the World Wide Web.[42] This statement coincides with academic discussions that assume nostalgia is partially induced by present uncertainty, creating a yearning for the comfort of the past.[43] Fittingly, there is a host of nostalgic references in contemporary popular culture: the ongoing reprisals of television shows (starting with the *Full House* reboot, *Fuller House*, in 2016); the aforementioned remake of *She's All That*; the frequent sampling of past songs in contemporary music; and even Ariana Grande's video for "thank u, next," which paid homage to films like *Mean Girls*, *Bring It On*, and *Legally Blonde*.

There's undoubtedly more to this idea of nostalgia than can be adequately interrogated within the final paragraphs of this book. However, whether or not the 1990s and first years of the 2000s were as "good" as the current cultural narratives would have us believe, they have become a cultural repository for a better time that people are yearning for. Yet I might suggest that the period wasn't as good as it's remembered; as I've shown throughout this book, the narratives we were provided were always a fantasy—even if that is cold comfort at the current moment.

At the risk of concluding this book on a bleak note, I don't have any profound prescriptions for how to fix this, and, as I wrote in the introduction, that was not my intent with the book. Instead, I have shown that for over a decade, between the mid-1990s and late aughts, teens and young adults were sold a particular version of the future steeped in privilege and consumer culture and that promoted a sense of aspiration and optimism. Only a subset of the population could ever fit into the promoted ideals—and many were excluded explicitly or implicitly because they inhabited the wrong bodies—yet the overarching narrative was that the *correct* consumption practices would prove fruitful in the long run. It was blind trust in consumer culture, and only in hindsight can we see how misguided the belief truly was.

It is vital to remember that affective cultural moments, like the era of privileged frivolity, do not last forever; the depressed 1970s gave way to the high-flying 1980s and then the aspirational 1990s. As such, it's difficult to tell what's on the horizon, although as I finish this book in the fall of 2023, there are signs that the cultural mood has shifted yet again, now away from wealthy and corporate interests. Recently, Hollywood writers and actors struck and won various concessions, as did autoworkers. Both railworkers and UPS drivers came close to striking but won concessions without needing to. Overall, union support is up after decades of stagnation, wages are finally outpacing inflation, and US unemployment has been near record lows.[44] Moreover, the Biden administration is working to help those with student debt, an acknowledgment of the financial stress younger adults are experiencing.[45] Further, young voters are seemingly more active and engaged than millennials were, and as older generations become less of an overall share of the voting population, perhaps we will make a change in the nick of time.[46]

The moral of the story for elder millennials is that no one is coming to save us, and truthfully, it may already be too late for us to change paths quickly enough to achieve the success we were sold as practically inevitable. Yet by engaging with political processes, pushing for change, and holding our elected officials accountable, we can hopefully right the ship for future generations. It'll take continued passion, interest, and involvement, but without it, we'll certainly never realize the lives we were promised.

NOTES

Preface

1. Hall, "Cultural Studies," 285–86.
2. Lipovetsky, *Empire of Fashion*, 7.
3. Lipovetsky, *Empire of Fashion*, 249–52.
4. Thing Bad (@Merman_Melville), Twitter, February 22, 2021. https://web.archive.org /web/20230613204313/https://twitter.com/Merman_Melville/status/13640006707 60669184.

Chapter One

1. Kristie Rohwedder, "The Greatest New Year's Eve Party Anthem Ever," *Bustle*, December 30, 2014, www.bustle.com/articles/56169-26-moments-from-jennifer-lopezs-waiting -for-tonight-music-video-that-shaped-my-expectations-for-new.
2. Roth et al., *'90s*; Raftery, *Best. Movie. Year. Ever.*; Klosterman, *Nineties*; Nathan S. Webster, "1999: Our Last Innocent, Giddy Summer," *Daily Beast*, May 25, 2015, www.thedailybeast.com/1999-our-last-innocent-giddy-summer.
3. Klosterman, *Nineties*, 337.
4. Jed Oelbaum, "Reasonable People Disagree about the Post-Gen X, Pre-Millenial Generation," Good, September 25, 2014, www.good.is/articles/generation-xennials.
5. Maney, *Bill Clinton*; Pimpare, *New Victorians*; Remnick, *New Gilded Age*.
6. Pimpare, *New Victorians*, 17–19; Remnick, *New Gilded Age*, xi–xii.
7. Stiglitz, *Roaring Nineties*.
8. Currid-Halkett, *Sum of Small Things*, 10–13.
9. Heath and Potter, *Nation of Rebels*, 188–200; Frank, "Why Johnny Can't Dissent," 31–45; White, "Killer App," 46–56; White, "Burn Down the House," 62–71.
10. Vanderbilt, "Advertised Life," 128–29.
11. Veblen, *Theory*, 49–69.
12. Gopnik, "Display Cases," 294.
13. Baudrillard, "From *Symbolic Exchange*," 421–23; Tseëlon, "Jean Baudrillard," 219–23. Tseëlon puts Baudrillard's discussion to work specifically regarding fashion and personal adornment.
14. Alex Kuczynski, "A Dark, Secluded Place," *New York Times*, July 7, 2005; Dan Nosowitz, "Something Borrowed, Something Blue," *BuzzFeed*, September 24, 2014, www.buzzfeed.com/dannosowitz/how-madewell-bought-and-sold-my-familys-history. Abercrombie & Fitch launched a sister brand, Ruehl No.925, which targeted a slightly older demographic but whose backstory—about German immigrants who opened a

leather business in New York City in the mid-1800s—is purely made up (Kuczynski). Similarly, in 2006, J.Crew brought the brand Madewell and developed a fictional story for it (Nosowitz).

15. Smith, *Rethinking*, 15–16; Quart, *Branded*, 85–89.

16. Hine, *Rise and Fall*, 8; Palladino, *Teenagers*; Massoni, *Fashioning Teenagers*; Quart, *Branded*.

17. Fashion has long been understood to help create identities; this period saw renewed academic interest in consumption related to identities and lifestyles. See Miles, *Youth Lifestyles*; and Chaney, *Lifestyles*.

18. Fukuyama, *End of History*, xii.

19. On consumer culture and American history, see Bishop, *More*; Lizabeth Cohen, *Consumer's Republic*; Cross, *All-Consuming Century*; Dickinson, *Suburban Dreams*; Glickman, *Consumer Society*; Frank, *Conquest of Cool*; Lange, *Meet Me*; Leach, *Land of Desire*; and Zukin, *Point of Purchase*. On teen consumption, see Miles, *Youth Lifestyles*; and Milner, *Freaks, Geeks*. On teen and youth media, see Bickford, *Tween Pop*; Davis and Dickinson, *Teen TV*; Jamieson and Romer, *Changing Portrayal of Adolescents*; Johnson, *Transgenerational Media Industries*; Kaveney, *Teen Dreams*; Ross and Stein, *Teen Television*; Shary, *Generation Multiplex*; Smith, *Rethinking*; Thornton, *Club Cultures*; Tropiano, *Rebels and Chicks*; and Wee, *Teen Media*. On cultural processes, see Dunn, *Identifying Consumption*; McCracken, *Culture and Consumption*; McCracken, *Culture and Consumption II*; and Daniel Miller, *Material Culture*. On brand culture, see Banet-Weiser, *Authentic*; Love, *Soda Goes Pop*; and Turow, *Breaking Up America*.

20. Glickman, *Consumer Society*, 1; Lizabeth Cohen, *Consumer's Republic*, 292–331; Hine, *Rise and Fall*, 8; Palladino, *Teenagers*; Massoni, *Fashioning Teenagers*.

21. McIntosh, "White Privilege."

22. Khan, *Privilege*. My use of "privilege" has some commonality with Khan's exploration of privilege developed through private boarding schools.

23. US Bureau of Labor Statistics, "Usual Weekly Earnings of Wage and Salary Workers Second Quarter 2023," news release no. USDL-23-1586, July 18, 2023, www.bls.gov /news.release/archives/wkyeng_07182023.htm; Badgett and Schneebaum, *Impact of Wage Equality*.

24. Dunn, *Identifying Consumption*; Zukin, *Point of Purchase*.

25. My view here is mainly in line with symbolic interactionist frameworks, whereby people treat their bodies as objects to be shaped by their inner selves.

26. Robin James, "What Is a Vibe?," *its her factory* (newsletter), January 29, 2021, https:// open.substack.com/pub/itsherfactory/p/what-is-a-vibe.

27. James, "What Is a Vibe?"

28. Magee, *Hegel Dictionary*, 262.

29. Robin James, "When Did 'Vibes' Become a Thing?" *its her factory* (newsletter), January 13, 2022, https://open.substack.com/pub/itsherfactory/p/when-did-vibes-become -a-thing. Klosterman also suggests that the 1990s saw the last gasps of a monoculture; while that might be the case, fashion history suggests that alternative styles of dressing have a long history before being properly recognized as subcultures in the 1950s and

'70s. While tangential to this book, the idea of a monoculture likely rested on power structures that sidelined or diminished the contributions and practices of marginalized groups.

30. Ahmed, *Queer Phenomology*, 119–20. James ("What Is a Vibe?") draws from Ahmed's work.

31. Saviolo and Marazza, *Lifestyle Brands*.

32. Lasswell, "Structure and Function," 38.

33. Theorists frequently see modernity as a period of time that coincided with industrialization and mass culture. Comparatively, postmodernity is defined by mediated imagery and subjective interpretations of the world. The rise of mass media in the mid-twentieth century, followed by the widespread adoption of "promotional culture," seemingly altered our relationship to consumption, inducing us to buy more for images rather than the functional quality of goods.

34. Andrew Van Dam, "The Unluckiest Generation in U.S. History," *Washington Post*, June 5, 2020.

35. Julian Mark, "'Unluckiest Generation' Falters in Boomer-Dominated Market for Homes," *Washington Post*, August 12, 2023.

36. Hall, introduction, 11–24. The selected texts also share commonality with Berlant's selection of texts in *Cruel Optimism* (11).

37. Aisha Harris, *Wannabe*, 78; Yang, Yu, and Wang, *Rise*.

38. Hall, "Encoding/Decoding"; Hebdige, *Subculture*. My view here has some similarities to cultural studies works by Hall and Hebdige; however, I am hesitant to prescribe meaning to subcultural identities. People can situate themselves in relation to the dominant narrative in any number of ways; however, the presence of the Abercrombie teen made it nearly impossible for elder millennial teens to ignore the narrative (although that would be a position nonetheless).

39. Deleuze and Guattari, *Thousand Plateaus*.

Chapter Two

1. *A&F Quarterly*, Summer 2001, 55; *A&F Quarterly: A Cool Yule*, Christmas 1997, 4–5, 44–45; *A&F Quarterly: Naughty or Nice*, Christmas 1998, 121, 86–87; *A&F Quarterly*, Summer 2001, 108–9, 112–13; *A&F Quarterly*, Summer 2002, 69; *A&F Quarterly*, Summer 2001, 69.

2. Laura Bird, "Beyond Mail Order: Catalogs Now Sell Images, Advice," *Wall Street Journal*, July 29, 1997.

3. Stacy Perman, "Abercrombie's Beefcake Brigade," *Time*, February 14, 2000, 62.

4. Hancock, "Chelsea on 5th Avenue."

5. "Our Story," Abercrombie & Fitch, accessed February 28, 2024, https://web.archive.org /web/20230910203851/https://corporate.abercrombie.com/about-us; "Sports Store Buys Chicago Interest," *New York Times*, November, 23, 1928, 50; Robert Hanley, "Abercrombie & Fitch Put Up for Sale; 6 Years of Losses Reported by Chain," *New York Times*, July 20, 1976; Robert Mcg. Thomas Jr., "An Old Sport, Abercrombie & Fitch Says It Must Close Its Historic Doors," *New York Times*, November 14, 1977; Isadore Barmash,

"Hundreds Stalk Bargains at Abercrombie Close Out," *New York Times*, November 18, 1977.

6. Robert F. Kelley, "Elaborate Plans Are Being Made for Cathedral Benefit Polo Games," *New York Times*, January 30, 1929; HK, "Along the Highways and Byways of Finance," *New York Times*, April 19, 1953; "Women's Tweeds Return, Soft and Light, in High Fashion Place from Spring and Fall," *New York Times*, March, 29, 1949; Gloria Emerson, "Sporting Goods Store, Once All-Male, Gives Distinct Niche to Women Now," *New York Times*, October 22, 1958; "New Face for Fashion at Abercrombie & Fitch," *New York Times*, September 11, 1965.

7. Hanley, "Abercrombie & Fitch Put Up for Sale"; Isadore Barmash, "Abercrombie & Fitch in Bankruptcy Step," *New York Times*, August 7, 1976; Thomas, "Old Sport"; Associated Press, "Taking a Step Back to Luxury," *Dallas Morning News*, November 21, 1976, 15; Barmash, "Hundreds Stalk Bargains."

8. Barmash, "Hundreds Stalk Bargains"; Associated Press, "Oshman's to Acquire Abercrombie," *Dallas Morning News*, April 15, 1978, 46; Isadore Barmash, "New Guise for Abercrombie's," *New York Times*, November 9, 1982; United Press International, "Oshman's to Revive Abercrombie & Fitch," *Dallas Morning News*, July 26, 1978, 35; Pamela G. Hollie, "Abercrombie's Reborn on Coast," *New York Times*, September 12, 1979.

9. Barmash, "New Guise for Abercrombie's"; "Abercrombie President Leaves after Shake-Up," *New York Times*, May 24, 1983; "Abercrombie's Return to City," *New York Times*, May 10, 1984; John Duka, "New Stores with Old Reputations," *New York Times*, January 27, 1985. Duka points out that what era was ending was "never quite clear" and asks, "Was it one in which gentlemen, when they were not relaxing at the club, were in the veld shooting springbok, and when they were doing neither, they were at Abercrombie's confident that they could find the accouterments needed for each pursuit? Or was it the era in which men only dreamed of clubs and velds and went to Abercrombie's to buy the store's famous leather rhinoceroses, confident that they would not be attacked by a cordon of young women spraying perfume at them?"

10. Duka, "New Stores"; John J. O'Connor, "Tapping into America's Turbulent Past," *New York Times*, April 13, 1986; "Dream West," IMDb, accessed February 29, 2024, www.imdb.com/title/tt0090422/plotsummary; "Oshman's Calls Off Abercrombie Sale," *New York Times*, December 25, 1987; "Abercrombie Chain Bought," *New York Times*, January 15, 1988; Donna Steph Hansard, "Limited to Purchase Abercrombie & Fitch," *Dallas Morning News*, January 16, 1988, 12F.

11. Isadore Barmash, "Abercrombie & Fitch Chief Sees Growth Opportunities," *New York Times*, January 31, 1989; Jennifer Steinhauer, "Can Ann Taylor Dust Itself Off? A Retailer Is Paying a High Price for a Big Detour in Strategy," *New York Times*, December 2, 1995; Stephanie Storm, "A Promotion to Chief at Limited's Lerner Unit," *New York Times*, February 20, 1992.

12. Benoit Denizet-Lewis, "The Man behind Abercrombie & Fitch," *Salon*, January 24, 2006, www.salon.com/2006/01/24/jeffries/.

13. Denizet-Lewis, "Man behind Abercrombie & Fitch."

14. Denizet-Lewis, "Man behind Abercrombie & Fitch"; Perman, "Abercrombie's Beefcake

Brigade"; Lauren Goldstein, "The Alpha Teenager," *Fortune*, December 20, 1999, https://web.archive.org/web/20190825030927/https://archive.fortune.com/magazines/fortune/fortune_archive/1999/12/20/270530/index.htm; Robert Berner, "Flip-Flops, Torn Jeans and Control," *BusinessWeek*, May 29, 2005, www.bloomberg.com/news/articles/2005-05-29/flip-flops-torn-jeans-and-control.

15. Denizet-Lewis, "Man behind Abercrombie & Fitch"; Berner, "Flip-Flops, Torn Jeans."

16. Burleigh B. Gardner and Sidney J. Levy, "The Product and the Brand," *Harvard Business Review*, March–April 1955; Sidney J. Levy, "Symbols for Sale," *Harvard Business Review*, July–August 1959, 117–24; Lury, *Brands*; Wigley, Nobbs, and Larsen, "Marking the Marque." The symbolic constructs created by brand messages have long been associated with brand image, as described by Gardner and Levy, Levy, and more recently Wigley, Nobbs, and Larsen, who have delineated various tangible communications that are assembled by consumers and other parties into intangible constructs including image, personality, and lifestyle.

17. Perman, "Abercrombie's Beefcake Brigade."

18. Pettinger, "Brand Culture"; Walters, "Mall Models," 2.

19. Denizet-Lewis ("Man behind Abercrombie & Fitch") writes that the look was neutered by "perennial *boyhood*."

20. Matthew Shaer, "Why Abercrombie Is Losing Its Shirt," *New York Magazine*, February 9, 2014, www.thecut.com/2014/02/why-abercrombie-is-losing-its-shirt.html.

21. Hancock, "Chelsea on 5th Avenue"; Perman, "Abercrombie's Beefcake Brigade"; Denizet-Lewis, "Man behind Abercrombie & Fitch."

22. Goldstein, "Alpha Teenager."

23. Denizet-Lewis, "Man behind Abercrombie & Fitch."

24. Denizet-Lewis, "Man behind Abercrombie & Fitch."

25. McBride, *Why I Hate Abercrombie & Fitch*; Klayman, *White Hot*.

26. Denizet-Lewis, "Man behind Abercrombie & Fitch." The offensive T-shirt promoted by Abercrombie & Fitch read "Two Wongs can make it white," riffing on a stereotyped accent and an industry in which many Asian immigrants work.

27. Goldstein, "Alpha Teenager."

28. Perman, "Abercrombie's Beefcake Brigade"; Hancock, "Chelsea on 5th Avenue."

29. Isabelle Kohn, "Sex, Lies and Cheap Cologne: An Oral History of Abercrombie & Fitch's Softcore Porn Mag," *MEL Magazine*, August 14, 2020, https://melmagazine.com/en-us/story/sex-lies-and-cheap-cologne-an-oral-history-of-abercrombie-fitchs-softcore-porn-mag.

30. Kohn, "Sex, Lies"; Cole Kazdin, "Have Yourself a Horny Little Christmas," *Salon*, November 26, 2003, www.salon.com/2003/11/26/abercrombie/; Jeannine Stein, "Nudity? A&F Quarterly Had It Covered," *Los Angeles Times*, June 29, 2001, https://www.latimes.com/archives/la-xpm-2001-jun-29-cl-16389-story.html.

31. Engel, "Marketing Everyday Life."

32. *A&F Quarterly: On the Road*, Back to School 1998, 164–65; Kohn, "Sex, Lies," on the drinking game; *A&F Quarterly: New York*, Back to School 2000, 112, 115; *A&F Quarterly*, Christmas 2003, 89, 279. See also Suzanne Kapner, "Too Racy for Retail: A&F

Pulls Its Naughty Catalog," *New York Post*, December 2, 2003, https://nypost.com /2003/12/02/too-racy-for-retail-af-pulls-its-naughty-catalog/. Kapner suggests the interview in question was advocating for oral sex, when in actuality the sex educator is responding to a humorous question referencing the hit song "You Oughta Know" by Alanis Morissette.

33. *A&F Quarterly: A Very Emerson Christmas*, Christmas 2000, 3.

34. According to the magalog, Whitney attends the San Francisco Arts Institute, likely a fictional reference to the San Francisco Art Institute.

35. *A&F Quarterly: A Very Emerson Christmas*, Christmas 2000, 261–63.

36. *A&F Quarterly: A Very Emerson Christmas*, Christmas 2000, 180–82.

37. *A&F Quarterly: A Very Emerson Christmas*, Christmas 2000, 24.

38. *A&F Quarterly: A Very Emerson Christmas*, Christmas 2000, 25.

39. *A&F Quarterly: A Very Emerson Christmas*, Christmas 2000, 116–17.

40. *A&F Quarterly: Go Play*, Summer 2000, 210–13; *A&F Quarterly: Wild and Willing*, Spring Break 2000, 173, 207, 265; *A&F Quarterly: New York*, Back to School 2000, 112.

41. McBride, *Why I Hate Abercrombie & Fitch*, 64.

42. McBride, *Why I Hate Abercrombie & Fitch*, 86.

43. Yu, "2000s," 189.

44. Abercrombie & Fitch Co., 2009 Annual Report; Abercrombie & Fitch Co., 2014 Annual Report.

45. Abercrombie & Fitch Co., 2007 Annual Report; Abercrombie & Fitch Co., 2014 Annual Report.

46. Jena McGregor, "Abercrombie & Fitch CEO Mike Jeffries Steps Down," *Washington Post*, December 9, 2014, https://www.washingtonpost.com/news/on-leadership/wp /2014/12/09/abercrombie-fitch-ceo-mike-jeffries-steps-down/.

Chapter Three

1. Raftery, *Best. Movie. Year. Ever.*

2. Radner, *Neo-feminist Cinema*, 2.

3. Considine, *Cinema of Adolescence*; Driscoll, *Teen Film*; Shary, *Generation Multiplex*; Kaveney, *Teen Dreams*; Smith, *Rethinking*; Tropiano, *Rebels and Chicks*.

4. Altman, *Film/Genre*; Neale, "Questions of Genre"; Staiger, "Hybrid or Inbred"; Tudor, "Genre."

5. Driscoll, *Teen Film*, 3; Wee, *Teen Media*, 47.

6. My approach aligns with that of Buckingham, *Youth on Screen*.

7. Considine, *Cinema of Adolescence*, 2–4; Driscoll, *Teen Film*, 10–25; Kaveney, *Teen Dreams*, 11–48; Nelson, *"Breakfast Club,"* 5; Doherty, *Teenagers and Teenpics*; Shary, *Generation Multiplex*, 8–9.

8. Amanda Ann Klein, *American Film Cycles*, 4, 97–99; Grindon, "Cycles and Clusters," 53. See also Altman, *Film/Genre*, 59–68, on cycles.

9. Rightfully, Hughes's *Sixteen Candles* (1984) has been criticized for its racist portrayal of Long Duk Dong, but as Jeff Yang notes, all of Hughes's films are racially problematic. Yang, Yu, and Wang, *Rise*, 22.

10. Driscoll, *Teen Film*, 48; Shary, *Generation Multiplex*, 300–302; Driscoll, afterword,

307–8; Kaveney, *Teen Dreams*, 11–48. Kaveney's discussion of the films of John Hughes is a particularly insightful read on contemporary teen cinema. While it's likely incorrect to say Hughes created the genre, it is probably accurate to say Hughes's films defined the genre for many.

11. McErin (@coleen_eileen), "When Clueless came out, 11 yo me vowed to have a closet like Cher's one day. Instead I have a laundry basket with 17 pairs of black leggings," Twitter, March 21, 2021, https://web.archive.org/web/20220325141247/https://twitter .com/colleen_eileen/status/1372244402060558346. An episode of *Articles of Interest* also documents the practical problems with a computerized closet, namely that people don't have enough clothing to need it; Avery Trufelman, "The Clueless Closet," *Articles of Interest*, podcast, March 29, 2023, 34:44, www.articlesofinterest.co/podcast/episode /2abe2e85/the-clueless-closet.

12. Radner, *Neo-feminist Cinema*, 20–21.

13. Shary, *Generation Multiplex*, 260–61.

14. Bourdieu, *Distinction*, 300–304.

15. Jeffers McDonald, *Hollywood Catwalk*.

16. Dunn, *Identifying Consumption*, 75–89, 122–24; Zukin, *Point of Purchase*, 35–38.

17. Shary (*Generation Multiplex*, 261–63) suggests that the story arc in *American Pie* is essentially "redemptive," a classification I would disagree with. Admittedly, there is something like equality in the film, which acknowledges that women and men can both be interested in sex and even takes stock of the differences in cultural context, yet being embarrassed because you were unable to perform is not an adequate or appropriate rejoinder for the scene.

18. Hall, "Encoding/Decoding"; Jen Chaney, "*Clueless* Is a Great Teen Movie. It's Also a Satire about the White and Wealthy," *Vulture*, July 8, 2020, www.vulture.com/article /clueless-is-a-great-teen-movie-its-also-a-satire.html.

19. Elisabeth Egan, "Why 'Clueless' Still Matters: Jen Chaney Explains in 'As If!,'" *Washington Post*, July 10, 2015, https://www.washingtonpost.com/; Kathryn Lindsay, "All the Words from *Clueless* That Prove Cher Is Basically Shakespeare," *Refinery29*, June 19, 2020, www.refinery29.com/en-us/2020/06/9843110/clueless-slang-words-meaning.

20. Palladino, *Teenagers*, 100–102. See also Hine, *Rise and Fall*, 23–24, on money in teen life.

21. Drew DeSilver, "After Dropping in 2020, Teen Summer Employment May Be Poised to Continue Its Slow Comeback," Pew Research Center, June 21, 2022, www.pewresearch .org/short-reads/2022/06/21/after-dropping-in-2020-teen-summer-employment-may -be-poised-to-continue-its-slow-comeback.

22. Arguably *But I'm a Cheerleader* (1999) could fit with these films; it starred Natasha Lyonne, who was also in *American Pie*, and features a lesbian storyline, but the film deals with conversion therapy and is more of an adult-oriented film about teenagers rather than a film targeted toward teens. Kaveney (*Teen Dreams*) came to a similar conclusion in her study.

23. Rebecca Bellan, "$23 Billion Education Funding Report Reveals Less Money for City Kids," Bloomberg.com, March 27, 2019, www.bloomberg.com/news/articles/2019-03 -27/why-city-kids-get-less-money-for-their-education; Currid-Halkett, *Sum of Small Things*, 46–60.

24. Small et al., "School Policy and Environment."

25. Craik, *Uniforms Exposed*, 71.

26. Kann et al., "Youth Risk Behavior Surveillance."

27. Joseph M. Anderson, "The Wealth of Families: Analysis of Recent Census Data" (US Census Bureau working paper no. SEHSD-WP1999-16, Washington, DC, November 10, 1999); Teri Morisi, "Teen Trends," *Commissioner's Corner* (blog), US Bureau of Labor Statistics, April 13, 2017, www.bls.gov/blog/2017/teen-trends.htm.

28. Raftery, *Best. Movie. Year. Ever.*, 75.

Chapter Four

1. Paul R. La Monica, "Summer Girls No Longer Shop at Abercrombie & Fitch," CNN.com, August 30, 2016, https://money.cnn.com/2016/08/30/investing/abercrombie-fitch-hollister-sales-earnings/.

2. J. Freedom du Lac, "Everything in Its Place—Pop Go the Brand Names!," *Sacramento Bee*, August 31, 1999, E1.

3. Fiske, *Understanding Popular Culture*, 98–101.

4. Warner, *Fashion on Television*.

5. Allen, *Intertextuality*, 1–3.

6. Hackley and Hackley, "Advertising at the Threshold"; Aronczyk, "Portal or Police?" Aronczyk makes the connection that brands are a form of paratextuality but argues that brands are ultimately more powerful than media paratexts because they do not need source material for meaning *and* can usurp and reshape meaning at a given time.

7. "The Best Summer Songs of All Time," *Rolling Stone*, June 25, 2022, www.rollingstone.com/music/music-lists/best-summer-songs-of-all-time-43407/; Brittany Spanos et al., "75 Greatest Boy Band Songs of All Time," *Rolling Stone*, July 24, 2020, www.rollingstone.com/music/music-lists/boy-band-songs-greatest-1033317/; Rob Harvilla, "How 'Summer Girls' Explains a Bunch of Hits—and the Music of 1999," *Ringer*, July 29, 2019, www.theringer.com/music/2019/7/29/8934482/lfo-summer-girls-1999-music-abercrombie-fitch-song.

8. Du Lac, "Everything in Its Place"; Sheela Raman, "Rich Cronin's Comeback," Boston.com, July 7, 2005, http://archive.boston.com/news/globe/living/articles/2005/07/07/rich_cronins_comeback/.

9. Aisha Harris, a former culture reporter and editor for the *New York Times*, told Rob Harvilla that the song was her first introduction to Abercrombie & Fitch, too; Harvilla, "How 'Summer Girls' Explains."

10. Du Lac, "Everything in Its Place."

11. For clarity, I'm using the term "band" to refer to LFO; however, "boy band" or "singing group" is probably more appropriate because they were not playing instruments.

12. Similar styles can be found in *A&F Quarterly: Spring Fever*, Spring Break 1999, 42.

13. Benoit Denizet-Lewis, "The Man behind Abercrombie & Fitch," *Salon*, January 24, 2006, www.salon.com/2006/01/24/jeffries/.

14. Savas Abadsidis, "Young at Heart," *A&F Quarterly: Spring Fever*, Spring Break 1999, 88–95; Grant Bixby, "Beachcoming," *A&F Quarterly: Spring Fever*, Spring Break 1999,

81; Adam Branch, "Baja Nights," *A&F Quarterly: Spring Fever*, Spring Break 1999, 138–45; John Gilles, "Sands of Time," *A&F Quarterly: Spring Fever*, Spring Break 1999, 252–53.

15. Patrick Carone, "Fit to Be Thaid," *A&F Quarterly: Summer Dreams*, Summer 1999, 60–63; Gary Kon, "Pool Sharks," *A&F Quarterly: Summer Dreams*, Summer 1999, 159.

16. On intertextuality being common in popular culture, see Fiske, *Understanding Popular Culture*.

17. Janice Miller, *Fashion and Music*, 23–24; Vernallis, *Experiencing Music Video*, x; Vernallis, "Strange People, Weird Objects"; Straw, "Popular Music and Postmodernism"; Arnold et al., *Music/Video*.

18. The intertextual elements present in both *A&F Quarterly* and various music videos of the time were so pronounced that it is difficult to document it all without being overly repetitive. A nonexhaustive list of the crossovers: Spaghetti-strap camisoles appeared in *A&F Quarterly: Wild and Willing*, Spring Break 2000, 76; *A&F Quarterly: Go Play*, Summer 2000, 15; and in the music videos for Jennifer Paige's "Crush"; Backstreet Boys' "As Long As You Love Me"; Mandy Moore's "Candy"; and Vitamin C's "Graduation (Friends Forever)." Men's ribbed sweaters appeared in *A&F Quarterly: New York*, Back to School 2000, 155; *A&F Quarterly: A Very Emerson Christmas*, Christmas 2000, 46–47; and in the music videos for Britney Spears's "From the Bottom of My Broken Heart"; 98°'s "Because of You"; and 'N Sync's "Music of My Heart" and "Thinking of You (I Drive Myself Crazy)." Classic convertibles also appeared in the music videos for Paige's "Crush"; LFO's "Summer Girls" and "Girl on TV"; and Christina Aguilera's "Genie in a Bottle." Other "classic" cars were seen in the music videos for Hoku's "Another Dumb Blonde"; Jennifer Love Hewitt's "How Do I Deal"; Backstreet Boys' "As Long as You Love Me"; and in *A&F Quarterly: About Love . . .* , Spring Break 2002, 112–23. A Volkswagen Beetle appeared in *A&F Quarterly: On the Road*, Back to School 1998, 14–15; Moore's "Candy"; and Vitamin C's "Graduation (Friends Forever)." Jeeps were in *A&F Quarterly: A Very Emerson Christmas*, Christmas 2000, 260–63; Britney Spears's ". . . Baby One More Time"; and Jordan Knight's "Give It to You." Microphones were seen in *A&F Quarterly: New York*, Back to School 2000, 195; *A&F Quarterly: About Love . . .* , Spring Break 2002, 103; Hewitt's "How Do I Deal"; and 'N Sync's "Tearin' Up My Heart." Surfboards made several appearances, including in *A&F Quarterly: Spring Fever*, Spring Break 1999, cover, 65–75, 248; *A&F Quarterly: Wild and Willing*, Spring Break 2000, 174, 204–5, 209; *A&F Quarterly: Go Play*, Summer 2000, 21, back cover; and in the music videos for Backstreet Boys' "As Long As You Love Me"; and Hoku's "Another Dumb Blonde." Beaches were in nearly every spring break and summer issue of the magalog, but for reference, they were featured in *A&F Quarterly: Spring Fever*, Spring Break 1999, 135; *A&F Quarterly: Paradise Found*, Summer 2002, 2–36; and in the music videos for 98°'s "I Do (Cherish You)"; and Britney Spears's "Sometimes" and "Don't Let Me Be the Last to Know." A carnival photo shoot was in *A&F Quarterly: Go Play*, Summer 2000, 74–92, and in the music video for Knight's "Give It to You." New York was the topic of *A&F Quarterly: New York*, Back to School 2000, and was featured in the music video for 'N Sync's "Merry Christmas, Happy Holidays."

19. "MTV Timeline," MTV.com, accessed February 28, 2024, https://web.archive.org/web/20140329085559/http://thepub.viacom.com/sites/mtvpress/Shows/mtv-timeline.

20. Karen Heller, "The Man Who Would Be . . . Dick Clark," *Philadelphia Inquirer*, August 27, 2000, I1; Ben Sisario, "Totally Over: Last Squeals for 'TRL,'" *New York Times*, November 17, 2008, www.nytimes.com/2008/11/18/arts/television/18trl.html.

21. *Frontline*, season 19, episode 5, "The Merchants of Cool," directed by Barak Goodman, aired February 27, 2001, on PBS.

22. Ross and Stein, *Teen Television*, 14–15.

23. In "The Merchants of Cool," a WB executive spells out the network's realization that sex sold.

24. Wee, *Teen Media*, 47.

25. Ross and Stein, *Teen Television*, 5.

26. Wee, *Teen Media*, 52–53.

27. Wee, *Teen Media*, 54–55.

28. Joe Flint, "WB's New Prep-School Drama Gives a Starring Role to Coke," *Wall Street Journal*, July 12, 2000.

29. *Beverly Hills, 90210*, season 1, episode 1, "Pilot Part 2," directed by Tim Hunter, aired October 4, 1990, on Fox.

30. McKinley, *"Beverly Hills, 90210"*; Brooker, "Living on *Dawson's Creek*."

31. *Dawson's Creek*, season 1, episode 1, "Dawson's Creek," directed by Steve Miner, aired January 20, 1998, on the WB.

32. *Dawson's Creek*, season 1, episode 9, "Road Trip," directed by Steven Robman, aired March 17, 1998, on the WB.

33. Daniel Victor, "Mary Kay Letourneau, Teacher Who Raped Student and Then Married Him, Dies at 58," *New York Times*, July 7, 2020, www.nytimes.com/2020/07/07/obituaries/mary-kay-letourneau-dead.html. Outside of the teen genre, in the first season of *Friends*, Monica sleeps with a high school senior thinking he is in college, although this is played up for laughs. *Friends*, season 1, episode 22, "The One With the Ick Factor," directed by Robby Benson, aired May 4, 1995, on NBC.

34. Bindig, *"Dawson's Creek,"* 61.

35. James S. Murphy, "The Real College Admissions Scandal," *Slate*, June 14, 2021, https://slate.com/news-and-politics/2021/06/private-schools-competitive-college-advantage-problems.html.

36. Chris Molanphy, "The Give Me a Sign Edition," *Hit Parade*, podcast, November 30, 2018, 1:13:47, https://slate.com/culture/2018/11/how-a-teenaged-britney-spears-made-a-generational-hit.html. This episode noted that the original idea for the " . . . Baby One More Time" music video was an outer space theme, but Spears intervened to set the video in a high school.

Chapter Five

1. Bunch, *After the Ivory Tower*, 15.

2. McMillan Cottom, *Lower Ed*; Shumar, *College for Sale*; Tuchman, *Wannabe U*.

3. Bunch, *After the Ivory Tower*, 131.

4. Melanie Hanson, "Average Cost of College and Tuition," Education Data Initiative, June 25, 2023, https://educationdata.org/average-cost-of-college.

5. Often, complaints of "student as consumer" act to deflect criticism, and that could not be further from my point. Instead, my contention pertains to the type of higher education experience we're selling to students and to what effects. Sara Ahmed, "Against Students," *New Inquiry*, June 29, 2015, https://thenewinquiry.com/against-students/.

6. Aatish Bhatia, Clair Cain Miller, and Josh Katz, "Study of Elite College Admissions Data Suggests Being Very Rich Is Its Own Qualification," *New York Times*, July 24, 2023.

7. Driscoll, *Teen Film*, 3.

8. "The Skulls," Box Office Mojo, accessed January 20, 2023, www.boxofficemojo.com /title/tt0192614/?ref_=bo_se_r_1.

9. *Van Wilder* made $21.3 million domestically and $16.9 internationally and spawned two sequels. "National Lampoon's Van Wilder," Box Office Mojo, accessed February 29, 2024, www.boxofficemojo.com/title/tt0283111.

10. "Top 100—Lowest Acceptance Rates," *US News and World Report*, accessed February 27, 2024, www.usnews.com/best-colleges/rankings/lowest-acceptance-rate. Harvard, MIT, Princeton, and Stanford rank among the schools with the lowest acceptance rates, at 4 percent, while Cornell and the University of Pennsylvania, the most accepting Ivies, accepted 7 percent in 2023. "The Pennsylvania State University–University Park," *US News and World Report*, accessed February 27, 2024, www.usnews.com/best-colleges /penn-state-6965; "University of Maryland, College Park," *US News and World Report*, accessed February 27, 2024, www.usnews.com/best-colleges/university-of-maryland -2103; "Michigan State University," *US News and World Report*, accessed February 27, 2024, www.usnews.com/best-colleges/michigan-state-2290; "Arizona State University," *US News and World Report*, accessed February 27, 2024, www.usnews.com/best -colleges/arizona-state-university-1081; "Colleges with the Highest Acceptance Rates— Top 100," *US News and World Report*, accessed February 27, 2024, www.usnews.com /best-colleges/rankings/highest-acceptance-rate. See also Alia Wong, "College-Admissions Hysteria Is Not the Norm," *Atlantic*, April 10, 2019, www.theatlantic.com /education/archive/2019/04/harvard-uchicago-elite-colleges-are-anomaly/586627/.

11. US Census Bureau, "Census Bureau Releases New Education Attainment Data," press release, February 24, 2022, https://www.census.gov/newsroom/press-releases/2022 /educational-attainment.html.

12. Bunch, *After the Ivory Tower*, 100.

13. Quart, *Branded*, 143–63.

14. Bunch, *After the Ivory Tower*, 132.

15. Shumar, *College for Sale*, 23–25; Tuchman, *Wannabe U*, 49.

16. Tuchman, *Wannabe U*, 10, 117–21; Bunch, *After the Ivory Tower*, 151.

17. Sophie Kasakove, "The College Admissions Scandal: Where Some Defendants Are Now," *New York Times*, October 9, 2021.

18. McMillan Cottom, *Lower Ed*, 173–74.

19. Anna Helhoski and Eliza Haverstock, "How Borrower Defense to Repayment Works,"

NerdWallet, May 9, 2023, www.nerdwallet.com/article/loans/student-loans/borrower
-defense-repayment; Jillian Berman, "What the Supreme Court's Decision to Let
$6 Billion in Student Loan Relief Move Forward Means for Borrowers," MarketWatch,
April 17, 2023, www.marketwatch.com/story/what-the-supreme-courts-decision-to
-let-6-billion-in-student-loan-relief-move-forward-means-for-borrowers-579c1ea2.

20. Melanie Hanson, "Student Loan Debt Statistics," Education Data Initiative, July 17,
2023, https://educationdata.org/student-loan-debt-statistics.

21. Melissa Korn and Andrea Fuller, "'Financially Hobbled for Life': The Elite Master's
Degrees That Don't Pay Off," *Wall Street Journal*, July 8, 2021.

22. Bunch, *After the Ivory Tower*, 233.

23. In *Accepted*, Hoyt is shown in a prep-style button-down from Hollister, while Bartleby
frequently underhandedly insults his fraternity, including calling the members
antisemitic.

Chapter Six

1. In the opening scene, the group leaves an airport as screaming fans watch them depart.
It's reminiscent of the arrival of the Beatles in 1964 and has similarities to the Backstreet Boys' music video for "I Want It That Way." (In the video, released in 1999, the
group sings on an airport tarmac in front of a jet. The video is interspersed with scenes
from the group in the airport, garnering attention as they walk through.)

2. Horkheimer and Adorno, "Culture Industry." This is perhaps the best-known criticism
asserting that popular culture products are endlessly replaceable.

3. As an aside, I first watched *Josie and the Pussycats* years after its original release and was
shocked by the prominence of brand placements throughout the film.

4. Smarandescu and Shimp, "Drink Coca-Cola," 715–26.

5. "Josie and the Pussycats," Box Office Mojo, accessed February 27, 2024, www.boxoffice
mojo.com/title/tt0236348.

6. Jarett Wieselman, "7 Things You Didn't Know about 'Josie and the Pussycats,'" *Buzz-
Feed*, September 14, 2017, https://www.buzzfeednews.com/article/jarettwieselman
/7-things-you-didnt-know-about-josie-and-the-pussycats; Ilana Kaplan, "'Josie and
the Pussycats': Inside the 16th Anniversary Reunion and Concert," *Billboard*, September 26, 2017, www.billboard.com/music/pop/josie-and-the-pussycats-reunion
-concert-7980736/.

7. Naomi Klein, *No Logo*.

8. Quart, *Branded*.

9. Naomi Klein, *No Logo*, 182–90; Quart, *Branded*.

10. *Frontline*, season 19, episode 5, "The Merchants of Cool," directed by Barak Goodman,
aired February 27, 2001, on PBS.

11. Frank, *Conquest of Cool*, 9.

12. Frank and Weiland, *Commodify Your Dissent*.

13. Heath and Potter, *Nation of Rebels*, 322.

14. Quart (*Branded*, 7) links the increased role brands play in teens' lives to the development of *Seventeen* as well.

15. Quart, *Branded*, 77–95.

16. *Daria*, season 1, episode 5, "Malled," directed by Ken Kimmelman, aired March 31, 1997, on MTV.

17. *Daria*, season 1, episode 6, "This Year's Model," directed by Karen Disher and Ray Kosarian, aired April 7, 1997, on MTV.

18. Quart, *Branded*, 215–24.

19. Kalefa Sanneh, "The Rap against Rockism," *New York Times*, October 31, 2004, www.nytimes.com/2004/10/31/arts/music/the-rap-against-rockism.html.

20. As late as 2014, the lead singer of Maroon 5, Adam Levine, stated that he was more interested in being a celebrity than getting a particular message out and was derided for it; Jessica Pressler, "Adam Levine Doesn't Care if You Like Him (But He'd Really Prefer That You Did)," *GQ*, June 24, 2014, https://www.gq.com/story/adam-levine.

21. *Frontline*, season 19, episode 5, "The Merchants of Cool"; Quart, *Branded*, 41–45; Malcolm Gladwell, "The Cool Hunt," *New Yorker*, March 10, 1997, www.newyorker.com/magazine/1997/03/17/the-coolhunt-malcolm-gladwell.

22. Eric Sundermann, "Inside Gathering of the Juggalos," *SPIN*, August 17, 2010, \www.spin.com/2010/08/inside-gathering-juggalos/; Camille Dodero, "Live from Insane Clown Posse's Gathering of the Juggalos," *Village Voice*, September 8, 2010, https://www.villagevoice.com/live-from-insane-clown-posses-gathering-of-the-juggalos/.

23. Heath and Potter, *Nation of Rebels*, 129–32. My use of "alternative lifestyle" is intended literally, not as a euphemism for the LGBTQ+ community.

24. *Music Box*, season 1, episode 1, "Woodstock 99: Peace, Love and Rage," directed by Garrett Price, aired July 23, 2001, on HBO; Rob Sheffield, "'Woodstock '99' Documentary: A Long Day's Journey into 'Break Stuff,'" *Rolling Stone*, July 22, 2021, https://www.rollingstone.com/tv-movies/tv-movie-reviews/woodstock-99-documentary-review-hbo-1200593/; Amanda Petrusich, "Woodstock '99 and the Rise of Toxic Masculinity," *New Yorker*, July 30, 2021, https://www.newyorker.com/culture/cultural-comment/woodstock-99-and-the-rise-of-toxic-masculinity; Craig Jenkins, "We're Still Getting Woodstock '99 Wrong," *Vulture*, July 29, 2021, https://www.vulture.com/2021/07/hbo-woodstock-99-peace-love-and-rage-documentary-review.html.

25. Dave Holmes, "I Was at Woodstock '99, and Yes, Everyone *Was* That Angry," *Esquire*, July 23, 2021.

26. Marc Hogan, "The Nightmare of Woodstock '99 Persists in HBO's New Documentary," *Pitchfork*, July 22, 2021, https://pitchfork.com/thepitch/hbo-woodstock-99-documentary-review; Gil Kaufman, "Woodstock '99 Death Toll Rises to Three," MTV.com, July 28, 1999, https://web.archive.org/web/20220813085512/https://www.mtv.com/news/ii7mvg/woodstock-99-death-toll-rises-to-three.

27. Petrusich, "Woodstock '99."

28. See Klosterman's *The Nineties* for a recent example.

Chapter Seven

1. Although this is a direct quote from the film, the students in question are, at best, juniors, making the "always" relatively hyperbolic. However, it speaks to how high school portrayals make it seem permanent.

2. Klosterman, *Nineties*, 331–37; Nathan S. Webster, "1999: Our Last Innocent, Giddy

Summer," *Daily Beast*, May 25, 2015, www.thedailybeast.com/1999-our-last-innocent
-giddy-summer.

3. Klosterman, *Nineties*, 337.

4. George W. Bush, address to a joint session of Congress and the American people, September 20, 2001, transcript, White House Archives, https://georgewbush-whitehouse
.archives.gov/news/releases/2001/09/20010920-8.html.

5. George W. Bush, remarks to airline employees at Chicago O'Hare International Airport, September 27, 2001, transcript, White House Archives, https://georgewbush
-whitehouse.archives.gov/news/releases/2001/09/20010927-1.html.

6. Emily Stewart, "How 9/11 Convinced Americans to Buy, Buy, Buy," *Vox*, September 9,
2021, www.vox.com/the-goods/22662889/september-11-anniversary-bush-spend
-economy.

7. Lizabeth Cohen, *Consumer's Republic*, 112–33; Glickman, *Consumer Society*, 8.

8. Melnick, *9/11 Culture*, 18.

9. Melnick, *9/11 Culture*, 128–29; Godfrey and Hamad, "Save the Cheerleader"; Will
Paskin, "Another 24 Hours," *Slate*, May 5, 2014, https://slate.com/culture/2014/05
/new-24-miniseries-live-another-day-starring-kiefer-sutherland-reviewed.html; Adam
Green, "Normalizing Torture on '24,'" *New York Times*, May 22, 2005, www.nytimes
.com/2005/05/22/arts/television/normalizing-torture-on-24.html.

10. Brett Martin, *Difficult Men*, 13; Hope Reese, "Why Is the Golden Age of TV So Dark?,"
Atlantic, July 11, 2013, www.theatlantic.com/entertainment/archive/2013/07/why-is
-the-golden-age-of-tv-so-dark/277696/; Esther Zuckerman, "America Just Can't Ditch
Its Anti-heroes," *Atlantic*, June 21, 2013, www.theatlantic.com/culture/archive/2013/06
/tony-soprano-anti-heroes/314000/; Meghan Lewit, "Bad Husband, Good Wife, Good
TV: The Fascinating Rise of Antihero Marriages," *Atlantic*, April 30, 2013, https://
www.theatlantic.com/entertainment/archive/2013/04/bad-husband-bad-wife-good
-tv-the-fascinating-rise-of-antihero-marriages/275347/; Darren Franich, "16 Ultimate
Antiheroes," *Entertainment Weekly*, July 16, 2012, https://ew.com/gallery/16-ultimate
-tv-antiheroes/.

11. While Wee (*Teen Media*, 2010) suggests that the teen genre expanded to a particular
type of media product that prioritized personal growth and relationships rather than
making teens the center of the action, as discussed in chapter 1, the roots of being a
"teen" were primarily constructed from magazines and advertising. See, e.g., Palladino,
Teenagers; Massoni, *Fashioning Teenagers*; and Hine, *Rise and Fall*.

12. On femininity in this context, see De Grazia, introduction, 2–3.

13. Trencansky, "Final Girls"; Wee, "Resurrecting and Updating"; Rios, "Joey Potter."

14. "Mean Girls," Box Office Mojo, accessed February 27, 2024, www.boxofficemojo.com
/release/rl3395520001.

15. Anya Meyerowitz, "*Mean Girls* Fans, This Deleted Scene Might Have You Seeing
Regina in a Whole New Light," *Glamour UK*, May 13, 2022, https://www.glamour
magazine.co.uk/article/mean-girls-deleted-scene. While deleted from the movie, it was
kept as part of the *Mean Girls* musical, also written by Fey, which ran on Broadway
from 2018 to 2020.

16. *John Tucker Must Die* made $14 million its first weekend, for a total of $41 million domestically and $68.8 million worldwide; "John Tucker Must Die," Box Office Mojo, accessed February 27, 2024, www.boxofficemojo.com/title/tt0455967/.

17. Other authors have attributed the distinction of being the final film in the cycle to *Easy A*, which I discuss in chapter 9, but that film feels distinct in its themes and storytelling.

18. David von Drehle, "For 'Shock and Awe' Author, Concern," *Washington Post*, March 22, 2003, www.washingtonpost.com; "Shock and Awe: The Idea behind the Buzzwords," *Washington Post*, March 30, 2003, www.washingtonpost.com. "Shock and awe" is the colloquial, public term for "decisive or overwhelming force," which is intended to surprise and overwhelm an opponent, thus ending a war quickly. News reports latched on to this terminology, using it hundreds of times in February and March 2003.

19. *Saved!* was produced with a budget of $5 million but made $8.9 million domestically and $10.27 million worldwide. "Saved!," Box Office Mojo, accessed February 27, 2024, www.boxofficemojo.com/title/tt0332375/.

20. Elyse Pham, "Here's How Pop Culture Has Perpetuated Harmful Stereotypes of Asian Women," Today.com, April 1, 2021, www.today.com/popculture/here-s-how-pop -culture-has-perpetuated-harmful-stereotypes-asian-t213676.

21. Quart, *Branded*, 78–82.

Chapter Eight

1. "The Devil Wears Prada," Box Office Mojo, accessed February 27, 2024, www.box officemojo.com/title/tt0458352/.

2. Driscoll, *Teen Film*, 3; Wee, *Teen Media*, 47.

3. "Teen Choice Awards: 2003 Awards," IMDb, accessed February 29, 2024, https://web .archive.org/web/20230715080117/https://www.imdb.com/event/ev0000644/2003/1/; "Teen Choice Awards: 2004 Awards," IMDb, accessed February 27, 2024, https://web .archive.org/web/20220721190807/https://www.imdb.com/event/ev0000644/2004 /1/; "Teen Choice Awards: 2005 Awards," IMDb, accessed February 27, 2024, https:// web.archive.org/web/20231030225230/https://www.imdb.com/event/ev0000644 /2005/1; Teen Choice Awards: 2006 Awards," IMDb, accessed February 24, 2024, https://web.archive.org/web/20230715080113/https://www.imdb.com/event/ev0000 644/2006/1/; "Teen Choice Awards: 2007 Awards," IMDb, accessed February 27, 2024, https://web.archive.org/web/20221112234017/https://www.imdb.com/event /ev0000644/2007/1/.

4. McCracken, *Transformations*; McGee, *Self-Help, Inc.*, 16–17; McDonald, *Hollywood Catwalk*, 199–217.

5. McDonald, *Hollywood Catwalk*, 82–95; McGee, *Self-Help, Inc.*, 171–74.

6. *Sweet Home Alabama* topped the box office the weekend it opened with $35.6 million and would earn $127.2 million domestically and $180.6 million worldwide during its theatrical run. "Sweet Home Alabama," Box Office Mojo, accessed February 27, 2024, www.boxofficemojo.com/title/tt0256415/.

7. On academic attention, see McDonald, *Hollywood Catwalk*; and Radner, *Neo-feminist*

Cinema, both of which have chapters dedicated to *The Devil Wears Prada*. On "creative industries," see Hartley et al., *Key Concepts*. The term is borrowed from policies in the United Kingdom. Thirteen industries officially fall under the categorization, according to Hartley et al.: advertising, architecture, art and antiques, computer games/leisure software, crafts, design, designer fashion, film and video, music performing arts, publishing, software, television, and radio.

8. *Waiting . . .* made $6 million on its opening weekend and $16.1 million domestically and $18.6 million globally during its release. "Waiting . . . ," Box Office Mojo, accessed February 27, 2024, www.boxofficemojo.com/title/tt0348333/.

9. While some of the actions of the characters in *Waiting . . .* are harmful and would even classify as sexual harassment, others are just personal traits that would not be looked down on in a different setting or when done by someone with a higher-profile job. In short, at least some of this criticism is steeped in classism.

10. Bourdieu, *Distinction*, 323–26.

11. US Bureau of Labor Statistics, "All Employees, Leisure and Hospitality (USLAH)," retrieved from FRED, Federal Reserve Bank of St. Louis, on February 27, 2024, https://fred.stlouisfed.org/series/USLAH.

12. US Bureau of Labor Statistics, "All Employees, Food Services and Drinking Places (CES7072200001)," retrieved from FRED, Federal Reserve Bank of St. Louis, on February 27, 2024, https://fred.stlouisfed.org/series/CES7072200001; US Bureau of Labor Statistics, "All Employees, Retail Trade (USTRADE)," retrieved from FRED, Federal Reserve Bank of St. Louis, February 27, 2024, https://fred.stlouisfed.org/series/USTRADE.

13. US Bureau of Labor Statistics, "All Employees, Publishing Industries (CES5051100001)," retrieved from FRED, Federal Reserve Bank of St. Louis, on February 27, 2024, https://fred.stlouisfed.org/series/CES5051100001.

14. US Bureau of Labor Statistics, "All Employees, Information (USINFO)," retrieved from FRED, Federal Reserve Bank of St. Louis, on February 27, 2024, https://fred.stlouisfed.org/series/USINFO.

15. Becker and Lowery, "Monitoring the U.S. Journalism."

16. US Bureau of Labor Statistics, "Occupational Employment and Wages, 2008," news release no USDL 09-0457, May 1, 2009, https://www.bls.gov/news.release/archives/ocwage_05012009.pdf; "Wage Statistics for 2008," Social Security Administration, accessed February 27, 2024, https://www.ssa.gov/cgi-bin/netcomp.cgi?year=2008.

17. US Bureau of Labor Statistics, "Average Hourly Earnings of All Employees, Information (CES5000000003)," retrieved from FRED, Federal Reserve Bank of St. Louis, on January 20, 2024, https://fred.stlouisfed.org/series/CES5000000003. According to the bureau, the average hourly salary for information workers was $28.17; assuming a forty-hour workweek and fifty-two weeks a year, that equates to $58,593.60 annually.

Chapter Nine

1. Ben Sisario, "Totally Over: Last Squeals for 'TRL,'" *New York Times*, November 17, 2008, www.nytimes.com/2008/11/18/arts/television/18trl.html.

2. *Total Request Live*, special episode, "Total Finale Live," directed by Steve Paley, aired November 16, 2008, on MTV.

3. Robert Lloyd, review of *Total Request Live*, special episode, "Total Finale Live," *Los Angeles Times*, November 17, 2008, www.latimes.com/archives/blogs/show-tracker /story/2008-11-17/review-trls-total-finale-live.

4. Jon Pareles, "Critics' Choice: New CDs Britney Spears," *New York Times*, December 1, 2008; Samantha Schnurr, "Justin Timberlake Explains Why NSYNC's Breakup Wasn't 'Big News' to the Band," *E! News*, October 5, 2020, www.eonline.com/news/1194941 /justin-timberlake-explains-why-nsyncs-breakup-wasnt-big-news-to-the-band; Kalefa Sanneh, "The Solo Beyoncé: She's No Ashanti," *New York Times*, July 6, 2003, www .nytimes.com/2003/07/06/arts/music-the-solo-beyonce-she-s-no-ashanti.html; Jon Caramanica, "A Young Outsider's Life Turned Inside Out," *New York Times*, September 5, 2008, www.nytimes.com/2008/09/07/arts/music/07cara.html.

5. Dana Rubinstein, "Aeropostale to Take Over Old MTV Studio Space in Times Square," *Observer*, January 12, 2010, https://observer.com/2010/01/aeropostale-to-take-old-mtv -studio-space-in-times-square/; Sharon Edelson, "Aeropostale Lands in Times Square," *Women's Wear Daily*, October 21, 2010, https://wwd.com/feature/aeropostale-lands-in -times-square-3347540-1233492/.

6. Alex Vadukul, "Virgin Megastore's Last Days: Farewell to NYC's Big Record Shop," *Rolling Stone*, June 12, 2009, www.rollingstone.com/music/music-news/virgin -megastores-last-days-farewell-to-nycs-big-record-shop-83707/.

7. William Neuman, "In New York, Broadway as Great Walk Way," *New York Times*, February 26, 2009, https://www.nytimes.com/2009/02/27/nyregion/27broadway .html; Ben Fried, "Bloomberg: The Transformation of Broadway Here to Stay," *Streets- blog NYC*, February 11, 2010, https://nyc.streetsblog.org/2010/02/11/bloomberg-the -transformation-of-broadway-is-here-to-stay.

8. Smith (*Rethinking*) argues that *Easy A* is nostalgia for earlier teen movies, while Kakla- manidou ("*Easy A*") situates the film as the last high school teen comedy.

9. Rich Cohen, "The Ballad of Downward Mobility," *Atlantic*, August 28, 2022, www .theatlantic.com/ideas/archive/2022/08/downward-economic-mobility-boomer -generation-x-debt/671260/; Tami Luhby, "Many Millennials Are Worse Off Than Their Parents—a First in American History," CNN.com, January 11, 2020, www.cnn .com/2020/01/11/politics/millennials-income-stalled-upward-mobility-us/index.html.

10. Carrie Bell, "'Twilight' Premiere: Hysteria and Happy Campers," *Entertainment Weekly*, November 21, 2008, https://ew.com/article/2008/11/21/twilight-premiere -hysteria-and-happy-campers/.

11. Jillian Mapes, "Katy Perry Dedicates Leaked 'Firework' Video to LGBT Campaign," *Billboard*, October 28, 2010, www.billboard.com/music/music-news/katy-perry -dedicates-leaked-firework-video-to-lgbt-campaign-952410/.

12. Muri Assunção, "12 Times Lady Gaga Showed Love for the LGBTQ Community," *Billboard*, September 20, 2018, www.billboard.com/culture/pride/lady-gaga-12-times -showed-love-for-lgbtq-community-8475993/.

13. James Montgomery, "Ke$ha Regrets Nothing, Not Even Drinking Her Own Pee,"

MTV.com, June 3, 2013, www.mtv.com/news/m7u3gi/kesha-crazy-beautiful-life
-drink-pee.

14. Smith, *Rethinking*, 138–40.

15. Smith, *Rethinking*, 138–40.

16. Kaklamanidou, *"Easy A,"* 30.

17. Reviews of *Confessions of a Shopaholic*, Rotten Tomatoes, accessed January 20, 2024,
www.rottentomatoes.com/m/confessions_of_a_shopaholic/reviews; "Confessions
of a Shopaholic," Box Office Mojo, accessed February 27, 2024, www.boxofficemojo
.com/title/tt1093908/.

18. "Bridesmaids," Box Office Mojo, accessed January 20, 2024, www.boxofficemojo.com
/title/tt1478338/.

19. Like the films discussed in chapter 8, *Bridesmaids* may not be typical teen fare, but it
was nominated for Teen Choice Awards and broadly fits the same themes.

20. *Pitch Perfect* made $65.2 million domestically and $115.6 million worldwide and
spawned two sequels. "Pitch Perfect," Box Office Mojo, accessed January 20, 2024,
www.boxofficemojo.com/title/tt1981677/.

21. Pimpare, *New Victorians*; Remnick, *New Gilded Age*; Paul Krugman, "Gilded Once
More," *New York Times*, April 27, 2007, www.nytimes.com/2007/04/27/opinion
/27krugman.html.

22. Louis Uchitelle, "The Richest of the Rich, Proud of a New Gilded Age," *New York
Times*, July 15, 2007, www.nytimes.com/2007/07/15/business/15gilded.html. See also
Emmanuel Saez and Gabriel Zucman, "The Explosion in U.S. Wealth Inequality Has
Been Fueled by Stagnant Wages, Increasing Debt and a Collapse in Asset Values for the
Middle Class," London School of Economics Phelan US Centre, accessed July 19, 2022,
https://blogs.lse.ac.uk/usappblog/2014/10/29/the-explosion-in-u-s-wealth-inequality
-has-been-fuelled-by-stagnant-wages-increasing-debt-and-a-collapse-in-asset-values
-for-the-middle-classes/.

23. Pew Research Center, *Lost Decade*.

24. Christopher Ingraham, "The Staggering Millennial Wealth Deficit, in One Chart,"
Washington Post, December 3, 2019, https://www.washingtonpost.com/business
/2019/12/03/precariousness-modern-young-adulthood-one-chart/.

25. Olivia Rockman and Catarina Saraiva, "Millennials Are Running Out of Time to
Build Wealth," Bloomberg.com, June 3, 2021, www.bloomberg.com/features/2021
-millennials-are-running-out-of-time.

26. Andrew Van Dam, "The Unluckiest Generation in US History," *Washington Post*,
June 5, 2020, www.washingtonpost.com/business/2020/05/27/millennial-recession
-covid/.

27. David Hope and Julian Limberg, "The Economic Consequences of Major Tax Cuts
for the Rich" (working paper, London School of Economics International Inequalities
Institute, December 2020); David Hope and Julian Limberg, "Footing the COVID-19
Bill: Economic Case for Tax Hike on the Wealth," *Conversation*, December 16, 2020,
https://theconversation.com/footing-the-covid-19-bill-economic-case-for-tax-hike
-on-wealthy-151945.

28. Jay Shambaugh and Ryan Nunn, "Why Wages Aren't Growing in America," *Harvard*

Business Review, October 24, 2017, https://hbr.org/2017/10/why-wages-arent-growing -in-america; Drew DeSilver, "For Most US Workers, Real Wages Have Barely Budged in Decades," Pew Research Center, August 7, 2018, www.pewresearch.org/short-reads /2018/08/07/for-most-us-workers-real-wages-have-barely-budged-for-decades.

29. Alina Selyukh, "Paycheck-to-Paycheck Nation: Why Even Americans with Higher Income Struggle with Bills," NPR.com, December 16, 2020, www.npr.org/2020/12 /16/941292021/paycheck-to-paycheck-nation-how-life-in-america-adds-up.

30. Steven Russolillo, "Irrational Exuberance: Alan Greenspan's Call, 20 Years Later," *Wall Street Journal*, December 3, 2016, www.wsj.com/articles/irrational-exuberance-alan -greenspans-call-20-years-later-1480773602.

31. Parker, *Boomerang Generation*.

32. Filipovic, *OK Boomer*.

33. Malcolm Harris, *Kids These Days*.

34. Hayes, *Twilight of the Elite*; Bunch, *After the Ivory Tower*; Alter, *We've Been Waiting*; Duca, *How to Start*.

35. Christopher Kurz, Geng Li, and Daniel J. Vine, "Are Millennials Different?" (Finance and Economic Discussion Series 2018–080, Federal Reserve, Washington, DC, November 2018), http://doi.org/10.17016/FEDS.2018.080.

36. Filipovic, *OK Boomer*, 8–11.

37. Stuart A. Thompson (@stuartathompson), Twitter, March 25, 2022, https://web .archive.org/web/20220325183850/https://twitter.com/stuartathompson/status/150742 6672013885451.

38. Sunny Moraine (@dynamicsymmetry), Twitter, February 13, 2022, https://web.archive .org/web/20220214013357/https://twitter.com/dynamicsymmetry/status/1493035 221163425800.

39. The thread begins with Sunny Moraine (@dynamicsymmetry), "Okay, I actually want to talk about this for a second, regarding millennials and how really goddamn difficult it is for us to make sense of our own age sometimes," Twitter, October 1, 2018, https:// web.archive.org/web/20220516004600/https://twitter.com/dynamicsymmetry /status/1046873895494664192.

40. Jack Jenkins (@jackmjenkins), "Extreme shifts happen in all gens, but the chaotic intensity of the Elder* Millennial experience is arguably underestimated," Twitter, February 23, 2022, https://web.archive.org/web/20220223145033/https://twitter.com /jackmjenkins/status/1496496434023219200.

41. Charlotte Cowles, "We Aren't Asking for the Moon," *New York Times*, July 11, 2022, www.nytimes.com/interactive/2022/07/11/style/economic-anxiety-millennials.html.

42. Kyle Chayka, "Pokémon and the First Wave of Digital Nostalgia," *New Yorker*, December 3, 2021, www.newyorker.com/culture/infinite-scroll/pokemon-and-the-first-wave -of-digital-nostalgia.

43. Davis, *Yearning for Yesterday*, 141.

44. Justin McCarthy, "U.S. Approval of Labor Unions at Highest Point Since 1965," Gallup, August 30, 2022, https://news.gallup.com/poll/398303/approval-labor-unions -highest-point-1965.aspx; Courtenay Brown, "Jobs Boom at the State Level," *Axios*, July 24, 2023, www.axios.com/2023/07/24/states-jobs-unemployment-rate.

45. Tara Siegel Bernard, "Biden's New Student Loan Repayment Plan Is Open. Here's How to Enroll," *New York Times*, August 22, 2023, www.nytimes.com/2023/08/22 /your-money/student-loans-income-driven-repayment-save.html.

46. *PBS NewsHour*, "Higher Young Voter Turnout in Midterms Changes Approach to Major Political Issues," by John Yang and Saher Khan, aired November 24, 2022, on PBS, transcript, www.pbs.org/newshour/show/higher-young-voter-turnout-in -midterms-changes-approach-to-major-political-issues#transcript.

BIBLIOGRAPHY

Audiovisual Sources

Becker, Walt, dir. *National Lampoon's Van Wilder*. Santa Monica, CA: Lionsgate, 2002.

Berlanti, Greg, dir. *Love, Simon*. Los Angeles: Fox 2000 Pictures, 2018.

Beverly Hills, 90210. Created by Darren Star. Starring Jason Priestley, Shannen Doherty, Luke Perry, and Jennie Garth. Aired on Fox 1990–2000.

Cannon, Danny, dir. *I Still Know What You Did Last Summer*. Culver City, CA: Sony Pictures Entertainment: 1999.

Carter, Thomas, dir. *Save the Last Dance*. Los Angeles: MTV Films, 2001.

Cohen, Rob, dir. *The Skulls*. Universal City, CA: Universal Pictures, 2000.

Coolidge, Greg, dir. *Employee of the Month*. Santa Monica, CA: Lionsgate, 2006.

Dannelly, Brian, dir. *Saved!* Beverly Hills, CA: United Artists, 2004.

Daria. Created by Glenn Eichler and Susie Lewis. Starring Tracy Grandstaff, Wendy Hoopes, and Julian Rebolledo. Aired on MTV 1997–2002.

Dawson's Creek. Created by Kevin Williamson. Starring James Van Der Beek, Katie Holmes, Joshua Jackson, and Michelle Williams. Aired on the WB 1998–2003.

Elfont, Harry, and Deborah Kaplan, dirs. *Josie and the Pussycats*. Universal City, CA: Universal Pictures, 2001.

Feig, Paul, dir. *Bridesmaids*. Universal City, CA: Universal Pictures, 2011.

Friends. Created by David Crane and Marta Kauffman. Starring Jennifer Aniston, Courtney Cox, Lisa Kudrow, Matt LeBlanc, and Matthew Perry. Aired on NBC 1994–2004.

Frontline. Created by David Fanning. Starring Will Lyman and Sarah Childress. Aired on PBS 1983–present.

Gluck, Will, dir. *Easy A*. Culver City, CA: Screen Gems, 2010.

Gosnell, Raja, dir. *Never Been Kissed*. Los Angeles: Fox 2000 Pictures, 1999.

Hardwicke, Catherine, dir. *Twilight*. Santa Monica, CA: Summit Entertainment, 2008.

Hogan, P. J., dir. *Confessions of a Shopaholic*. Universal City, CA: Touchstone Pictures, 2009.

Iscove, Robert, dir. *She's All That*. Los Angeles: Miramax, 1999.

Junger, Gil, dir. *10 Things I Hate about You*. Burbank, CA: Touchstone Pictures, 1999.

King, Michael Patrick, dir. *Sex and the City*. Burbank, CA: New Line Cinema, 2008.

Klayman, Alison, dir. *White Hot: The Rise and Fall of Abercrombie & Fitch*. Los Gatos, CA: Netflix, 2022.

Kumble, Roger, dir. *Cruel Intentions*. Culver City, CA: Columbia Pictures, 1999.

Luketic, Robert, dir. *Legally Blonde*. Beverly Hills, CA: Metro-Goldwyn-Mayer, 2001.

Marshall, Garry, dir. *Pretty Woman*. Universal City, CA: Touchstone Pictures, 1990.

McKittrick, Rob, dir. *Waiting . . .* Santa Monica, CA: Lionsgate, 2005.

Moore, Jason, dir. *Pitch Perfect*. Universal City, CA: Universal Pictures, 2012.

Music Box. Documentary series created by Bill Simmons. Aired on HBO from 2021 to present.

O'Haver, Tommy, dir. *Get Over It*. Los Angeles: Paramount, 2001.

Pink, Steven, dir. *Accepted*. Universal City, CA: Universal Pictures, 2006.

Reed, Peyton, dir. *Bring It On*. Santa Monica, CA: Universal Pay Television: 2000.

Robbins, Brian, dir. *Varsity Blues*. Los Angeles: MTV Films, 1999.

Roth, Robin, Glenn Barden, Fred Hepburn, Sarah Hunt, Peter Lovering, Martin Pupp, and Jane Root, prods. *The '90s: The Last Great Decade?* Documentary miniseries narrated by Rob Lowe. Aired on National Geographic in 2014.

Sandel, Ari, dir. *The Duff*. Los Angeles: CBS Films, 2015.

Schultz, John, dir. *Drive Me Crazy*. Los Angeles: 20th Century Fox, 1999.

Stone, Charles, III, dir. *Drumline*. Los Angeles: 20th Century Fox, 2002.

Thomas, Betty, dir. *John Tucker Must Die*. Los Angeles: 20th Century Fox, 2006.

Total Request Live. Presented by Carson Daly, Damien Fahey, Hilarie Burton, Quddus, La La Vasquez, et al. Original run aired on MTV from 1998 to 2008.

Waters, Mark, dir. *He's All That*. Los Angeles: Miramax, 2021.

———, dir. *Mean Girls*. Los Angeles: Paramount Pictures, 2004.

Weitz, Paul, and Chris Weitz, dirs. *American Pie*. Universal City, CA: Universal Pictures, 1999.

Wilde, Olivia, dir. *Booksmart*. Los Angeles: 20th Century Fox, 2019.

Periodicals and Online News Sources

A&F Quarterly	*Glamour UK*	*Rolling Stone*
Axios	*GQ*	*Sacramento (CA) Bee*
Atlantic	*Harvard Business Review*	*Salon*
Billboard	*Los Angeles Times*	*Slate*
BusinessWeek	*MEL Magazine*	*SPIN*
Bustle	*New York Magazine*	*Streetsblog NYC*
BuzzFeed	*New York Post*	*Time*
Conversation	*New York Times*	*Village Voice*
Daily Beast	*New Yorker*	*Vox*
Dallas Morning News	*Observer*	*Vulture*
E! News	*Philadelphia Inquirer*	*Wall Street Journal*
Entertainment Weekly	*Pitchfork*	*Washington Post*
Esquire	*Refinery29*	*Women's Wear Daily*
Fortune	*Ringer*	

Books, Journal Articles, and Other Sources

Abercrombie & Fitch Co. 2007 Annual Report. www.annualreports.com/HostedData /AnnualReportArchive/a/NYSE_ANF_2007.pdf.

———. 2009 Annual Report. Form 10-K, filed with the Securities and Exchange Commission for fiscal year ended January 30, 2010. Commission file no. 1–12107. www .annualreports.com/HostedData/AnnualReportArchive/a/NYSE_ANF_2009.pdf.

———. 2014 Annual Report. Form 10-K, filed with the Securities and Exchange Commission for fiscal year ended January 31, 2015. Commission file no. 1–12107. www.annual reports.com/HostedData/AnnualReportArchive/a/NYSE_ANF_2014.pdf.

———. 2016 Annual Report. Form 10-K, filed with the Securities and Exchange Commission for fiscal year ended January 28, 2017. Commission file number 1–12107. www .annualreports.com/HostedData/AnnualReportArchive/a/NYSE_ANF_2016.pdf.

Ahmed, Sara. *Queer Phenomenology: Orientations, Objects, Others*. Durham, NC: Duke University Press, 2006.

Allen, Graham. *Intertextuality: The New Critical Idiom*. New York: Routledge, 2000.

Alter, Charlotte. *The Ones We've Been Waiting For: How a New Generation of Leaders Will Transform America*. New York: Penguin, 2020.

Altman, Rick. *Film/Genre*. London: BFI, 1999.

Arnold, Gina, Daniel Cookney, Kirsty Fairclough, and Michael Goddard. *Music/Video: Histories, Aesthetics, Media*. New York: Bloomsbury, 2017.

Aronczyk, Melissa. "Portal or Police? The Limits of Promotional Paratexts." *Critical Studies in Media Communication* 34, no. 2 (2017): 111–19. https://doi.org/10.1080/15295036.2017 .1289545.

Badgett, M. V. Lee, and Alyssa Schneebaum. *The Impact of Wage Equality on Sexual Orientation of Poverty Gaps*. Los Angeles: Williams Institute, 2015. https://williamsinstitute .law.ucla.edu/wp-content/uploads/Wage-Equality-LGB-Poverty-Gap-Jun-2015.pdf.

Banet-Weiser, Sarah. *Authentic: The Politics of Ambivalence in a Brand Culture*. New York: New York University Press, 2012.

Baudrillard, Jean. "From *Symbolic Exchange and Death*." In *From Modernism to Postmodernism: An Anthology*, edited by Lawrence Cahoone, 421–34. Malden, MA: Blackwell, 2003.

Becker, Lee B., and Wilson Lowery. "Monitoring the U.S. Journalism and Mass Communication Labor Market: Findings, History and Methods of an Ongoing Survey Project." *Australian Journalism Review* 22, no. 1 (2000): 20–36. https://web.archive.org/web /20100612020717/https://grady.uga.edu/annualsurveys/Supplemental_Reports /ausjreview.pdf

Berlant, Lauren. *Cruel Optimism*. Durham, NC: Duke University Press, 2011.

Bickford, Tyler. *Tween Pop: Children's Music and Public Culture*. Durham, NC: Duke University Press, 2020.

Bindig, Lori. *"Dawson's Creek": A Critical Understanding*. New York: Lexington Books, 2008.

Bishop, Ron. *More: The Vanishing of Scale in an Over-the-Top Nation*. Waco, TX: Baylor University Press, 2011.

Bourdieu, Pierre. *Distinction: A Social Critique of the Judgement of Taste*. Cambridge, MA: Harvard University Press, 1984.

Brooker, Will. "Living on *Dawson's Creek*: Teen Viewers, Cultural Convergence, and Television." *International Journal of Cultural Studies* 4, no. 4 (2001): 456–72. https:// doi.org/10.1177/136787790100400406.

Buckingham, David. *Youth on Screen: Representing Young People in Film and Television*. Medford, MA: Polity, 2021.

Bunch, Will. *After the Ivory Tower Falls*. New York: William Morrow, 2022.

Chaney, David. *Lifestyles*. New York: Routledge, 1996.

Cohen, Lizabeth. *A Consumer's Republic: The Politics of Mass Consumption in Postwar America*. New York: Vintage, 2003.

Cole, Daniel James, and Nancy Deihl. *The History of Modern Fashion*. London: Laurence King, 2015.

Considine, David M. *The Cinema of Adolescence*. Jefferson, NC: McFarland, 1985.

Craik, Jennifer. *Uniforms Exposed: From Conformity to Transgression*. New York: Berg, 2005.

Cross, Gary. *An All-Consuming Century: Why Commercialism Won in Modern America*. New York: Columbia University Press, 2000.

Currid-Halkett, Elizabeth. *The Sum of Small Things: A Theory of the Aspirational Class*. Princeton, NJ: Princeton University Press, 2017.

Davis, Fred. *Yearning for Yesterday: A Sociology of Nostalgia*. New York: Free Press, 1979.

Davis, Glyn, and Kay Dickinson. *Teen TV: Genre, Consumption and Identity*. London: BFI, 2004.

De Grazia, Victoria. Introduction to *The Sex of Things: Gender and Consumption in Historical Perspective*, edited by Victoria de Grazia and Ellen Furlough, 1–10. Los Angeles: University of California Press, 1996.

Deleuze, Giles, and Fèlix Guattari. *A Thousand Plateaus: Capitalism and Schizophrenia*. Minneapolis: University of Minnesota Press, 1987.

Dickinson, Greg. *Suburban Dreams: Imagining and Building the Good Life*. Tuscaloosa: University of Alabama Press, 2015.

Doherty, Thomas Patrick. *Teenagers and Teenpics: The Juvenilization of American Movies in the 1950s*. Boston: Unwin Hyman, 1988.

Driscoll, Catherine. Afterword to Shary, *Generation Multiplex*, 303–8.

———. *Teen Film: A Critical Introduction*. New York: Berg, 2011.

Duca, Lauren. *How to Start of Revolution: Young People and the Future of American Politics*. New York: Simon and Schuster, 2019.

Dunn, Robert. *Identifying Consumption: Subjects and Objects in Consumer Society*. Philadelphia: Temple University Press, 2009.

Engel, Stephen M. "Marketing Everyday Life: The Postmodern Commodity Aesthetic of Abercrombie & Fitch." *Advertising and Society Review* 5, no. 3 (2004). https://muse.jhu.edu/article/174080.

Ferguson, Kevin. *Eighties People: New Lives in the American Imagination*. New York: Palgrave Macmillan, 2016.

Filipovic, Jill. *OK Boomer, Let's Talk: How My Generation Got Left Behind*. New York: One Signal, 2020.

Fiske, John. *Understanding Popular Culture*. New York: Routledge, 2011.

Frank, Thomas. *The Conquest of Cool: Business Culture, Counterculture, and the Rise of Hip Consumerism*. Chicago: University of Chicago Press, 1997.

———. "Why Johnny Can't Dissent." In Thomas and Weiland, *Commodify Your Dissent*, 31–45.

Frank, Thomas, and Matt Weiland, eds. *Commodify Your Dissent*. New York: W. W. Norton, 1997.

Fukuyama, Francis. *The End of History and the Last Man*. New York: Free Press, 1992.

Glickman, Lawrence B. *Consumer Society in American History: A Reader*. Ithaca, NY: Cornell University Press, 1999.

Godfrey, Sarah, and Hannah Hamad. "Save the Cheerleader, Save the Males: Resurgent Protective Paternalism in Popular Film and Television after 9/11." In *The Handbook of Gender, Sex, and Media*, edited by Karen Ross, 157–73. Malden, MA: Wiley-Blackwell, 2011.

Gopnik, Adam. "Display Cases." In Remnick, *New Gilded Age*, 287–96.

Grindon, Leger. "Cycles and Clusters: The Shape of Film Genre History." In *Film Genre Reader*, 4th ed., edited by Barry Keith Grant, 42–59. Austin: University of Texas Press, 2012.

Hackley, Chris, and Amy Rungpaqka Hackley. "Advertising at the Threshold: Paratextual Promotion in the Era of Media Convergence." *Marketing Theory* 19, no. 2 (2019): 195–215. https://doi.org/10.1177/1470593118787581.

Hall, Stuart. "Cultural Studies and Its Legacies." In *Cultural Studies*, edited by Lawrence Grossberg, Cary Nelson, and Paula Treichler, 277–94. New York: Routledge, 1992.

———. "Encoding/Decoding." In *Media and Cultural Studies Keyworks*, edited by Meenakshi Gigi Durham and Douglas M. Kellner, 137–44. Malden, MA: Wiley-Blackwell, 2012.

———. Introduction to *Paper Voices: The Popular Press and Social Change, 1935–1965*, edited by A. C. H. Smith, Elizabeth Immirzi, and Trevor Blackwell, 11–24. Totowa, NJ: Rowman and Littlefield, 1975.

Hancock, Joseph H., II. "Chelsea on 5th Avenue: Hypermasculinity and Gay Clone Culture in the Retail Brand Practices of Abercrombie & Fitch." *Fashion Practice* 1, no. 1 (2009): 63–85. http://doi.org/10.2752/175693809X418702.

Harris, Aisha. *Wannabe: Reckonings with the Pop Culture That Shapes Me*. New York: HarperOne, 2023.

Harris, Malcolm. *Kids These Days: The Making of Millennials*. New York: Back Bay Books, 2017.

Hartley, John, Jason Potts, Stuart Cunningham, Terry Flew, and John Banks. *Key Concepts in the Creative Industries*. Thousand Oaks, CA: Sage, 2013.

Hayes, Chris. *The Twilight of the Elite: America after Meritocracy*. New York: Crown, 2012.

Heath, Joseph, and Andrew Potter. *Nation of Rebels: Why Counterculture Became Consumer Culture*. New York: HarperBusiness, 2004.

Hebdige, Dick. *Subculture: The Meaning of Style*. London: Methuen, 1979.

Hine, Thomas. *The Rise and Fall of the American Teenager*. New York: Harper Perennial, 1999.

Horkheimer, Max, and Theodor W. Adorno. "The Culture Industry: Enlightenment as Mass Deception." In *Media and Cultural Studies Keyworks*, edited by Meenakshi Gigi Durham and Douglas M. Kellner, 53–75. Malden, MA: Wiley-Blackwell, 2012.

Jamieson, Patrick E., and Daniel Romer. *The Changing Portrayal of Adolescents in the Media since 1950*. New York: Oxford University Press, 2008.

Jeffers McDonald, Tamar. *Hollywood Catwalk: Exploring Costume and Transformation in American Film*. New York: I. B. Tauris, 2010.

Johnson, Derek. *Transgenerational Media Industries*. Ann Arbor: University of Michigan Press, 2019.

Kaklamanidou, Betty. *"Easy A": The End of the High-School Teen Comedy?* New York: Routledge, 2018.

Kann, Laura, Steven A. Kinchen, Barbara I. Williams, James G. Ross, Richard Lowry, Jo Anne Grunbaum, and Lloyd J. Kolbe. "Youth Risk Behavior Surveillance—United States, 1999." In "Surveillance Summaries." Supplement, *Morbidity and Mortality Weekly Report* 49, no. SS-5 (2000): 1–96. www.cdc.gov/mmwr/preview/mmwrhtml/ss4905a1.htm.

Kaveney, Roz. *Teen Dreams: Reading Teen Film and Television from "Heathers" to "Veronica Mars."* New York: I. B. Tauris, 2006.

Khan, Shamus Rahman. *Privilege: The Making of an Adolescent Elite at St. Paul's School*. Princeton, NJ: Princeton University Press, 2012.

Klein, Amanda Ann. *American Film Cycles: Reframing Genres, Screening Social Problems and Defining Subcultures*. Austin: University of Texas Press, 2011.

Klein, Naomi. *No Logo*. New York: Picador, 2009.

Klosterman, Chuck. *The Nineties: A Book*. New York: Penguin, 2022.

Lange, Alexandra. *Meet Me by the Fountain: An Inside History of the Mall*. New York: Bloomsbury, 2022.

Lasswell, Harold D. "The Structure and Function of Communication in Society." In *The Communication of Ideas: A Series of Addresses*, edited by Lyman Bryson, 37–51. New York: Cooper Square, 1964.

Leach, William. *Land of Desire: Merchants, Power, and the Rise of a New American Century*. New York: Vintage, 1993.

Lipovetsky, Gilles. *The Empire of Fashion: Dressing Modern Democracy*. Princeton, NJ: Princeton University Press, 1994.

Love, Joanna K. *Soda Goes Pop: Pepsi-Cola Advertising and Popular Music*. Ann Arbor: University of Michigan Press, 2019.

Lury, Celia. *Brands: The Logos of the Global Economy*. New York: Routledge, 2004.

Magee, Glenn Alexander. *The Hegel Dictionary*. New York: Continuum, 2010.

Malin, Brent. *American Masculinity under Clinton: Popular Media and the Nineties "Crisis of Masculinity."* New York: Peter Lang, 2005.

Maney, Patrick J. *Bill Clinton: New Gilded Age President*. Lawrence: University of Kansas Press, 2016.

Martin, Brett. *Difficult Men: Behind the Scenes of a Creative Revolution; From "The Sopranos" and "The Wire" to "Mad Men" and "Breaking Bad."* New York: Penguin, 2013.

Massoni, Kelley. *Fashioning Teenagers: A Cultural History of "Seventeen" Magazine*. Walnut Creek, CA: Left Coast, 2010.

McBride, Dwight A. *Why I Hate Abercrombie & Fitch: Essays on Race and Sexuality*. New York: New York University Press, 2005.

McCracken, Grant. *Culture and Consumption*. Bloomington: Indiana University Press, 1988.

———. *Culture and Consumption II: Markets, Meaning, and Brand Management*. Bloomington: Indiana University Press, 2005.

———. *Transformations: Identity Construction in Contemporary Culture*. Bloomington: Indiana University Press, 2008.

McGee, Micki. *Self-Help, Inc.: Makeover Culture in American Life*. New York: Oxford University Press, 2005.

McIntosh, Peggy. "White Privilege: Unpacking the Invisible Knapsack." *Peace and Freedom*, July/August 1989, 10–12. Available online at https://nationalseedproject.org/Key-SEED-Texts/white-privilege-unpacking-the-invisible-knapsack.

McKinley, E. Graham. *"Beverly Hills, 90210": Television, Gender, and Identity*. Philadelphia: University of Pennsylvania Press. 1997.

McMillan Cottom, Tressie. *Lower Ed: The Troubling Rise of For-Profit Colleges in the New Economy*. New York: New Press, 2017.

McNelis, Tim. *US Youth Film and Popular Music: Identity, Genre, and Musical Agency*. New York: Routledge, 2017.

Melnick, Jeffrey. *9/11 Culture: America under Construction*. Malden, MA: Wiley-Blackwell, 2009.

Miles, Stephen. *Youth Lifestyles in a Changing World*. Philadelphia, PA: Open University Press, 2000.

Miller, Daniel. *Material Culture and Mass Consumption*. New York: Blackwell, 1987.

Miller, Janice. *Fashion and Music*. New York: Berg, 2011.

Milner, Murray, Jr. *Freaks, Geeks, and Cool Kids: American Teenagers, Schools, and the Culture of Consumption*. New York: Routledge, 2006.

Neale, Steve. "Questions of Genre." In *Film Genre Reader*, 4th ed., edited by Barry Keith Grant, 178–202. Austin: University of Texas Press, 2012.

Nelson, Elissa H. *"The Breakfast Club": John Hughes, Hollywood, and the Golden Age of the Teen Film*. New York: Routledge, 2019.

Palladino, Grace. *Teenagers: An American History*. New York: Basic Books, 1996.

Parker, Kim. *The Boomerang Generation: Feeling OK about Living with Mom and Dad*. Washington, DC: Pew Research Center, 2012. www.pewresearch.org/social-trends/2012/03/15/the-boomerang-generation.

Pettinger, Lynne. "Brand Culture and Branded Workers: Service Work and Aesthetic Labour in Fashion Retail." *Consumption Markets and Culture* 7, no. 2 (2004): 165–84. https://doi.org/10.1080/1025386042000246214.

Pew Research Center. *The Lost Decade of the Middle Class*. Washington, DC: Pew Research Center, 2012. www.pewresearch.org/social-trends/2012/08/22/the-lost-decade-of-the-middle-class.

Pimpare, Stephen. *The New Victorians: Poverty and Politics in Two Gilded Ages*. New York: New Press, 2004.

Quart, Alissa. *Branded: The Buying and Selling of Teenagers*. New York: Basic Books, 2003.

Radner, Hilary. *Neo-feminist Cinema: Girly Films, Chick Flicks, and Consumer Culture.* New York: Routledge, 2011.

Raftery, Brian. *Best. Movie. Year. Ever.: How 1999 Blew Up the Big Screen.* New York: Simon and Schuster, 2019.

Remnick, David. *The New Gilded Age: "The New Yorker" Looks at the Culture of Affluence.* New York: Random House, 2000.

Rios, Sofia. "Joey Potter: Final Girl Next Door." *Journal of Popular Film and Television* 43, no. 3 (2015): 136–47. https://doi.org/10.1080/01956051.2015.1043232.

Ross, Sharon Marie, and Louisa Ellen Stein. *Teen Television: Essays on Programming and Fandom.* Jefferson, NC: McFarland, 2008.

Saviolo, Stefania, and Antonio Marazza. *Lifestyle Brands: A Guide to Aspirational Marketing.* New York: Palgrave Macmillan, 2013.

Shary, Timothy. *Generation Multiplex: The Image of Youth in American Cinema since 1980.* Austin: University of Texas Press, 2014.

Shumar, Wesley. *College for Sale: A Critique of the Commodification of Higher Education.* Washington, DC: Falmer, 1997.

Small, Meg L., Sherry Everette Jones, Lisa C. Barrios, Linda S. Crossett, Linda L. Dahlberg, Melissa A. Albuquerque, David A. Sleet, Brenda Z. Greene, and Ellen R. Schmidt. "School Policy and Environment: Results from the School Health Policies and Programs Study 2000." *Journal of School Health* 71, no. 7 (2001): 325–34.

Smarandescu, Laura, and Terence A. Shimp. "Drink Coca-Cola, Eat Popcorn, and Choose Powerade: Testing the Limits of Subliminal Persuasion." *Marketing Letters* 26, no. 4: (2015): 715–26. https://doi.org/10.1007/s11002-014-9294-1.

Smith, Frances. *Rethinking the Hollywood Teen Movie: Gender, Genre and Identity.* Edinburgh, UK: Edinburgh University Press, 2019.

Staiger, Janet. "Hybrid or Inbred: The Purity Hypothesis and Hollywood Genre History." *Film Criticism* 22, no. 1 (1997): 5–20. www.jstor.org/stable/44018896.

Stiglitz, Joseph E. *The Roaring Nineties: A New History of the World's Most Prosperous Decade.* New York: W. W. Norton, 2003.

Straw, Will. "Popular Music and Postmodernism in the 1980s." In *Sound and Vision: The Music Video Reader,* edited by Simon Frith, Andrew Goodwin, and Lawrence Grossberg, 3–21. New York: Routledge, 1993.

Thornton, Sarah. *Club Cultures: Music, Media, and Subcultural Capital.* New York: Wiley and Sons, 1995.

Trencansky, Sarah. "Final Girls and Terrible Youth: Transgression in 1980s Slasher Horror." *Journal of Popular Film and Television* 29, no. 2 (2001): 63–73. https://doi.org/10.1080/01956050109601010.

Tropiano, Stephen. *Rebels and Chicks: A History of the Hollywood Teen Movie.* New York: Back Stage Books, 2006.

Tseëlon, Efrat. "Jean Baudrillard: Postmodern Fashion as the End of Meaning." In *Thinking through Fashion: A Guide to Key Theorists,* edited by Agnès Rocamora and Anneke Smelik, 215–32. New York: I. B. Tauris, 2016.

Tuchman, Gaye. *Wannabe U: Inside the Corporate University*. Chicago: University of Chicago Press, 2009.

Tudor, Andrew. "Genre." In *Film Genre Reader*, 4th ed., edited by Barry Keith Grant, 3–11. Austin: University of Texas Press, 2012.

Turow, Joseph. *Breaking Up America: Advertisers and the New Media World*. Chicago: University of Chicago Press, 1997.

Vanderbilt, Tom. "The Advertised Life." In Frank and Weiland, *Commodify Your Dissent*, 127–42.

Veblen, Thorstein. *The Theory of the Leisure Class*. New York: Oxford University Press, 2007.

Vernallis, Carol. *Experiencing Music Video: Aesthetics and Cultural Context*. New York: Columbia University Press, 2004.

———. "Strange People, Weird Objects: The Nature of Narrativity, Character, and Editing in Music Videos." In *Medium Cool: Music Videos from Soundies to Cellphones*, edited by Roger Beebe and Jason Middleton, 111–51. Durham, NC: Duke University Press, 2007.

Walters, Kyla. "Mall Models: How Abercrombie & Fitch Sexualizes Its Retail Workers." *Sexualization, Media, and Society* 2, no. 2. (2016): 1–5. https://doi.org/10.1177/23746238 16643283.

Warner, Helen. *Fashion on Television: Identity and Celebrity Culture*. New York: Bloomsbury, 2014.

Wee, Valerie. "Resurrecting and Updating the Teen Slasher: The Case of *Scream*." *Journal of Popular Film and Television* 34, no. 2 (2006): 50–61. https://doi.org/10.3200/JPFT .34.2.50-61.

———. *Teen Media: Hollywood and the Youth Market in the Digital Age*. Jefferson, NC: McFarland, 2010.

White, Keith. "Burn Down the House of Commons in Your Brand New Shoes." In Frank and Weiland, *Commodify Your Dissent*, 62–71.

———. "The Killer App: *Wired* Magazine, Voice of the Revolution." In Frank and Weiland, *Commodify Your Dissent*, 46–56.

Wigley, Stephen M., Karinna Nobbs, and Ewa Larsen. "Marking the Marque: Tangible Branding in Fashion Product and Retail Design." *Fashion Practice* 5, no. 2 (2013): 245–63. https://doi.org/10.2752/175693813X13705243201577.

Yang, Jeff, Phil Yu, and Phillip Wang, eds. *Rise: A Pop History of Asian America from the Nineties to Now*. New York: Mariner Books, 2022.

Yu, Phil. "The 2000s." In Yang, Yu, and Wang, *Rise*, 181–95.

Zukin, Sharon. *Point of Purchase: How Shopping Changed American Culture*. New York: Routledge, 2005.

INDEX